Lecture Notes in Artificial Intelligence 2700

Edited by J. G. Carbonell and J. Siekmann

Subseries of Lecture Notes in Computer Science

T0240731

Springer

Berlin
Heidelberg
New York
Hong Kong
London
Milan
Paris
Tokyo

Maria Teresa Pazienza (Ed.)

Information Extraction in the Web Era

Natural Language Communication
for Knowledge Acquisition
and Intelligent Information Agents

Springer

Series Editors

Jaime G. Carbonell, Carnegie Mellon University, Pittsburgh, PA, USA
Jörg Siekmann, University of Saarland, Saarbrücken, Germany

Volume Editor

Maria Teresa Pazienza
AI Research Group
Department of Computer Science, Systems and Production
Via del Politecnico 1
00133 Roma, Italy
E-mail: pazienza@info.uniroma2.it

Cataloging-in-Publication Data applied for

A catalog record for this book is available from the Library of Congress.

Bibliographic information published by Die Deutsche Bibliothek
Die Deutsche Bibliothek lists this publication in the Deutsche Nationalbibliografie;
detailed bibliographic data is available in the Internet at <http://dnb.ddb.de>.

CR Subject Classification (1998): I.2, H.3, H.2.8, H.4

ISSN 0302-9743
ISBN 3-540-40579-8 Springer-Verlag Berlin Heidelberg New York

Springer-Verlag Berlin Heidelberg New York
a member of BertelsmannSpringer Science+Business Media GmbH

http://www.springer.de

© Springer-Verlag Berlin Heidelberg 2003
Printed in Germany

Typesetting: Camera-ready by author, data conversion by PTP-Berlin GmbH
Printed on acid-free paper   SPIN: 10928653   06/3142   5 4 3 2 1 0

Preface

The number of research topics covered in recent approaches to Information Extraction (IE) is continually growing as new facts are being considered. In fact, while the user's interest in extracting information from texts deals mainly with the success of the entire process of locating, in document collections, facts of interest, the process itself is dependent on several constraints (e.g. the domain, the collection dimension and location, and the document type) and currently it tackles composite scenarios, including free texts, semi- and structured texts such as Web pages, e-mails, etc.

The handling of all these factors is tightly related to the continued evolution of the underlying technologies.

In the last few years, in real-world applications we have seen the need for scalable, adaptable IE systems (see M.T. Pazienza, "Information Extraction: Towards Scalable Adaptable Systems", LNAI 1714) to limit the need for human intervention in the customization process and portability of the IE application to new domains. Scalability and adaptability requirements are still valid impacting features and get more relevance into a Web scenario, wherein intelligent information agents are expected to automatically gather information from heterogeneous sources.

In such an environment, the ability to manage different kinds of knowledge assumes an important role. As the problem of knowledge acquisition cannot be solved only by human intervention (with the increased dimension and distribution of collections it becomes too costly and time consuming), the process of automatic knowledge acquisition becomes crucial to scale up the systems. See the contribution by R. Yangarber, "Acquisition of Domain Knowledge":

"Linguistic knowledge in Natural Language understanding systems is commonly stratified across several levels. This is true of Information Extraction as well. Typical state-of-the-art Information Extraction systems require syntactic-semantic patterns for locating facts or events in text; domain-specific word or concept classes for semantic generalization; and a specialized lexicon of terms that may not be found in general-purpose dictionaries, among other kinds of knowledge.

The objective of IE, as considered here, is to analyze text written in plain natural language, and to find facts or events in the text. The facts and events are formally expressed as multi-argument (n-ary) relations, whose arguments are entities, corresponding to objects in the real world. Information Extraction systems typically operate within a specific domain, and need to be adapted for every new domain of interest. Adaptation for a particular domain entails the collection of knowledge that is needed to operate within that domain.

There has been an observable trend in these approaches, moving from the labor-intensive manual methods of customization, toward automatic methods of knowledge acquisition; further, among the automatic methods, moving from fully-

supervised methods, which require large amounts of annotation, toward unsupervised or minimally supervised methods."

A further support to speed up the localization of *facts-of-interest* in texts descends from *terminology awareness*. There is a demand for reliable methods both to identify key terms or phrases characterizing texts and to link them with other texts and knowledge sources. See the contribution by B. Daille, "Terminology Mining":

"Terminology mining is a major step forward in terminology extraction and covers acquisition and structuring of the candidate terms.

The computation methods used for terminology mining depend on the data to be processed: raw texts or texts enhanced with linguistic annotations, and the use or not of pre-existing knowledge sources.

In terminology mining, references are made to the acquisition of complex terms, the discovering of new terms, but also the structuring of the acquired candidate terms. Among others, it is possible to adopt lexicality, criteria of the linguistic well-formedness of complex terms and their variations expressed in terms of syntactic structures.

We need to underline, for terminology extraction purposes, the crucial part of the handling of term variations in building a linguistic structuring, detecting advanced lexicalisation and obtaining an optimised representatives of the candidate term occurrences. Then we must analyse the implemented computational methods: shallow parsing, morphological analysis, morphological rule learning and lexical statistics."

Due to the fact *terms* are tightly connected to *concepts*, the latter plays a relevant role in characterizing the content of texts and, consequently, in relating them with other information sources. We have to focus on the aspect of the representativeness of a term to provide a mathematically sound formulation of its relatedness to concepts. See the contribution by T. Hisamotsu and J. Tsujii, "Measuring Term Representativeness":

"Although conventional methods based on tf-idf and its variants used intensively in IR systems have also been used to identify terms in texts on the network, the empirical nature of such measures suggests that we should not use them in far more dynamic and heterogeneous situations such as those possible on the network.

Unlike conventional IR systems, we deal with many diverse text types with different lengths and subject fields, and we can not rely on the carefully calibrated parameters that the performances of these empirical measures are highly dependent on.

In order to understand why some empirical measures work well in certain applications but perform rather poorly in other application environments, we first have to disentangle the integrated nature of these measures and identify a set of new measures whose mathematical properties can be understood. Since the termhood comprises several different dimensions, each dimension should be understood in terms of its mathematical properties, and then different measures that represent different aspects of termhood can be combined to accomplish goals specific to given application environments."

Information agents are emerging as a very important approach for building next generation value-added services. Among other uses, information agents could be profitable for automatically gathering information from heterogeneous sources. See the contribution by N. Kushmerick, "Finite-State Approaches to Web Information Extraction":

"It is possible to view information extraction as a core enabling technology for a variety of information agents. We therefore focus specifically on information extraction, rather than tangential (albeit important) issues, such as how agents can discover relevant sources or verify the authenticity of the retrieved content, or caching policies that minimize communication while ensuring freshness.

Scalability is the key challenge to automatic information extraction. There are two relevant dimensions. The first dimension is the ability to rapidly process large document collections. IE systems generally scale well in this regard because they rely on simple shallow extraction rules, rather than sophisticated (and therefore slow) natural language processing. The second and more problematic dimension is the number of distinct sources.

IE is challenging in this scenario because each source might format its content differently, and therefore each source could require a customized set of extraction rules. Machine learning is the only domain-independent approach to scaling along this second dimension. The use of machine learning could enable adaptive information extraction systems that automatically learn extraction rules from training data in order to scale with the number of sources."

To be successful, Information Agents should also be able to deal with linguistic problems. *Linguistic knowledge* is weighted to fruitfully support *intelligent agents* in the activities of filtering, selecting, and classifying a large amount of information daily available on the Web. Due to the unavailability of generic ontologies, intelligent agents behaviour is far from being semantically based. Meanwhile, it appears evident that it is important to take into account semantic aspects to obtain more precise results for IE systems.

Intelligent agents involved in the extraction process could be helpful in the process of mediation among several (possibly domain-specific) ontologies underlying different texts from which information could be extracted. See the contribution by M.T. Pazienza and M. Vindigni, "Agent Based Ontological Mediation in IE Systems":

"Different components should be considered when dealing with documents content. In fact different levels of problems arise related to the two existing communication layers: lexical and conceptual. A group of interacting agents could be seen as a small cooperative society requiring a shared language and communication channels in order to circulate ideas, knowledge and background assumptions. General abilities for language processing may be considered as part of the agent knowledge: differences in formal representation may be overcome by means of transposition – conversion mechanisms."

In the context of knowledge sharing we can refer to ontology as the means for specifying a conceptualisation. That is an ontology may be a description of concepts and relationships that can exist for an agent community for the purpose of enabling knowledge sharing and reuse, thus supporting ontological commitments (e.g. an agreement to use a vocabulary to put queries and make assertions in a way that is consistent – but not complete – with respect to the underlying theory)."

As a consequence of the easier access to textual information, there is a wider interest in not being limited to extract information in the context of a predefined application domain. *Open domain questioning* fascinates the new frontier of research in information extraction. See the contribution by D. Moldovan, "On the Role of the Information Retrieval and Information Extraction in Question Answering Systems":

"Question Answering, the process of extracting answers to natural language questions is profoundly different from Information Retrieval (IR) or Information Extraction (IE). IR systems allow us to locate relevant documents that relate to a query, but do not specify exactly where the answers are. In IR, the documents of interest are fetched by matching query keywords to the index of the document collection. By contrast, IE systems extract the information of interest provided the domain of extraction is well defined. In IE systems, the information of interest is in the form of slot fillers of some predefined templates. The QA technology takes both IR and IE a step further, and provides specific and brief answers to open domain questions formulated naturally."

In a future agent-based adaptive Web information Extraction framework, possibly dialoguing with the user, we could think of *virtual agents* with linguistic abilities for interaction purposes. See the contribution by M. Cavazza, "Natural Language Communication with Virtual Actors":

"The development of realistic virtual actors in many applications, from user interfaces to computer entertainment, creates expectations on the intelligence of these actors including their ability to understand natural language. Specific technical aspects in the development of language-enabled actors could be highlighted. The embodied nature of virtual agents leads to specific syntactic constructs that are not unlike sublanguages: these can be used to specify the parsing component of a natural language interface. However, the most specific aspects of interacting with virtual actors consist in mapping the semantic content of users' input to the mechanisms that support agents' behaviours. A generalisation of speech acts can provide principles for this integration.

Virtual agents are embodied in a physical (although virtual) environment: apart from the properties of any specific task they have to carry, this embodiment is at the heart of understanding the requirements for NLP. The embodiment of virtual agents requires that their understanding of language is entirely translated into actions in their environment."

Hereafter, throughout the various sections, all the previously cited research topics will be dealt with and deeply analyzed. The papers represent the authors' contribution to SCIE 2002, the "Summer Convention on Information Extraction," held in Frascati (Rome, Italy), in July 2002, attended by a very qualified international audience that participated actively to the technical discussions. Comments from the participants have been considered in some cases during updating and some further details were introduced.

It emerges that new technological scenarios are forcing IE research activities to move in new directions. Meanwhile question answering is being proposed as a new frontier. We shall see ...

June 2003

Maria Teresa Pazienza
Program Chair
SCIE 2002

Organization

SCIE 2002 – Summer Convention on Information Extraction – was organized by the AI research group (Maria Teresa Pazienza, Roberto Basili, Michele Vindigni and Fabio Zanzotto among others) of the University of Roma Tor Vergata (Italy), and was hosted by ESA – the European Space Agency – at the ESRIN establishment, its premises in Frascati, Italy. Special thanks to the staff of the European Space Agency (ESA) at ESRIN for valuable support in the organization of SCIE 2002.

Sponsoring Institutions

SCIE 2002 was partially supported by the following institutions:

AI*IA, Artificial Intelligence Italian Association, Italy
ESA, European Space Agency
DISP, Department of Computer Science, Systems and Production, University of Roma Tor Vergata, Italy
MIUR Ministero dell'Istruzione, dell'Universitá e della Ricerca, Italy
ENEA, Ente Nazionale Energie Alternative, Italy
NOUS Informatica srl., Italy

Table of Contents

Information Extraction in the Web Era

Acquisition of Domain Knowledge

Roman Yangarber

Courant Institute of Mathematical Sciences
New York University, New York, USA
roman@cs.nyu.edu
www.cs.nyu.edu/roman

Abstract. Linguistic knowledge in Natural Language understanding systems is commonly stratified across several levels. This is true of Information Extraction as well. Typical state-of-the-art Information Extraction systems require syntactic-semantic *patterns* for locating facts or events in text; domain-specific word or concept *classes* for semantic generalization; and a specialized *lexicon* of terms that may not be found in general-purpose dictionaries, among other kinds of knowledge.

We describe an approach to unsupervised, or minimally supervised, knowledge acquisition. The approach is based on bootstrapping a comprehensive knowledge base from a small set of seed elements. Our approach is embodied in algorithms for discovery of patterns, concept classes, and lexicon, from raw un-annotated text.

We present the results of knowledge acquisition, and examine them in the context of prior work. We discuss problems in evaluating the quality of the acquired knowledge, and methodologies for evaluation.

1 Customization for Information Extraction

This chapter focuses on event-level Information Extraction (IE), and its lower-level enabling components. The objective of IE, as considered here, is to analyze text written in plain natural language, and to find facts or events in the text. The facts and events are formally expressed as multi-argument (n-ary) relations, whose arguments are entities, corresponding to objects in the real world.

Information Extraction systems typically operate within a specific domain, and need to be adapted for every new domain of interest. Adaptation for a particular domain entails the collection of knowledge that is needed to operate within that domain. Experience indicates that such collection cannot be undertaken by manual means only—i.e., by enlisting domain experts to provide expertise, and computational linguists to induct the expertise into the system,—as the costs would compromise the enterprise. This is known as the acquisition bottleneck.

Hence, attention has centered on the process of knowledge acquisition for NLP in general, and for IE in particular. There has been an observable trend in these approaches, moving from the labor-intensive manual methods of customization, toward automatic methods of knowledge acquisition; further, among the automatic methods, moving from fully-supervised methods, which require large amounts of annotation, toward unsupervised or minimally supervised methods.

M.T. Pazienza (Ed.): SCIE 2002, LNAI 2700, pp. 1–28, 2003.

The present chapter focuses on the last category.

After reviewing the basics of event-level IE (section 1.1), we present learning algorithms for two knowledge acquisition tasks: discovery of patterns (section 2) and of classes of lexical items (section 3), two kinds of knowledge necessary for IE. We discuss how these approaches fit into a general framework in section 4, and examine its relation to prior work and implications for on-going research.

1.1 Basics

We briefly review some standard terminology. In MUC-style IE[1], the term *subject domain* denotes a class of textual documents to be processed, e.g., "business news" or "medical reports." By a *scenario* we mean the specific topic of interest within the domain, i.e., the set of facts to be extracted. An example of a scenario is "Management Succession,"[2] which focuses on high-level corporate executives leaving or assuming their posts (see section 2).

Each fact, or *event*, in this scenario can be viewed as a row in a table (or element of a relation, in database terminology); the fields (slots) of the table include the name of the executive, her/his post or title, the name of the company, and a binary-valued slot indicating whether the person is assuming or leaving the post.

IE systems commonly use a sequence of finite-state transducers (e.g., [2, 18]), which apply regular-expression patterns to the text, to mark phrases of increasing complexity with syntactic/semantic information. At the clause level, the system typically applies *event patterns*, e.g.:

```
np(C-Company) vg(V-Appoint) np(C-Person) 'as'? np(C-Post)
```

This pattern matches a noun phrase of semantic type C-Company[3], followed by a verb group of type V-Appoint, etc. The class V-Appoint appears in the system's concept hierarchy (similar to WordNet, [24]) and contains the lexical entries {*appoint, name, elect*}; C-Post contains, e.g., {*president, chairman, vice president*}. This pattern creates an event by matching on text segments like:

"IBM, Inc. named John B. Smith, Jr. vice president."

The patterns comprise a domain-specific knowledge base that is essential for the system's operation: gaps in patterns translate directly into gaps in coverage. Finding all the ways in which these events are phrased is critical to the task.

Another example of a scenario is "Infectious Disease Outbreaks" (see section 3), about the spread of epidemics of infectious diseases throughout the world. For this scenario the system will have patterns like:

```
np(C-Disease) vg(V-Afflict) np(C-Person)
```

---

[1] See, e.g., [26,27], which also describe evaluation of performance of IE systems, and the IR-based concepts of recall and precision.

[2] The topic of MUC-6, the 6th Message Understanding Conference, [26].

[3] NPs of type C-Company and C-Person are identified in an earlier stage by a Named Entity tagger.

to match clauses like "[...since Tuesday] Ebola has killed 5 people [in Uganda...]" The class C-Disease should contain as many names of infectious diseases as possible. A complete domain-specific lexicon is crucial for good coverage: gaps in the lexicon translate directly into gaps in coverage.

Our goal is to populate knowledge bases automatically, for each new scenario or domain, based on minimal input from the user. We first consider the task of learning event patterns.

2   Learning Event Patterns

2.1   Prior Work

We begin with a taxonomy of methods for learning event patterns for IE.

Semi-automatic Methods. Some earlier systems can be classed as semi-automatic, as they require interaction between the user and the system. PET, [39,40], is an example of an interactive toolkit for generalizing examples in text into extraction patterns.

AutoSlog, from the University of Massachusetts, [22,31] uses a corpus annotated with extraction templates for inducing a "concept dictionary"—the pattern base. A human checker weeds out undesirable patterns from the output. Cardie, in [9], proposes an integrated environment for IE, where the user iteratively filters the results from an automatic algorithm for pattern learning.

Supervised Methods. [13,23] present methods for automatically converting a corpus *annotated* with extraction examples into extraction patterns. [23, 15] report on experiments with HMMs. RAPIER, in [7,8], builds symbolic rules for identifying slot fillers using Inductive Logic Programming (ILP). These approaches do not reduce the user's burden of *finding* good examples to annotate. They shift the portability bottleneck from the problem of building patterns to that of finding good candidates.

These learning algorithms require relatively large amounts of annotated training data, even for relatively simple extraction tasks. For example, the automatically trained UMASS system, [13], performed well when trained on the large MUC-4 corpus (1500 articles), but suffered a substantial drop in performance on MUC-6 training (100 articles). One reason for the need for large training corpora is that most such systems learn template-filling rules in terms of individual lexical items. Later work from NTT, [33], describes a system capable of specializing and generalizing rules using a pre-existing hierarchy of word classes.

Active Learning. Automatic learning from an annotated corpus can quickly pick up the most common patterns, but requires a large corpus to achieve good coverage of the less frequent patterns. Because of the typically skewed distribution of patterns in a corpus—with a few patterns appearing frequently, followed by a long tail of rare patterns,—the user who undertakes exhaustive annotation of examples for automatic learning finds him/herself annotating the same examples over and over again.

The idea behind *Active Learning* is to cut down the number of examples the user must annotate, by selecting suitable candidates for annotation. [34,37]

select for annotation those examples which match patterns that are similar to good patterns, or examples which match uncertain patterns (supported by few examples). This results in gains in learning efficiency.

Learning from Un-Annotated Corpora. Research on unsupervised learning from un-annotated corpora relates most closely to ours. DIPRE [6], and Snowball [1], modeled after DIPRE, use bootstrapping to populate a *binary* relation in a database, e.g., *book/author* or *organization/location-of-headquarters*. The algorithm starts with a small set of seed pairs, and searches a large un-annotated corpus, like the Web, for contexts in which the seed pairs appear. Given these contexts, it finds additional pairs, and the process repeats.

This approach takes advantage of facts which are stated in the corpus repeatedly and in different forms, but it relies on the fact that the relation is *functional* (i.e., many-to-one).

AutoSlog-TS, [32], uses supervised learning for automatic filling of slots in event templates; the method uses an annotated corpus and some syntactic heuristics for locating candidate slot fills. Meta-bootstrapping, [30], a descendant method, finds word classes relevant to a scenario, and patterns for locating these word classes.

In [32] all possible patterns (a word and its immediate syntactic context) are generated for a collection of relevant and non-relevant documents. Patterns are then ranked based on their frequency in the relevant vs. the non-relevant parts of the collection, preferring patterns which occur more often in the relevant documents. The top-ranked patterns turn out to be effective extraction patterns for the task.

This work differs from ours in several respects. First, AutoSlog's patterns do not cover entire events, after the fashion of MUC Scenario Template task. For "Terrorist Attack" events, each pattern produced by AutoSlog-TS and meta-bootstrapping can identify a single slot in isolation, e.g., the *victim* or the *weapon* slot. Combining these slots into complete events is treated as a separate problem. We focus directly on discovering relational, *event-level* patterns, for filling multiple slots.

Second, AutoSlog-TS relies on a pre-classified corpus—all documents in the collection are judged "relevant" or "non-relevant." Meta-bootstrapping uses an un-classified corpus containing a high proportion of relevant documents. These requirements are lifted in our work.

Classifying documents by hand, although much easier than tagging *events* for supervised training, is still a time-consuming and error-prone form of supervision. In one experiment, it took us 5 hours to classify a corpus of 150 short documents (1–2Kb each). The procedure we propose requires no relevance judgements and works on a balanced corpus, where the proportion of relevant documents is small.

2.2   Pattern Discovery

We now present an outline of a procedure for acquisition of event patterns, ExDisco.[4] Details will follow in section 2.3. The procedure is *unsupervised* in that it does not require an annotated or a pre-classified corpus.

ExDisco is an iterative process, gaining small improvements at each step. It is motivated, in part, by an important observation made by Riloff, [32], that "[...] domain-specific expressions will appear substantially more often in relevant texts than irrelevant texts." I.e., *if* we partition a corpus into relevant vs. non-relevant subsets, *then* we can assume that patterns which are strongly correlated with the relevant subset will be good patterns for the domain.

We make a second key observation: the duality between the space of documents and the space of patterns.

Principle of Duality:

I. Relevant documents are strong indicators of good patterns.
II. Conversely, good patterns are strong indicators of relevant documents.

Part I is a restatement of the quote from [32]. Part II, its converse, is also intuitively true. Starting with a set of good patterns and documents, this principle allows us to find new patterns and documents, in a bootstrapping chain.

Algorithm (ExDisco).

0. **Given:**
   a) A large corpus of *un-annotated* and *un-classified* documents, U.
   b) Initialize the set of accepted scenario patterns: $Accept_0 \leftarrow$ a trusted set of *seed* patterns, chosen by the user. The seed can be quite small—two or three patterns may suffice.
1. **Partition:** The seed patterns induce a split on the corpus: for any document, either some patterns match it, or no patterns match. The corpus (universe) of documents, U, is partitioned into the "relevant" sub-corpus, R, vs. the "non-relevant," $\overline{R} = U - R$. Documents are assigned *relevance weights* between 0 and 1 (documents matched by a pattern in $Accept_0$ receive a weight of 1).
2. **Search for new candidate patterns:**
   a) Convert each sentence in the corpus into a candidate pattern.[5]
   b) From among the relevant documents consider those candidate patterns, p, which meet the *density* criterion:

$$\frac{|H \cap R|}{|H|} \gg \frac{|U \cap R|}{|U|} = \frac{|R|}{|U|} \qquad (1)$$

where $H = H(p)$ is the set of documents where p matches. The key idea is to select the patterns strongly correlated with the relevant documents, i.e., patterns which occur much more densely among the relevant documents than among the non-relevant ones.

---

[4] First described in [41,42]; discussion in [44].
[5] Cf. sec. 6, syntactic analysis.

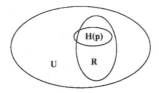

Fig. 1. Pattern Correlation with Relevant Documents

c) Select the pattern, $\bar{p}$, most correlated with R, and add it to the growing set of accepted patterns:

$$Accept_{i+1} \leftarrow Accept_i \cup \{\bar{p}\}$$

3. **Repeat:** The expanded pattern set induces a new partition on the corpus. Repeat from step 1, until a stopping criterion is fulfilled.

The intuition behind inequality in (1) can be visualized in Figure 1. The right side of the inequality is an estimate of the prior probability of relevance; this is how often we expect to find a relevant document in the corpus. The left side is an estimate of the conditional probability that a document is relevant, given that the pattern p has matched it.

During a given iteration, the right side is fixed; finding the best pattern amounts to maximizing the left side. This forms the basis for pattern scoring.

2.3   Methodology

Before applying the discovery procedure, we subject the corpus to several pre-processing steps.

Pre-processing: Name Normalization. First we apply a Named Entity (NE) Recognizer[6], and replace each proper name with a class label, e.g. *C-Person, C-Company, C-Location*. Proteus also replaces out-of-dictionary items (OODs)—numeric expressions, percentages, currency values, dates, etc., with a category label, e.g., *C-Number, C-Date*. Factoring NEs and OODs is *essential* to the discovery algorithm, since it increases redundancy in the text for finding repeated patterns.

Pre-processing: Syntactic Analysis. After name normalization, we run the corpus through a syntactic parser.[7] The parser performs several levels of syntactic normalization, to maximize commonality among the patterns in the text.

---

[6] From the Proteus IE system, [19].

[7] We use a general-purpose dependency parser, based on the FDG formalism [36], which was developed at the University of Helsinki and Conexor Oy.

First, the parser transforms clausal variants, such as the passive and relative, into a common form (active), and attempts to resolve some relative pronouns. As a result, the clauses "IBM hired John," "John was hired by IBM" and "... John, who was hired by IBM" yield identical structure.

Second, it reduces all inflected forms to the corresponding *base* forms, by stripping auxiliaries, tense, number, case, and so on.

The experiments described here use only key information from the parse trees. Each clause is transformed into a *primary tuple* consisting of:

- subject (only the *head* of the subject NP),
- verb (the head of the verb chain),
- direct object.[8]

These primary tuples are used as patterns in ExDisco. Examples:
"The board has appointed J. Smith as president" → *[board-appoint-C-person].*
"John Smith will remain the acting chairman" → *[C-person-remain-chairman].*

Generalized Patterns and Concept Classes. Primary tuples may not repeat in the corpus with sufficient frequency to obtain reliable statistics. For this reason, each primary tuple is generalized, to produce three *generalized patterns*:

$$[S - V - O] \Longrightarrow \begin{cases} [* - V - O] \\ [S - * - O] \\ [S - V - *] \end{cases}$$

with one of the arguments replaced by a wild-card. In the search for best pattern, Step 2, ExDisco actually searches for the best generalized pattern.

ExDisco uses the possible values of the missing argument to construct a new concept class, by grouping together the values which appear in the corpus. For example, the algorithm decides that the best generalized candidate is [*company-*-person*], a pattern with a missing verb. It would then form a concept class for the verbs which occur in the corpus with this subject–object pair: e.g., [*company-*{hire,fire,expel...}*-person*].

The algorithm does not admit *all* possible values of the missing role into the new concept class, since indiscriminate inclusion might yield irrelevant tuples, like as [*company-sue-person*] or [*company-congratulate-person*]. Each value for the missing role gives rise to a primary tuple, and ExDisco chooses only values corresponding to primary triples that have high correlation scores, i.e. those that are strongly correlated with the relevant documents. Note, therefore, that together with the best pattern, the algorithm also learns a new class of concepts, (see section 4.1)

Several researchers have explored induction of semantic classes through analysis of syntactic co-occurrence, [30,29,12,20], but in our case, the contexts are limited to selected syntactic constructs, which are relevant to the scenario.

---

[8] If present; otherwise we use the object/subject complement or the co-predicative, [28].

Pattern Ranking. ExDISCO ranks all patterns (generalized tuples) according the strength of their correlation with the relevant sub-corpus. We define the *correlation score* function, $Score(p)$ as:[9]

$$Score(p) = \frac{Sup'(p)}{|H|} \cdot \log Sup'(p) \qquad (2)$$

where, as in (1), $H = H(p)$ are documents where p matched, and

$$Sup'(p) = |H \cap R| \qquad (3)$$

is a measure of *support*[10] for p among the relevant documents. The first factor in (2) accounts for the pattern's accuracy—the conditional probability that a document d is relevant, given that the pattern p matches d.

At the end of each iteration, the system selects the pattern with the highest correlation score, and adds it to the trusted set.[11] The documents which the top-scoring pattern matched are given new relevance scores.

Internal Model of Document Relevance. At the start of the algorithm, the seed patterns are considered as ground truth, so the documents they match receive relevance 1 and the rest receive relevance 0:

$$Rel_0(d) = \begin{cases} 1 & \text{if } d \in H(p), p \in Accept_0 \\ 0 & \text{otherwise} \end{cases}$$

However, ExDISCO does not have complete confidence in the patterns accepted on subsequent iterations. On iteration $i + 1$, the accepted pattern p_{i+1} receives a confidence measure, the precision of p_{i+1}, computed as the *average* relevance of the documents that p_{i+1} matched:

$$Prec(p_{i+1}) = \frac{1}{|H(p)|} \cdot \sum_{d \in H(p)} Rel_i(d) \qquad (4)$$

where $Rel_i(d)$ is the relevance of d from the previous iteration.

The algorithm also maintains an internal model of document relevance, between 0 and 1. In general, for each document, the relevance starts at zero and increases monotonically. After a new pattern is accepted, the relevance scores of the documents are re-adjusted as follows. Suppose a document d is matched by some of the currently accepted patterns, $K(d) = \{p_j\}$. These patterns determine the new relevance of d by the following "voting" scheme:

---

[9] This is similar to the measure used in [32]

[10] This is *binary* support: each document matched by p contributes 1 if it's relevant, and 0 if it's not. We will refine the notion of support shortly.

[11] We use two additional *support criteria*: discard frequent patterns with $|H \cap U| > \alpha|U|$ as uninformative, and rare patterns for which $|H \cap R| < \beta$ as noise. We used $\alpha = 0.1$ and $\beta = 2$.

$$Rel_{i+1}(d) = 1 - \prod_{p \in K(d)} \left(1 - Prec(p)\right) \tag{5}$$

This equation can be interpreted as follows. Precision of p, as computed in (4), estimates the probability that a document that p matches is relevant. Then the product term in (5) is the probability that the document d is *not* relevant, given that all the patterns in $K(d)$ match it. One minus that is the probability that d is relevant.

We can refine the notion of support in (3), by defining *continuous* support as

$$Sup(p) = \sum_{d \in H(p)} Rel(d) \tag{6}$$

where each document in $H(p)$ contributes its relevance value, rather than 0 or 1. We have $Sup(p) \le Sup'(p)$, and $Sup(p) = Sup'(p)$ if $p \in Accept_0$.

The algorithm uses a weighted version of voting, to account for variation in their support:

$$Rel_{i+1}(d) = 1 - \sqrt[\overline{w}]{\prod_{p \in K_d} \left(1 - Prec(p)\right)^{w_p}} \tag{7}$$

where the weight w_p accounts for the cumulative support for p:

$$w_p = \log Sup(p), \text{ and } \overline{w} = \max_p w_p$$

$\overline{w}$ is the largest weight. The formula for pattern score in (2) actually uses $Sup(p)$, *cumulative relevance* of the documents matched by p, rather than $Sup'(p)$, the count of the relevant documents. The recursive formulas, (4) and (5), or (7), capture the duality between patterns and documents. This is the core of the approach.

2.4 Evaluation

We discuss experiments with EXDISCO on several scenarios, in the domains of business news and general news. For business news, we used a corpus of $\approx 10,000$ articles from the Wall Street Journal (WSJ), between 1992 and 1994. The parsed corpus yielded 440,000 clausal tuples, of which 215,000 were distinct. For general news, we used a corpus of 14,000 articles from Associated Press (AP), from 1989.

In the experiments we ran the algorithm until it started learning irrelevant patterns, usually after 80-100 iterations.

Management Succession. EXDISCO was tested extensively on Management Succession, since this scenario comes with pre-existing extraction systems (Proteus, [18]), and high-quality original MUC-6 "Training" and "Test" corpora (cf. [26]), each containing 100 WSJ articles with event annotations. Table 1 shows some of the discovered patterns; the seed patterns are marked with †; examples of "bad" patterns are underlined. In the seeds, *C-Company* or *C-Person*

Table 1. Seed pattern set for "Management Succession"

† C-Company V-Appoint C-Person
† C-Person V-Resign —

person–succeed–person
person–{be,become}–president
person–become–{chairman,officer,president,executive}
person–retire–
person–serve–{company,board,<u>sentence</u>}
person–{run,leave,join,<u>say</u>,own,head,found,start,remain,rejoin}–company
person–assume–{post,title,responsibility,control,duty}
person–replace–person
person–step_down–[as-officer]
person–{relinquish,assume,hold,accept,retain,take,resign,leave}–post
company–name–{chairman,president,successor}
*–hire–person
person–run–{company,operation,<u>campaign</u>,organization,business}
person–hold–{position,title,post,<u>stake</u>,<u>share</u>,job,meeting}
person–{hold,retain,resign,fill}–position
person–take–{control,helm,<u>care</u>,<u>action</u>,office,retirement,job,post, duty,responsibility}

‡ company–bring–person–[in]–[as+officer]
‡ person–{come,return}–[to+company]–[as+officer]
‡ person–rejoin–company–[as+officer]
‡ person–tap–person–[to+be+officer]
‡ person–{continue,remain,stay}–[as+officer]
‡ person–pursue–interest

denotes a semantic class of named entities of the corresponding type; *V-Appoint* is a list of verbs { *appoint, elect, promote, name, nominate* }, and *V-Resign* = { *resign, depart, quit* }.

Evidently, ExDisco discovers useful patterns.[12] We can get a simple measure of performance by comparing patterns found by ExDisco with the manually constructed pattern base in Proteus, at the time of the MUC-6 competition. Proteus used approximately 75 clause-level patterns, with 32 distinct verbs. Using 8 of the verbs in the seed, ExDisco found 80% of the remaining ones (19 of 24). However, it also found many patterns—with 14 *new* verbs—which the original developers of Proteus did not find, but which are strongly relevant to the scenario. These are marked in the table with ‡.

We should note that in search for patterns, in preparation for MUC-6, the designers of Proteus studied not only the 100-document Training corpus, but also a large number of additional documents, retrieved with an IR engine.

---

[12] It is sobering to observe that the pattern *[person–serve–sentence]* is found by the algorithm to be strongly correlated with this scenario.

We should also note that in the MUC-6 competition, Proteus achieved the highest score over all participants.

Patterns discovered by EXDISCO for several other scenarios are shown in the Appendix.

Quantitative Evaluation. The output of EXDISCO is $Accept_n$, the set of patterns discovered after n iterations. These patterns can be incorporated into an IE system, to perform event extraction. However, evaluating the quality of $Accept_n$ directly is difficult.

Note, for example, that the precision measure, $Prec(p)$, is not helpful. A pattern may have low precision but still be very important for the scenario: e.g., the pattern *[person–die–]*, which matches clauses like "15 people have died [in *Location*...]," would be useful in multiple scenarios, including Infectious Disease Outbreaks, Terrorist Attacks, and Natural Disasters, yet it would have low precision.

Therefore, in [42], we introduced an *indirect* evaluation for the discovered patterns: rather than focusing on the pattern set $Accept_n$, we focus on how well EXDISCO is estimating the true relevance of the documents.

Text Filtering. In MUC, in addition to evaluating how well an IE system extracts *events*, we also evaluated how well it extracts *documents*. This treats the IE system as an IR engine: a document is relevant if *any* relevant event is found in it, and non-relevant otherwise. Then we compute the system's recall and precision at the level of documents, rather than events. This is called *text filtering*. The idea is to evaluate EXDISCO as a text filter.

To do that, we can say that EXDISCO classifies each document d by assigning to it an *external* relevance measure as:

$$Rel_i^*(d) = \begin{cases} 1 & \text{if } Rel_i(d) \geq \theta \\ 0 & \text{if } Rel_i(d) < \theta \end{cases}$$

with the threshold, θ, chosen empirically.[13] I.e., if after i iterations, the algorithm's internal model of relevance of a document d exceeds the threshold, its external relevance is 1, else it is zero.

Then if we have a set of documents $D \subset U$ which are manually classified as relevant/non-relevant, we can calculate recall and precision for EXDISCO's relevance judgements.

Figure 2 shows the results on text filtering for the MUC-6 task. We tested EXDISCO against the two MUC-6 corpora, Training and Test, using only the document relevance/non-relevance information from the answer keys.[14]

The recall/precision plot starts with the seed patterns in table 1. Recall grows steadily with reasonable precision until bad patterns invade the system and improvement stops. Note, again, this is an indirect evaluation of the patterns.

---

[13] We analyzed different thresholds, and $\theta = 0.5$ worked well.

[14] Both corpora are included in the 10,000 articles on which EXDISCO was trained. The judgements were used only for evaluation, and were *not* seen by the algorithm.

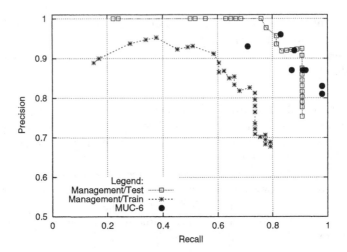

Fig. 2. Management Succession

The figure also shows the text filtering results of the MUC-6 participant systems on the Test corpus. ExDisco attains values well within the range of these IE systems, which were heavily supervised or manually coded.

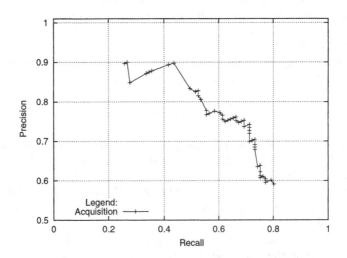

Fig. 3. Mergers/Acquisitions

Figure 3 shows the performance of text filtering on the Mergers & Acquisition task, using the seeds in table 4 in the Appendix. ExDisco was trained on the same WSJ corpus as for Management Succession. We retrieved a test set of 200 documents using an IR keywords, and judged their relevance manually.

Table 2. Performance on slot filling for "Management Succession"

	Training			Test		
Pattern Base	*Recall*	*Precision*	*F*	*Recall*	*Precision*	*F*
Seed	38	83	52.60	27	74	39.58
ExDisco	62	80	69.94	52	72	60.16
Union	69	79	73.50	57	73	63.56
Manual-MUC	54	71	61.93	47	70	56.40
Manual-NOW	69	79	73.91	56	75	64.04

Event Extraction. As a final quantitative evaluation, ExDisco was tested on the event extraction task. We started with a version of Proteus which was used in MUC-6, in 1995, and has been improved since then. We removed all scenario-specific clause and nominalization patterns.[15]

Then we *manually* incorporated patterns learned by ExDisco into the Proteus knowledge base, and ran IE on the MUC-6 Training and Test corpora. The extracted events were scored for recall and precision, as shown in table 2.

The baseline is the *Seed* pattern base, using the seed patterns from table 1. This results in an F-measure[16] of 52.60, for the Training corpus.

If we add the relevant patterns learned by ExDisco, the F-measure goes up to almost 70F. For comparison, *Manual-MUC*—Proteus's 1995 official result—was just under 62F. This pattern base was prepared for the MUC-6 Training corpus during one month by two computational linguists. *Manual-Now* shows the current performance of the Proteus system, which is just under 74F points. The base called *Union* combines the patterns from ExDisco and *Manual-Now*.

The results are encouraging: the IE engine performs at least as well with the patterns discovered by ExDisco as it did with manual tuning.

3   Learning Generalized Names

Next we present NOMEN, an algorithm for learning *generalized names* from text, [43]. NOMEN uses bootstrapping similarly to ExDisco to acquire patterns and name instances. The algorithm makes use of competing evidence to boost learning of several categories of names simultaneously.

We apply the algorithm in the context of the "Infectious Disease Outbreaks" scenario, [17], for tracking epidemics of infectious diseases throughout the world.[17]

---

[15] Non-clausal patterns can also create scenario events, e.g., "Mr Smith, former president of IBM," will create a *departure* event. These patterns were kept in, and they contribute to the relatively high baselines.

[16] *F-measure* is the harmonic mean of recall and precision, defined in, e.g., [26].

[17] This research grew out of an Integrated Feasibility Experiment on Biological Infectious Outbreaks (IFE-BIO), a project to build an IE system for this scenario.

3.1   Generalized Names

A fundamental knowledge base in IE is the domain-specific lexicon—lexical items that may not appear in general-purpose dictionaries. Several classes of names would help coverage for the Disease Outbreak scenario, e.g., disease names, biological *agents*—organisms that cause disease, such as viruses and bacteria; *vectors*—organisms or animals capable of transmitting infection; and *drugs* used in treatment. We call these *generalized names*.

Generalized names differ from conventional proper names (PNs), and exhibit certain properties that make their identification more complex.

The main feature of proper names in English, with very few exceptions, is capitalization. This makes PNs simple to identify. This clue is unavailable for generalized names, as they are often not capitalized—"mad cow disease", "tuberculosis", or partially capitalized—"Ebola haemorrhagic fever", "E. coli", "(new) variant Creutzfeldt-Jacob disease." The generalized name can modify the head of a noun phrase—"Bacillus anthracis infection", "the seven dengue cases." The boundaries of these names are less clear-cut than those of the classic NEs.

Why Learning?   Reliance on fixed specialised, domain-specific lists or gazetteers may be unsatisfactory for several reasons:

1. Comprehensive lists are not easy to obtain.

2. Even when one can obtain a list, it is necessarily incomplete, since new names (locations, diseases) continually enter the literature, and they are usually the most topical and the most interesting ones for extraction.

3. Text typically contains sufficient information for a human reader to infer the category of a name. This makes discovering names in text a challenging problem for AI in its own right.

In the next section we introduce an algorithm for *simultaneous* learning of several categories of names, the *target* categories. We compare the algorithm to prior work (sec. 3.4), and discuss results and evaluation (sec. 3.5 and 3.6).

3.2   Name Discovery

Algorithm (NOMEN).

0. **Given:**
   a) A large training corpus, tagged with lemmas and parts of speech.
   b) The user provides seeds for each target category. E.g., we select 10 common diseases, locations, and several other categories.

   The set of accepted names, *AcceptName*, is initialized with the seeds.
1. **Tagging:** For every accepted name, mark the corpus by placing *left* and *right* tags for the category around each occurrence of the name—e.g., `<disease>` and `</disease>`.
2. **Pattern Generation:** For each tag T inserted in the corpus in Step 1, generate a *literal* pattern p using a context window of width w around T:

$$p = [\, l_{-3}\ l_{-2}\ l_{-1}\ < T >\ l_{+1}\ l_{+2}\ l_{+3}\,]$$

where $l_{\pm i}$ form the *context* of p—the lemmas of the surrounding words. Note, the tag of the pattern, $Tag(p) = T$, has a *direction*, either "left" or "right", $Dir(p) \in \{left, right\}$, and a category, $Cat(p)$. E.g., if $Tag(p) = $ `</disease>`, then $Dir(p) = right$ and $Cat(p) = disease$.

Each pattern matches on only one side of a name instance, either its beginning or end. These patterns together form the set of *potential* patterns, Φ.

3. **Pattern Matching:** For every pattern $p \in \Phi$, match p against the entire training corpus. At the location where the context of p matches, p predicts the presence of either the left or the right boundary of a name in text. Call this position pos_a. NOMEN then applies a noun group (NG) regular expression[18] to find the location where the corresponding *partner* boundary of the name would be, say, at position pos_b.

For example, suppose a pattern p matches the text:

$$\dots \textit{distribute the } \langle_1 yellow \quad fever\rangle_2 \, vaccine\rangle_3 \textit{ to the areas } \dots$$

at $pos_a = 2$ and $Dir(p) = right$; then $pos_b = 1$. If, instead, $pos_a = 1$ and $Dir(p) = left$, then $pos_b = 3$. (Note, the RE search proceeds in the direction opposite to $Dir(p)$.)

Now, we check whether the NG between positions pos_a and pos_b has already been accepted as a name in some target category; the result can be:

- *positive*: The NG has already been accepted as a name in the category $Cat(p)$;
- *negative*: The NG has already been accepted as a name in a different category, $C' \neq Cat(p)$;
- *unknown*: The NG has not yet been accepted as a name in any category.

The *unknown* case is where a new candidate of the category $Cat(p)$ may potentially be discovered.

4. **Pattern Acquisition:** For each pattern $p \in \Phi$, record its positive $pos(p)$, negative $neg(p)$, and unknown $unk(p)$ matches, and compute $Score(p)$ as a function of these statistics.

The scoring function favors patterns which select names of the correct category more often than names of incorrect or unknown categories; it also favors patterns which select a greater number of *distinct* names in $AcceptName$. Add the n best-scoring patterns for each target category to the set of *accepted* patterns, $AcceptPat$.

5. **Pattern Application:** Apply each accepted pattern $p \in AcceptPat$ to the entire corpus, use the noun-group RE to recover the NGs as in step 3, and consider the NGs in the *unknown* case—the *candidate* instances.

Group all identical candidate instances of a name into one *candidate type*, and let Ψ be the list of the distinct candidate types. E.g., the accepted patterns may find several different instances of "Ebola" in the corpus, but "Ebola" will appear only once in Ψ.

---

[18] Using regular-expression heuristics, as in terminology discovery [14,21]; e.g., the simple noun-group RE `[Adj* Noun+]`.

6. **Candidate Acquisition:** Compute a score for each candidate type $t \in \Psi$, based on
   - how many *different* patterns in *AcceptPat* match an instance of type t,
   - how reliable these patterns are.

   For each target category, add the m best-scoring candidate types to the set *AcceptName*.
7. **Repeat:** from Step 1, until no more names can be learned.

3.3   Methodology

Pre-processing. The training corpus is passed through a lemmatizer and a part-of-speech (POS) tagger. The lemmatizer uses the Comlex dictionary of English to produce lemmas for inflected surface forms, [16]. The statistical POS tagger is trained on the WSJ (possibly sub-optimal for mail texts about epidemics). Unknown and foreign words are marked as *noun* by the tagger, and are not lemmatized.

Generalized Patterns. Literal patterns generated in Step 2 may not repeat in the corpus with sufficient frequency to obtain reliable statistics. Therefore, for each literal pattern p we create several generalized patterns, where each $l_{\pm i}$ may be replaced by its generalization—a wild-card.[19]

$$[\, l_{-3}\, l_{-2}\, l_{-1} < \mathrm{T} > l_{+1}\, l_{+2}\, l_{+3}\,] \Longrightarrow \begin{cases} [\, l_{-3}\, l_{-2}\, l_{-1} < \mathrm{T} > *\ *\ *\,] \\ [\, *\ \ l_{-2}\, l_{-1} < \mathrm{T} > *\ *\ *\,] \\ \ \ ... \\ [\, *\ \ *\ \ * < \mathrm{T} > l_{+1}\, l_{+2}\, l_{+3}\,] \\ [\, *\ \ *\ \ * < \mathrm{T} > l_{+1}\, l_{+2}\ *\,] \\ \ \ ... \end{cases}$$

The set of candidate patterns Φ includes the literal and the generalized patterns.

Pattern Ranking. In Step 4, each pattern $p \in \Phi$ produced instance-based lists of matches, $pos(p)$, $neg(p)$, and $unk(p)$. For scoring the patterns in Φ, we first define the corresponding *type-based* sets:

- $pos^*(p)$ = set of *distinct* names of category $Cat(p)$ from *AcceptName* that p matched.
- $neg^*(p)$ = set of distinct names of a wrong category.
- $unk^*(p)$ = set of distinct NGs of unknown type.

We then define the *accuracy* and *confidence* measures for patterns as:

$$acc^*(p) = \frac{|pos^*|}{|pos^*| + |neg^*|}$$

$$conf^*(p) = \frac{|pos^*|}{|pos^*| + |neg^*| + |unk^*|}$$

---

[19] In the currently implemented simple scheme, the only allowed generalization is a wild-card. It is also possible to generalize $l_{\pm i}$ to the corresponding parts of speech.

Patterns with accuracy below a precision threshold $acc(p) < \theta_{prec}$, are removed from Φ. The remaining patterns are ranked according to the following score:

$$Score(p) = conf^*(p) \cdot \log |pos^*(p)| \qquad (8)$$

(Note the similarity to Eq. 2.) In the first term, higher confidence implies that we take less risk if we acquire the pattern, since acquiring the pattern affects the unknown population. The second term, measures diversity of support for p, favoring patterns which select a greater number of distinct names in $AcceptName$.

Candidate Ranking. To rank the candidate types, in Step 6, for every $t \in \Psi$ we consider the set of patterns in $AcceptPat$ which match on some instance of t. Let's call this set M_t. If $|M_t| < 2$, the candidate is discarded.[20] Otherwise, we compute $Rank(t)$ based on the quality of M_t:

$$Rank(t) = 1 - \prod_{p \in M_t} \left(1 - conf^*(p)\right) \qquad (9)$$

This formula combines evidence similarly to Eq. (5). On one hand, it favors candidates matched by a greater number of patterns; on the other hand, the term $conf^*(p)$ assigns more credit to the more reliable patterns.

3.4   Prior Work

Supervised Methods. Initially NE classification centered on methods using statistical learning from tagged corpora, Bayesian learning, ME, e.g., [38,3,5].

A high-performance supervised algorithm $(LP)^2$, [10], learns surface-based contextual rules separately for the left and the right side of an instance. Separating the two sides allows the learner to accept weaker rules. Several correction phases compensate for errors by removing uncertain items and preventing them from polluting the pool of good seeds.

Unsupervised Methods. The "universal concept spotter", [35], can in principle learn generic noun-phrases as well as proper names—a step toward our notion of generalized names. It uses a bootstrapping algorithm, starting from a few seeds, but does not employ negative or competing evidence.

DL-CoTrain and CoBoost, [11], are algorithms for classifying proper names as Person, Organization or Location, appearing in a few syntactic contexts. Because they use a syntactically analyzed corpus, the patterns can benefit from a wider context, which is hard to get from local surface-level information.

AutoSlog-TS, [30], is designed to learn concepts which fill slots in events, which in principle can include generalized names. The algorithm does not use competing evidence. It uses syntactic heuristics which mark whole noun phrases

---

[20] Note, this means that the algorithm is in principle unlikely to learn a candidate which occurs only once in the corpus. It can happen, if the unique occurrence is flanked by accepted patterns on both sides.

as candidate instances, whereas NOMEN also attempts to learn names that appear as modifiers inside a noun phrase.

Terminology acquisition is a field with a vast literature on supervised as well as unsupervised methods. The goals of terminology identification and classification partially overlap with ours. The topic is covered in B. Daille's and J. Tsujii's contributions in this volume.

3.5   Evaluation

We tested NOMEN on text from the ProMed mailing list, a global forum where medical professionals share information regarding infectious outbreaks and epidemics. In this section, we discuss experiments with a training corpus 26,000 sentences long, or about 1,400 documents (3.2Mb) from January to July 1999.

To measure performance, we constructed three reference lists as follows. First, the *manual list* of infectious diseases was hand-compiled from multiple sources[21], yielding 2,492 names.

Next, the *recall list* is automatically derived from the manual list by searching the training corpus for names that surface more than once[22], yielding 322 names. The *precision list* is constructed from the manual list by automatically generating and adding a list of acronyms, 3,588 items in all. This is done because the manual list might contain, say, "bovine spongiform encephalopathy", but not "BSE".

The manual, recall and precision lists for locations are constructed in the same way. We then judge the recall of NOMEN against the recall list, and precision against the precision list.

The algorithm parameters are set as follows: the number of seeds is 10 per category, including the negative category; the pattern precision threshold $\theta_{prec} = 0.80$; $n = m = 5$ for the top retained patterns and name types.

Ten common names of each target category are used as seeds: cholera, dengue fever, Japanese encephalitis, anthrax, etc., for diseases; location seeds include United States, Australia, Malaysia, China, etc.

We further introduce two additional categories: a category of symptoms, and a *negative-evidence* category for terms that do not belong to any class we are trying to learn.[23] The effect of these is discussed in section 3.6.

NOMEN was trained on the 26,000-sentence corpus, until it stopped learning new names. The curves in Figure 4 show performance on disease and location names. E.g., by the last iteration, about 70% of diseases (from the recall list of 322 items) were learned, at 50% precision—half of the learned names were not on the precision list.

These precision measures, however, are understated: we find that NOMEN is frequently penalized for finding correct answers, because it is not possible to get

---

[21] Using the disease IE database [17], the Gideon disease database, and Web search.

[22] This is justified because the current algorithm is unlikely to discover names that occur only once. It is possible to plot separately how well names are learned if they appear at least once, at least twice, and so on.

[23] We used the 10 most frequently occurring nouns in the corpus as seeds, e.g., case, health, people, year.

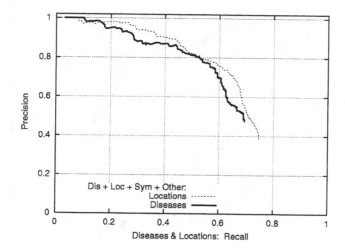

Fig. 4. Diseases and Locations

a full list for measuring precision. To quantify this effect, we manually examined the disease names learned by NOMEN and re-introduced those names that were *incorrectly* marked as errors, into the precision list only.

The updated graph for diseases is shown in Figure 5; at 70% recall the true precision is about 65%. Note, that precision is similarly understated for all type-based curves in this paper. This is a general problem of type-based evaluation.

We should also note that among the re-introduced names there were about 100 names which were missed in the manual compilation of reference lists. This is an encouraging result, since this is ultimately how the algorithm is intended to be used: for discovering new, previously unknown names.

3.6   Competing Categories

Figure 6 demonstrates the usefulness of competition among target categories. All curves show the performance of NOMEN on the *disease* category, when the algorithm is seeded only with diseases (the curve labeled *Dis*), when seeded with diseases and locations (*Dis+Loc*), and with symptoms, and the "other" category. The curves *Dis* and *Dis+Loc* are very similar. However, when more categories are added, precision and recall increase dramatically.

When only one category is being learned, $acc^*(p) = 1.0$ for all patterns p. The lack of an effective accuracy measure causes NOMEN to acquire unselective patterns that often match disease names but often match non-diseases as well (e.g., "... $< X >$ has been confirmed ..."). This hurts precision.

Recall also suffers, because (a) some selective patterns are neglected because they have lower confidence or coverage, and (b) the less selective patterns contaminate the seed set with non-diseases, which in turn generate useless patterns.

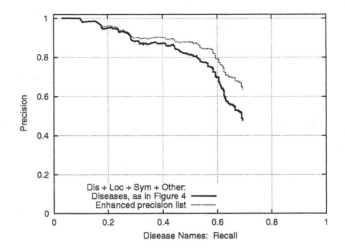

Fig. 5. Effect of Understated Precision

DL-CoTrain, [11], also makes use of competing categories— person, organization, and location; these categories cover 96% of all the name instances they target for classification. In our setting, the sought categories—diseases and locations—do not cover the bulk of potential candidates for generalized names—sequences matching [ADJ* N+]. Introducing a "negative" category helps the algorithm to cover more of the potential candidates, which boosts the utility of the accuracy measure.

3.7   Type- vs. Instance-Based Evaluation

The results in Figures 4–6 are not directly commensurate with those in the literature mentioned in section 3.4 (e.g., [35,11]), because of a difference in evaluation strategies. The difference relates to the *token-type* dichotomy.

Evaluation in the prior work is *instance*-based (or "token-based"), i.e., the learner gets credit or penalty—i.e., gains recall points or loses precision points—for identifying an instance of a name correctly or incorrectly, for every occurrence of the name in the corpus. Usually recall and precision are measured against a small *test* set, in which all instances have been labeled manually.[24]

By contrast, our evaluation is *type*-based. It is intended to measure how many different disease names the algorithm identifies correctly and incorrectly, irrespective of how many times each name appears in the corpus.

To conduct an instance-based evaluation, more compatible with the mentioned prior work, we manually tagged *all* diseases and locations in a 500-sentence test sub-corpus. We then measured recall and precision of the same run as in

---

[24] E.g., in [35], all instances of organizations are labeled for testing in 10 articles. DL-CoTrain, [11], is trained on 89,000 candidate strings targeted for categorization, and tested against 1,000 manually tagged occurrences, with about 90% accuracy.

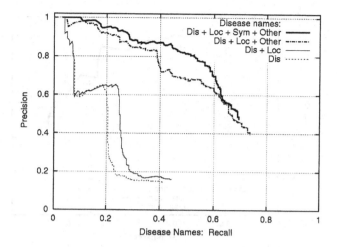

Fig. 6. Effect of Competing Categories: Disease names

Table 3. Evaluation of Disease Recall

Iteration	Type-Based	Instance-Based
0	0.03	0.35
20	0.18	0.68
40	0.31	0.85
60	0.42	0.85
300	0.69	0.86

Figure 4 against this test corpus. The scoring was done according to the standard MUC NE scoring scheme, with results shown in Figure 7.

Another way to contrast type-based and instance-based evaluation is in Table 3, which summarizes recall values across the iterations. The instance-based evaluation can barely distinguish between an algorithm that learns 31% of the types vs. one that learns 69% of the types. The algorithm continues to learn many new, infrequent *types* until iteration 340, but this is not borne out by the instance-based evaluation.

4   A General Framework

The learning algorithms presented in sections 2 and 3 deal with rather different problems. Yet, they are similar in several crucial respects, which we shall summarize in this section.

The general procedure for knowledge acquisition gradually builds up a classifier, composed of a set of *rules*, to identify and/or label a set of *datapoints* in the corpus.

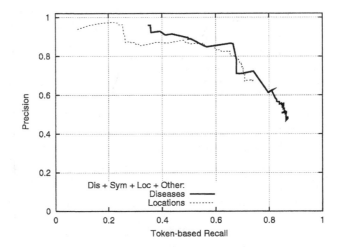

Fig. 7. MUC-style scoring: Instance-based

In the case of ExDisco the datapoints are documents, and among them we seek those which relate to a given query, e.g., management succession. In the case of Nomen, the datapoints are nouns or noun phrases (i.e., the name types), e.g., names of infectious diseases.

The objective is to find a set of rules that partitions a set of potential candidate datapoints into those belonging to the class of interest vs. the rest; let's call these "relevant" vs. "non-relevant."

By a *rule* we mean a contextual pattern which can identify and classify datapoints. A rule may be a pattern appearing in text, or it may be the immediate context of a lexical item.

We focus on situations where the following principle is satisfied:

Principle of Duality:

I. In the corpus, more than one rule applies to (or can be used to identify) each datapoint, and more than one datapoint is identified by each rule;
II. moreover, "good" rules indicate relevant datapoints, and relevant datapoints indicate good rules.

In such situations we apply the following bootstrapping procedure to grow two sets simultaneously—the set of good rules and the set of relevant datapoints:

0. **Pre-process** a large un-annotated natural language corpus; use pre-existing NLP tools to automatically annotate the text, in order to factor out features that are irrelevant for the discovery of the rules and datapoints.
1. **Seed** selection: the user chooses an *accepted* set of characteristic rules or datapoints of the target class.
2. **Partition**: split the set of potential datapoints into the relevant vs. the non-relevant subsets. In case where the seeds are datapoints, the relevant set is

simply the seed set. In case when the seeds are rules, we tag all datapoints matched by the rules as relevant, and that induces the partition.

3. **Rank rules**: search for best candidate rules. We choose those rules that are much more likely to co-occur with the relevant datapoints. We select the top-ranking rule(s) and add it to the set of accepted rules.

4. **Re-calculate relevance of datapoints**: compute accuracy measures for each pattern. Rank datapoints based on the combined quality of the set of patterns which match them. Choose the best datapoint(s) and induct them into the set of accepted datapoints.

5. **Repeat** from Step 2, until a stopping criterion is satisfied.

Notes: The general statement makes no reference to the specific type of knowledge we are trying to acquire. However, the actual algorithms which embody this general methodology will make heavy reference to the specific nature of the rules and datapoints.

The nature of the rules and datapoints will dictate, for example, what kind of pre-processing is suitable prior to learning. It is crucial to factor out irrelevant features, to maximally leverage the mutual redundancy between rules and datapoints.

In this abstract form, the process may result in an expansive search, i.e., the quality of the rules and datapoints may quickly degrade due to contamination from bad examples. It is crucial that the expansion be carefully controlled.

One mechanism for control is the assignment of *graded relevance* to datapoints, as demonstrated in EXDISCO. Inducting datapoints into an "accepted" set is equivalent to assigning a binary relevance judgement to the datapoints. (That is actually what happens in the version of NOMEN presented here.)

Rather than labeling datapoints with a binary judgement, EXDISCO maintains a cautious internal confidence measure for each datapoint, and reserves judgement until an appropriate time—e.g., once the confidence has surpassed an acceptable threshold.

The confidence of a datapoint mutually depends on characteristics of the rules which match the datapoint: their accuracy, their generality, and their total number.

Thus, a natural extension to NOMEN is moving from assignment of binary labels to datapoints, toward assignment of graded relevance, as in EXDISCO.

Relation to Co-Training. Acquiring knowledge simultaneously on more than one level has been investigated previously. The main innovation in such approaches is that the acquisition of knowledge on one level serves to inform the acquisition on the other levels.

We should note that the type of mutual learning described in this paper is somewhat different from the co-training framework, as presented, e.g., in [4,25]. In co-training, learning centers on:

a. acquiring a set of datapoints; e.g., segments of text containing names, [11], or web pages relevant to a query [4], and

b. *disjoint views* with *redundantly sufficient* features; here these features are exemplified by internal and external contextual cues.

A key idea in co-training is that the algorithm simultaneously trains, or refines, two or more independent recognizers, rather than one. Each recognizer utilizes only one of the views on the datapoints. The recognizers can start out weak, but, as a result of learning, will strengthen each other, by labeling a growing number of datapoints based on the independent sets of evidence that they provide to each other.

In the framework we have outlined, each algorithm trains a *single* recognizer for the dataset: the recognizer is the growing set of rules, and the dataset is the pool of datapoints. Rather than assigning relevance labels to the datapoints, however, the algorithm assigns a measure of its *confidence* in its classification of the datapoint.

4.1   Further Work

The expressive power of the patterns is somewhat limited, in both algorithms.

In EXDISCO, the use of generalized *S-V-O* triples may be too restrictive. In some scenarios events may be more naturally expressed inside a nominalized clause or a noun phrase: e.g., "The number of Ebola-related *deaths* reached 10..."

In NOMEN, using a small window of tokens surrounding a tag limits the amount of contextual information available to the learner.

We expect that using richer syntactic/contextual patterns will help performance.

In EXDISCO, along with a set of scenario-specific patterns, the algorithm yields a rich set of concept classes, i.e., sets of terms that are semantically and functionally related in the given scenario. These concept classes, discovered as a by-product of pattern learning, can be utilized for generalizing other patterns discovered on previous or subsequent iterations. Preliminary experiments are yielding promising results.

5   Conclusion

This chapter presented a procedure for unsupervised acquisition of domain-specific semantic knowledge. We examined in detail two instances of the procedure: acquisition of semantic patterns, and of large open classes of names or domain-specific terms. These types of knowledge are essential for Information Extraction.

We also discussed the respective merits of different evaluation strategies for these methods. As the accuracy of these methods improves, they are likely to prove increasingly useful in the process of building systems for IE, as well as for other NLP tasks.

Acknowledgements. Kind thanks to Winston Lin for performing the experiments with NOMEN, and to Silja Huttunen and Ralph Grishman for their assistance.

This research is supported by the Defense Advanced Research Projects Agency as part of the Translingual Information Detection, Extraction and Summarization (TIDES) program, under Grant N66001-001-1-8917 from the Space and Naval Warfare Systems Center San Diego, and by the National Science Foundation under Grant IIS-0081962. This paper does not necessarily reflect the position or the policy of the U.S. Government.

References

[1] E. Agichtein and L. Gravano. 2000. Snowball: Extracting relations from large plain-text collections. In *Proc. 5th ACM Intl. Conf. Digital Libraries (DL'00)*.

[2] D. Appelt, J. Hobbs, J. Bear, D. Israel, M. Kameyama, and M. Tyson. 1993. SRI: Description of the JV-FASTUS System used for MUC-5. In *Proc. 5th Message Understanding Conf. (MUC-5)*, Baltimore, MD. Morgan Kaufmann.

[3] D. Bikel, S. Miller, R. Schwartz, and R. Weischedel. 1997. Nymble: a high-performance learning name-finder. In *Proc. 5th Applied Natural Language Processing Conf.*, Washington, DC.

[4] A. Blum and T. Mitchell. 1998. Combining labeled and unlabeled data with co-training. In *Proc. 11th Annl. Conf Computational Learning Theory (COLT-98)*, New York. ACM Press.

[5] A. Borthwick, J. Sterling, E. Agichtein, and R. Grishman. 1998. Exploiting diverse knowledge sources via maximum entropy in named entity recognition. In *Proc. 6th Workshop on Very Large Corpora*, Montreal, Canada.

[6] S. Brin. 1998. Extracting patterns and relations from the world wide web. In *WebDB Workshop at 6th Intl. Conf. Extending Database Technology, EDBT'98*.

[7] M. E. Califf and R. J. Mooney. 1998. Relational learning of pattern-match rules for information extraction. In *Working Notes of AAAI Spring Symposium on Applying Machine Learning to Discourse Processing*, Menlo Park, CA. AAAI Press.

[8] M. E. Califf. 1998. *Relational Learning Techniques for Natural Language Information Extraction*. Ph.D. thesis, Department of Computer Sciences, University of Texas, Austin, TX.

[9] C. Cardie and D. Pierce. 1998. Proposal for an interactive environment for information extraction. Technical Report TR98-1702, Cornell University.

[10] F. Ciravegna. 2001. Adaptive information extraction from text by rule induction and generalisation. In *Proc. 17th Intl. Joint Conf. on AI (IJCAI 2001)*, Seattle, WA.

[11] M. Collins and Y. Singer. 1999. Unsupervised models for named entity classification. In *Proc. Joint SIGDAT Conf. on EMNLP/VLC*, College Park, MD.

[12] I. Dagan, S. Marcus, and S. Markovitch. 1993. Contextual word similarity and estimation from sparse data. In *Proceedings of the 31st Annual Meeting of the Assn. for Computational Linguistics*, pages 31–37, Columbus, OH.

[13] D. Fisher, S. Soderland, J. McCarthy, F. Feng, and W. Lehnert. 1995. Description of the UMass system as used for MUC-6. In *Proc. 6th Message Understanding Conf. (MUC-6)*, Columbia, MD. Morgan Kaufmann.

[14] K. Frantzi, S. Ananiadou, and H. Mima. 2000. Automatic recognition of multi-word terms: the C-value/NC-value method. *Intl. Journal on Digital Libraries*, 2000(3):115–130.

[15] D. Freitag and A. McCallum. 1999. Information extraction with HMMs and shrinkage. In *Proceedings of Workshop on Machine Learning and Information Extraction (AAAI-99)*, Orlando, FL.

[16] R. Grishman, C. Macleod, and A. Meyers. 1994. Comlex Syntax: Building a computational lexicon. In *Proc. 15th Int'l Conf. Computational Linguistics (COLING 94)*, Kyoto, Japan.

[17] R. Grishman, S. Huttunen, and R. Yangarber. 2002. Event extraction for infectious disease outbreaks. In *Proc. 2nd Human Language Technology Conf. (HLT 2002)*, San Diego, CA.

[18] R. Grishman. 1995. The NYU system for MUC-6, or where's the syntax? In *Proc. 6th Message Understanding Conf. (MUC-6)*, Columbia, MD. Morgan Kaufmann.

[19] R. Grishman. 1997. Information extraction: Techniques and challenges. In M.T. Pazienza, editor, *Information Extraction*. Springer-Verlag, LNAI.

[20] L. Hirschman, R. Grishman, and N. Sager. 1975. Grammatically-based automatic word class formation. *Information Processing and Management*, 11(1/2):39–57.

[21] J.S. Justeson and S.M. Katz. 1995. Technical terminology: Some linguistic properties and an algorithm for identification in text. *Natural Language Engineering*, 1(1):9–27.

[22] W. Lehnert, C. Cardie, D. Fisher, J. McCarthy, E. Riloff, and S. Soderland. 1992. University of Massachusetts: MUC-4 test results and analysis. In *Proc. Fourth Message Understanding Conf.*, McLean, VA. Morgan Kaufmann.

[23] S. Miller, M. Crystal, H. Fox, L. Ramshaw, R. Schwartz, R. Stone, R. Weischedel, and the Annotation Group. 1998. Algorithms that learn to extract information; BBN: Description of the SIFT system as used for MUC-7. In *Proceedings of the Seventh Message Understanding Conference (MUC-7)*, Fairfax, VA.

[24] G.A. Miller. 1995. Wordnet: a lexical database for English. *Communications of the ACM*, 38(11):39–41.

[25] T. Mitchell. 1999. The role of unlabeled data in supervised learning. In *Proceedings of the Sixth International Colloquium on Cognitive Science*, San Sebastian, Spain.

[26] 1995. *Proceedings of the 6th Message Understanding Conference (MUC-6)*, Columbia, MD. Morgan Kaufmann.

[27] 1998. *Proceedings of the 7th Message Understanding Conference (MUC-7)*, Fairfax, VA. www.itl.nist.gov/iaui/894.02/related_projects/muc/.

[28] J. Nichols. 1978. Secondary predicates. *Proceedings of the 4th Annual Meeting of Berkeley Linguistics Society*.

[29] F. Pereira, N. Tishby, and L. Lee. 1993. Distributional clustering of English words. In *Proceedings of ACL-93*, Columbus, OH.

[30] E. Riloff and R. Jones. 1999. Learning dictionaries for information extraction by multi-level bootstrapping. In *Proc. 16th Natl. Conf. on AI (AAAI-99)*, Orlando, FL.

[31] E. Riloff. 1993. Automatically constructing a dictionary for information extraction tasks. In *Proc. 11th Annl. Conf. Artificial Intelligence*. The AAAI Press/MIT Press.

[32] E. Riloff. 1996. Automatically generating extraction patterns from untagged text. In *Proc. 13th Natl. Conf. on AI (AAAI-96)*. The AAAI Press/MIT Press.

[33] Y. Sasaki. 1999. Applying type-oriented ILP to IE rule generation. In *Proc. Workshop on Machine Learning and Information Extraction (AAAI-99)*, Orlando, FL.

[34] S. Soderland. 1999. Learning information extraction rules for semi-structured and free text. *Machine Learning*, 44(1-3):233–272.

[35] T. Strzalkowski and J. Wang. 1996. A self-learning universal concept spotter. In *Proc. 16th Intl. Conf. Computational Linguistics (COLING-96)*, Copenhagen, Denmark.

[36] P. Tapanainen and T. Järvinen. 1997. A non-projective dependency parser. In *Proc. 5th Conf. Applied Natural Language Processing*, Washington, D.C. ACL.

[37] C.A. Thompson, M.E. Califf, and R.J. Mooney. 1999. Active learning for natural language parsing and information extraction. In *Proc. 16th International Conf. on Machine Learning*. Morgan Kaufmann, San Francisco, CA.

[38] T. Wakao, R. Gaizauskas, and Y. Wilks. 1996. Evaluation of an algorithm for the recognition and classification of proper names. In *Proc. 16th Int'l Conf. on Computational Linguistics (COLING 96)*, Copenhagen, Denmark.

[39] R. Yangarber and R. Grishman. 1997. Customization of information extraction systems. In Paola Velardi, editor, *International Workshop on Lexically Driven Information Extraction*, Frascati, Italy. Università di Roma.

[40] R. Yangarber and R. Grishman. 1998. NYU: Description of the Proteus/PET system as used for MUC-7 ST. In *MUC-7: 7th Message Understanding Conf.*, Columbia, MD.

[41] R. Yangarber, R. Grishman, P. Tapanainen, and S. Huttunen. 2000a. Unsupervised discovery of scenario-level patterns for information extraction. In *Proc. Conf. Applied Natural Language Processing (ANLP-NAACL'00)*, Seattle, WA.

[42] R. Yangarber, R. Grishman, P. Tapanainen, and S. Huttunen. 2000b. Automatic acquisition of domain knowledge for information extraction. In *Proc. 18th Intl. Conf. Computational Linguistics (COLING 2000)*, Saarbrücken, Germany.

[43] R. Yangarber, W. Lin, and R. Grishman. 2002. Unsupervised learning of generalized names. In *Proc. 19th Intl. Conf. Computational Linguistics (COLING 2002)*, Taiwan.

[44] R. Yangarber. 2000. *Scenario Customization for Information Extraction*. Ph.D. thesis, New York University, New York, NY.

Appendix

This section contains a sample of ExDisco's output for several scenarios. Seed patterns are marked with †. Concept classes used in the seeds are given below.

Mergers and Acquisitions. Patterns are shown in table 4. The seed uses the class *V-Buy* = { buy, purchase }. *C-Company* means a NE of type company.

Corporate Lawsuits. Patterns in table 1. The class *V-Sue* = { sue, litigate }.

Natural Disasters. Classes used in patterns:

- *C-Disaster* = { earthquake, tornado, flood, hurricane, landslide, snowstorm, avalanche },
- *V-Damage* = { hit, destroy, ravage, damage },
- *C-Urban* = { street, bridge, house, home }.

Table 4. Patterns for "Mergers and Acquisitions"

†   *–V-Buy–C-Company
†   C-Company–merge–*

*–complete–purchase
company–express–interest
company–seek–partner
company–acquire–{business,company,stake,interest}
company–{acquire,have,own,take[over],pay,drop,sell}–company
company–{have,value,acquire}–asset
{company,unit,bank}–have–asset
*–expect–transaction
acquisition–be–step
company–own–{company,station,stake,store,business}
company–{hold,buy,own,raise,pay,acquire,sell,boost,take,swap,retain}–stake
company–hold–{stake,percent,talk,interest,share,position}
company–buy–{stake,share}
company–have–{sale,asset,earning,revenue}
company–{issue,have,repurchase,own,sell,buy,hold}–share
company–{report,have,post,expect,record}–loss
company–report–{loss,earning,income,profit,increase,sale}
company–{become,hire,sell,control,invest,compete,make}–company

Table 5. Patterns for "Lawsuits" and "Natural Disasters"

Lawsuit patterns	*Natural Disaster patterns*
† *–V-Sue–C-Organization	C-Disaster–cause–*
† *–bring–suit	C-Disaster–V-damage–C-Urban
person–hear–case	quake–measured–[number]
plaintiff–seek–damage	quake–was–felt
group–charge–[that ...]	earthquake–shook–area
*–face–suit	earthquake–was–centered
company–appeal–	quake–struck–
person–marshal–argument	quake–was–considered
they–recoup–loss	quake–occurred–
they–alert–regulator	{quake,storm}–knocked[out]–power
company–abet–violation	damage–was–reported
lawsuit–allege–[that ...]	aftershock–injured–
suit–seek–[that ...]	aftershock–killed–people
assets–be–frozen	quake–registered–
{person,organization}–file–suit	it–caused–damage
{person,court}–reject–argument	quake–{killed,injured}–people
{person,court}–rule–[that ...]	
company–deny–{allegation,charge, wrongdoing}	
company–settle–charge	

Terminology Mining

Béatrice Daille

IRIN – Université de Nantes, 2, rue la Houssinière, BP 92208,
F-44322 Nantes Cedex 3, FRANCE
daille@irin.unvi-nantes.fr,
http://www.sciences.univ-nantes.fr/irin

Abstract. Terminology mining is a major step forward in terminology extraction and covers acquisition and structuring of the candidate terms. We presents a terminology mining method based on linguistic criteria and combined computational methods. In terminology mining, references are made to the acquisition of complex terms, the discovering of new terms, but also, the structuring of the acquired candidate terms. First, the linguistic specifications of terms are given for French and we define a typology of base-terms and their variations. We stress the crucial part of the handling of term variations to build a linguistic structuring, to detect advanced lexicalisation and to obtain an optimised representativity of the candidate term occurrences. Second, we move to the computational methods implemented: shallow parsing, morphological analysis, morphological rule learning and lexical statistics. Third, the system that identifies base terms and their variations, ACABIT (Automatic Corpus-Based Acquisition of Binary Terms) is introduced: its architecture, the languages it applies on and its functions. To conclude, a review of evaluation methods for terminology extraction is presented and results of the efficiency of ACABIT in evaluation campaigns are discussed.

1 Introduction

Terminology mining is a major step forward in terminology extraction. New insights show that the automatic identification of terminological units in a text must be improved regardless of the application: candidate terms need to be ranked, structured and filtered.

The terminology mining method presented in this paper is based on linguistic criteria: lexicality and lexicalisation rather than the unithood criteria [33]. The criteria of unithood which refers to the degree of strength or stability of syntagmatic combinaisons such as compound words is not pertinent enough for Romance languages such as French for which terms are liable to variation. We prefer to adopt lexicality, criteria of the linguistic well-formedness of complex terms and their variations expressed in terms of syntactic structures. The criteria of termhood which refers to the degree that a linguistic unit is related to a domain specific concept is not easily measured (contrary to unithood). Termhood can be estimated in a number of ways; by statistical scores [12], by classification

M.T. Pazienza (Ed.): SCIE 2002, LNAI 2700, pp. 29–44, 2003.

methods [11], etc. We estimate termhood both through linguistic clues reflecting lexicalisation, i.e. the stability of a complex term as denomination, and through statistical scores.

The computation methods used for terminology mining depend on the data to be processed: raw texts or texts enhanced with linguistic annotations, and the use or not of pre-existing knowledge sources [39]. Our approach uses an hybrid linguistic/statistical methodology which is applied on texts that have been segmented and annotated for part of speech and lemma. The ACABIT system which implements this approach is much more than a simple term extraction system: it detects new terms and structures the candidate terms thanks to their variations and could thus be considered as a first prototype to a new generation of terminology processing systems.

The plan of the article is as follows: First, we present the linguistic criteria used for terminology mining: lexicality, the well-formed syntactic structures of base terms and their variations, and lexicalisation, the automatic identification of linguistic clues denoting a naming character though term variations. Second, the computational methods are exposed: shallow parsing, morphological analysis, morphological rule learning, and lexical statistics. Third, the functionalities of the system ACABIT are given and evaluated through different experimentations.

2   Linguistic Specifications of Complex Terms

Complex terms are usually associated with the linguistic category of noun compounds. By examining the linguistic literature on compounding, it appears that there are as many definitions as linguistic schools. For example, [14] keeps the term "compound" for linguistic units linked through morphological rules such as *porte-avion (aircraft carrier)* while [26] refer to a complex sequence syntactically built, but which does not accept all the possible syntactic transformations of such sequence.

If there is no consensus on what is compounding, there is one on the syntactic structures of the potentially lexicalisable complex sequences which I shall call "base-terms". These syntactic structures or patterns are:

Noun1 Adj *emballage biodégradable (biodegradable package)*
Noun1 Noun2 *ions calcium (calcium ion)*
Noun1 Prep Noun2 *protéine de poissons (fish protein)*
Noun1 Prep Det Noun2 *chimioprophylaxie au rifampine (rifampicin chemo-prophylaxis)*
Noun1 à Vinf *viandes à griller (grill meat)*

The choice to concentrate on these structures, and not to take into account longer ones, is both linguistically and quantitatively motivated. From the linguistic point of view, the limitation on the length and the syntactic complexity of the sequence is a lexicalisation factor [13], on the other hand, as new terms are created from existing terms [27], it is possible to define linguistic operations that lead to longer terms [18]. From the quantitative point of view, these base-term structures are the most frequent ones both in texts and in terminological databases. For example, [51] indicates that the EDF thesaurus contains 25,1 % of the Noun Adjective structure, followed by the Noun1 Prep Noun2 structure (24,4 %). Only one structure of length 3 represents more than 2 %: the Noun1 Prep Noun2 Adjective structure (2,8 %).

These base structures are not frozen structures and accept variations. Terminology variation in texts is now a well-known phenomenon estimated from 15 % to 35 %, depending of the domain reflecting by the texts and the different kinds of variants handled. For acquisition, only term variants which can preserve the base-term semantics and thus refer to the same concept are taken into account. Two sequences such as *histamine présente dans le vin (histamine which is present in wine)* et *histamine du vin (histamine of the wine)* refer to the same term *histamine du vin (wine histamine)*; but, the sequences *produit à surgeler (product to be frozen)* and *produit surgelé (frozen product)* refer to two different terms.

We present now a typology of term variations for French:

Graphical case differences and presence of a optional hyphen inside the Noun1 Noun2 structure.

Inflexional orthographic variants gathering together inflexional variants that are predictable such as *conservations de produit (product preservations)* or unpredictable such as *conservation de produits (products preservation)*.

Shallow Syntactic. The shallow syntactic variations modify the function words of the base-terms. There are three kinds of internal syntactic variations:

is-1 variations of the preposition: *chromatographie en colonne (column chromatography)* ↔ *chromatographie sur colonne (chromatography on column)*;

is-2 optional character of the preposition and of the article: *fixation azote (nitrogen fixation)* ← *fixation d'azote (fixation of nitrogen)* → *fixation de l'azote (fixation of the nitrogen)*;

is-3 predicative variants: the predicative role of the adjective: *pectine méthylée (methylate pectin)* → *ces pectines sont méthylées (these pectins are metylated)*.

Syntactic. The shallow syntactic variations modify the internal structure of the base-terms:

S-1 Internal modification variants: insertion inside the base-term structure of
  − a modifier such as the adjective inside the Noun1 Prep Noun2 structure: *lait de brebis (goat's milk), lait cru de brebis (milk straight from the goat)*;
  − a nominal specifier inside the Noun Adj. These specifiers belongs to a closed list of nouns, so-called "pivot nouns" by [40], such as *type, origine, couleur (colour): protéine végétale (vegetable protein)* → *protéine d'origine végétale (protein of vegetable origin)*.

S-2 Coordinational variants: head or expansion coordination of base term structures and enumeration:
analyse de particules (particule analysis) → *analyse et le tri de particules (particle sort and analysis)*
alimentation humaine (human feeding) → *alimentation animale et humaine (human and animal feeding)*.

Morphosyntactic. The Morphosyntactic variations modify the internal structure of the base-terms and its components are liable to morphological modification (including derivation).

M-1 Morphology : the preposition inside a candidate term of Noun1 Prep Noun2 structure is equivalent to a prefix applying on Noun2: *pourrissement après récolte (rot after harvest)* ↔ *pourrissement post-récolte (post-harvesting rot)*;

M-2 Derivational morphology: a derivational variation that keeps the synonymy of the base term implies a relational adjective: *acidité du sang (acidity of the blood)* ↔ *acidité sanguine (blood acidity)*. This morphosyntactic variation could be associated with a syntactic variation: the sequence *alimentation destinée à l'homme et à l'animal (feeding destinated to man and to animal)* is a variation of *alimentation animale (animal feeding)*.

Paradigmatic. Paradigmatic variations rely on the substitution principle of distributional linguistics [29]. One or two words of the base term could be substituted by one of their synonyms without modifying the syntactic structure. These synonyms cannot be derived morphologically from the words of the base terms. These simple such as *épuisement du combustible (fuel expended)* ↔ *appauvrissement du combustible (fuel depletion)* or double such as *liaison d'alimentation* ↔ *ligne de distribution* substitutions have been studied by [28].

Anaphorical. Anaphorical variations make reference to a previous occurrence in the text of the base term:

D-1 elliptical anaphora refer to the head noun of the base term as a referential string, thus the noun *processus* could refer to the base term *processus enzymatique (enzymatic processus)* if the latter has been previously used. Other variations concern sequences analysed as base terms which refer to more complex terms: thus, *un procédé alimentaire (food process)* could refer to *un procédé de conservation alimentaire (food preservation process)* or to *un procédé de fermentation alimentaire (food fermentation process.*

D-2 acronyms: *synthèse organique (organic synthesis)* ↔ *SO* for which [42] proposes an algorithm to recognise the acronyms and their associated forms.

From a corpus of 430 000 tokens in the domain of agriculture, the following percentages of the different types of variations are observed:

Candidate terms	Syntactic variation			Morphological variation
	Coor + Modif	Coor	Modif	
11 246	61 (0,5 %)	458 (4 %)	1651 (14,7 %)	234 (2 %)
		19,2 %		2 %

Variation/New term? All the retained variations are those which could preserve synonymy with the base term. They can, of course, induce semantic discrepancies and can refer either to two base terms or to a base term and a "overcomposed term" [18]. Thus, two different prepositions lead to two base terms: *transmission par satellite (satellite transmission)* ≠ *transmission entre satellites (transmission between satellites)* and internal modification refers to a overcomposed term (S-1a): *huile essentielle de sapin (fir essence)* is an hyponym of *huile essentielle (essence)* and not a variation of *huile de sapin (fir oil)*. This problem comes within the terminology structuring and could be partly solved through linguistic clues:

1. if the morphological variation of *transmission entre satellites (transmission between satellites)* (*i.e. transmission inter-satellites*) has been encountered, then it could be deduced that *transmission par satellite (satellite transmission)* and *transmission entre satellites (transmission between satellites)* are two different terms;
2. if it is a relational adjective that modifies the base term, then a overcomposition by modification is encountered and not a variation by modification: with *huile essentielle de sapin (fir essence)*, *essentielle (essence)* is a relational adjective derived from the noun *essence*.

Simple Variation/Naming Variation. The naming property has been defined by [37] as a property to link an object to a linguistic sign within a stable referential association. Only the noun or the compound noun hold this naming property. The base term sequences are by nature potential candidate for lexicalisation; *i.e.* they hold a potential naming property. The morphological variation implies for the derived form of Noun Adj structure a more important naming potential than for the synonym form in Noun1 Prep Noun2 [15].

3   Automatic Discovery of Complex Terms

3.1   Partial Parsing

Partial analysis recognises non-recursive kernels of the sentence phrases ('chunks') and recovers surface syntactic information [1,2]. It is efficient compared to traditional parsers on unrestricted text and can be easily implemented with regular expressions integrated in a number of programming languages (Flex, Perl, JavaCC) or with finite state automatons. The grammar of a partial analysis includes two types of rules that apply on a tagged corpus annotated for part of speech and lemma:

1. **Chunk Patterns.** Chunks are expressed thanks to regular expressions constituted of part of speech categories and lexical forms (full forms or lemma). When at least one element of the expression belongs to a closed list of words, the term lexico-syntactic patterns is used. Chunk patterns precise explicitly the shape of the linguistic string searched for.
2. **Chink Patterns.** Chink refers to words that do not belong to the linguistic string searched for and identifies phrase boundaries. For example, one of the natural chink of a nominal phrase is a verb in an inflected tense. Chink patterns describe the chunk implicitly.

Chunk or Chink? Chunk and chink patterns are expressive enough to allow to describe the patterns of the base terms and their variations. Between chunk and chink patterns which one is the best? [36] claims that chinks patterns are more efficient than chunk to delimit sentence phrases. For candidate term extraction, the two methods seem equivalent from the point of view of the precision of the linguistic analysis. LEXTER [7] evaluates the precision of its chinks to delimit French nominal phrase to 95 %, NPTool [54] for English nominal phrases to 95 %, in [53] we evaluated the precision of our chunk patterns for term and variant recognition for French to 96 %.

Learning Approach/Linguistic Specification before Collecting. A unsupervised learning method has been used by [7] to recognise the term's chinks: only a productive head noun, *i.e.* which accepts several prepositional arguments built with the same preposition, is part of a complex term. In a first step, the program scans the text and collects all the noun occurrences followed by a preposition. In a second step, the cut-out is done only if a non productive noun has been encountered. This productivity does not reflect the term's lexicalisation, but rather the predicative character of the head noun. This opinion seems to be confirmed by [8] who applies this method on verbs to identify prepositional arguments. [46,5] learn nominal phrase patterns from already identified nominal phrase in corpora. They obtain several structures expressed in part-of-speech categories for English noun phrases. These unsupervised learning methods based on positive examples are not very relevant for learning term patterns which are well known and listed for many languages. They are more interesting to isolate lexico-syntactic patterns which denote a semantic relation [41].

3.2   Morphological Analysis

The morphological analysis uses general rules which allow the recovery of the morphological link from a derived form to another form. We present the schemata of the rules and a first experiment to learn them.

Morphological Rules. Derivational morphological analysis applies on a word a morphological rule extracted usually from a lexical database. In CELEX [10], derivational information is provided for each lemma through its morphological structure: for example, the morphological structure of *celebration* is *((celebrate [V]), (ion)([N\ V.])[N])*. This structure indicates that *celebration* is a noun built from the verb *celebrate* by suffixation using *ion*. But, if we need to calculate the verb *celebrate* from *celebration*, it is necessary to calculate the adding of the mutative suffix *-e* to the verb once the suffix *-ion* has been stripped [19]. Such databases are not available for French. To calculate the derivation, we define the following rule schemata:

$$A \rightarrow N : -S + M$$

where:

S is the relational suffix to be deleted from the end of an adjective. The result of this deletion is the stem **R**;
M is the mutative segment to be concatenated to **R** in order to form a noun.

For example, the rule [*-é +e*] says that if there is an adjective which ends with *é*, we should strip this ending from it and append the string *e* to the stem.

Morphological Rule Induction. Contrary to the learning of part of speech patterns of complex terms, the learning of morphological rules is crucial for French: only a few general derivation rules exist and they are not reproducible. Some experiments have been done to acquire derivational rules: for English [24, 25] respectively from dictionary and from corpora, for French [56] from a thesaurus. For information retrieval, [30] builds derivational families by segmenting words into stems and suffixes which occur together in two or more windows of length 5 or less. His hypothesis that two words share a common stem relies on the existence of identical context. Thus, *gene* and *genetic* have the common stem *gene*, *expression* and *expressed* have the common stem *express* if they appear in the following sequences: *genetic ... expression* et *gene ... expressed* . For French, we experiment a supervised learning method for morphological rules from corpora with making any context constraints. The goal was to obtain new morphological rules to rebuild from the relational adjective the base noun. We took as hypothesis that if the adjective ends by a relation suffix, it was possible to find in corpora its base noun and to induce a rebuilding rule. We used the Levenshtein's weighted distance [38] to find a common stem between a noun and a stripped adjective allowing alternants such as:

e/é *alphabet/aphabét-ique*
è/é *hygiène/hygién-ique*
e/i *pollen/pollin-ique*
x/c *thorax / thorac-ique*

[55] presents a recursive algorithm to calculate this distance.

$$dist(w_{1,i}, w'_{1,j}) =$$
$$\min(dist(w_{1,i-1}, w'_{1,j}) + q,$$
$$dist(w_{1,i}, w'_{1,j-1}) + q),$$
$$dist(w_{1,i-1}, w'_{1,j-1}) + p * dist(w_{i,i}, w'_{j,j}))$$

with $w_{n,m}$ being the substring beginning at the nth character and finishing after the mth character of the word w,

$$dist(x, y) = 1 \quad if \ x = y$$
$$= 0 \quad if \ x \neq y$$

and

q cost of the insertion/deletion of one character
p cost of the substitution of one character by another.

Generally, a substitution is considered as a deletion followed by an insertion, thus p = 2q. This learning method [16] is not satisfactory: if we restrict the Levenshtein's weighted distance to one substitution and one insertion, we obtain reliable rule such as [-*cique* +*x*] but we do not discover rules such as [-*ulaire*, +*le*] (*musculaire/muscle*)involving two substitutions. If we admit two substitutions, we get too much noise and the results are tedious to check.

3.3   Lexical Statistics

The 2x2 contingency tables are used in statistics to test the strength of the bond between two qualitative variables [23]. They can also be used to measure the association between two lexical forms in a set C of contexts. Each pair of lexical forms is associated to a contingency table:

	F_j	$F_{j'}$ with $j' \neq j$
F_i	a	b
$F_{i'}$ with $i' \neq i$	c	d

The values a, b, c et d resume the pair's occurrences:

a = the number of occurrences in C of the pair (F_i, F_j),
b = the number of occurrences in C of the pairs $(F_i, F_{j'})$ $F_{j'} \neq F_j$,
c = the number of occurrences in C of the pairs $(F_{i'}, F_j)$ $F_{i'} \neq F_i$,
d = the number of occurrences in C of the pairs $(F_{i'}, F_{j'})$ $F_{i'} \neq F_i$ et $F_{j'} \neq F_j$

The sum $a + b + c + d$, as N, is the total number of occurrences of all the pairs in C. The statistical literature proposes many scores which can be used to test the strength of the bond between the two variables of a contingency table, such as the association ratio, close to the concept of mutual information introduced by [12]:

$$IM = \log_2 \frac{a}{(a+b)(a+c)} \tag{1}$$

or the Loglike coefficient introduced by [21]:

$$Loglike = a \log a + b \log b + c \log c + d \log d - (a+b) \log(a+b)$$
$$-(a+c) \log(a+c) - (b+d) \log(b+d) \tag{2}$$
$$-(c+d) \log(c+d) + N \log N$$

The set C is composed of the set of textual sequences isolated by patterns for base terms and their variations. In order to improve the representativity of a pair, we build the contingency tables on lemmas. More exactly, we generalise to a set of lemmas when the candidate term accepted morphological or morpho-syntactical variations. This generalisation is legitimated by the hypothesis that there is an equiprobability of the appearances and preservation of synonymy. In [17], several statistical scores were evaluated and the Loglike coefficient was found to be one of the best to rank the more likely pairs of lemmas to be terms. The evaluation procedure is detailed in section ....

Which Order of Application for the Different Modules in the Mixed Approach? What should be applied first: linguistic filtering or lexical statistics? This question was debated in the CL community a few years ago. In their first experiment, [12] used the association ratio, close to mutual information (cf. formula 1) to identify associations between words on raw texts. They never throw back into question the fact that such associations are remarkable even if some of them are hardly interpretable. For their following experiments, such as identifying phrasal verbs, they first filter the linguistic sequences before applying the association ratio. Only [50] for the retrieval and identification of collocations[1] first uses the z-score [6] and never addresses the question as to whether its retained sequences are collocations even if its human expert disagrees. The common point between the first experiment of [12] and [50] lies in the linguistic vagueness of the searched elements which can not be precisely described. When a linguistic description is possible, it should be done before the statistical filtering so that all searched patterns are taken into account without frequency discrimination.

4 ACABIT: Direct Application and Evaluation

ACABIT is a term extractor which takes into account the linguistic specifications defined in section 2 and implements the computational method presented in section 3. It takes as input a tagged corpus with parts of speech and lemma which has been structured with XML tags to identify the main parts of the text: title, abstract and sentences.

ACABIT is used for two kinds of application:

Terminology Mining. Terminology mining refers to several functionalities of the programme:

1. To propose a list of candidate terms ranked from the most representative of the corpus to the least. This list could be used to build specialised dictionaries on a new domain;
2. To propose a list of candidate terms for which a morphological variation has been encountered and thus reflect a more advance lexicalisation. This list could be added to update an existing referential;

---

[1] [50] defined collocation as a sequence of adjacent words that frequently appear together.

3. To propose a list of candidate terms which are liable to variations in order to capture the dynamics of terms in a synchronic [32] or a diachronic [52] paradigm.

Automatic Indexing. Automatic Indexing is a subtask of information retrieval which assigns an indexing language to texts [47]. This indexing language consists of a set of descriptors which must reflect the textual document in a discriminatory and a no ambiguous way. There are two modes of indexing:

- **Controlled indexing** where indexes are occurrences of terms from a controlled vocabulary;
- **Free Indexing** where indexes are chosen without consideration for an authority list.

With free indexing, the descriptors, which are simple words, pose problems because of their ambiguity [48], contrary, key-phrase indexes are not ambiguous, but pose problems because of their variations [31]. ACABIT for free indexing proposes a rank list of multi-word terms for each text.

4.1   Evaluating Methods

Evaluating one or several tools for terminology extraction is not an easy task: generally, the tools include low-level processes using various lexical resources which act upon the quality of the extraction [34]. Moreover, the evaluation focuses on the quality of the extracted terms without taking into account other parameters such as speed, portability, robustness [43], or the partial structuring of the candidates. These evaluating methods rely on a corpus, a reference list and statistical measures.

Corpus. For terminology mining, the corpus should be monofield, homogeneous and representative of the level of the chosen specialisation [44]. By homogeneity, [45] refers to several criteria such as style or situational parameters. The data which compose the corpus should be well identified as to as its origin, its size, etc.

Reference List. The reference list which the results of the term extractors are compared with is of two types:

1. **Reference List.** This list could be built from a terminology bank or a specialised dictionary of the domain reflected by the corpus, by hand from the corpus itself by human experts, or using the two methods. In [17], the reference list is extracted from the Eurodicautom, the terminology data bank of the EEC, telecommunication section (6 000 terms). From the low overlap between the candidate terms and the terms of the reference list (300 terms), the list is complemented with a list of terms extracted directly from the corpus supported by two human experts of the telecommunication domain over three. [35] use two lists: the first one built from a dictionary, the second from the corpus.

2. **Human Evaluation.** Human evaluation is a non reproducible reference list and only valid for one tool. Since several tools are evaluated, it is impossible to judge if the expert has not been influenced by the preceding examined results. Ideally, an identical number of experts and tools would be necessary and all the systems should be evaluated by all the experts. Expert evaluation is so costly that it is restricted to samples. Human experts are also reluctant to wash on long lists, are influenced by the presentation and likely to change their opinion. Moreover, this method is not able to measure silence, except if the protocol specifies that the experts should pick up the missing terms not extracted by the system [20].

Linguistic Alignment. A reference list built from corpora seems to be *a priori* more suitable than human evaluation: cheaper, done for once, it allows repetition of the experiment and guarantees objective results. But, the form of the elements of the reference list should be compatible with the form of the elements submitted for evaluation. For terms, numerous problems occur because of term variations which does not allow the use of pattern matching. In [17], we chose to evaluate only terms sharing a common linguistic structure with those of the reference list. This method imposes a precise format to terms and masks numerous good candidate terms. Within the NTCIR'1 workshop's term recognition task, [35] chose not to limit the term structures and had defined different types of alignments: where T_R, T_{R1}, T_{R2} are terms of the reference list, T_E is a candidate term proposed by one of the systems:

F T_R fully matches T_E iff T_R is strictly equal to T_E ;

I T_E is included in T_R iff T_E is a sub-string of T_R ;

P T_R is included in T_E iff T_R is a sub-string of T_E ;

B (T_E is included in T_{R1}) and (T_{R2} is included in T_E) ;

A (*all inclusive*) (T_R is included in T_E) or (T_R fully matches T_E) or (T_E is included in T_R).

These different types of alignment allows us deduction, so that some systems show a tendency to extract only sub-strings of terms belonging to the reference list. These alignments are not fully satisfactory because they are based only on string length and do not treat all kind of variations. Within part-of-speech evaluation system task, [3] had developed alignment programmes to harmonise the different tag sets used by the different taggers. Such a programme could be developed for aligning terms and term variants: it could be based on supple equality of terms [22] defined from the Levenshtein's distance [38]. Thus, a term belonging to the reference list and a candidate term will be aligned if they are supply equal. This kind of alignment will accept all the variations of a term, even the distant variants, but will produce noise. Another possibility which takes into account the different types of variants is to use linguistic distances [52] developed to measure terminology evolution along time.

Measures. The measures generally used, precision and recall, have been borrowed from Information Retrieval [47]. Given L, the reference list:

$$Précision = \frac{number\ of\ extracted\ terms\ included\ in L}{number\ of\ extracted\ terms} \tag{3}$$

$$Recall = \frac{number\ of\ extracted\ terms\ included\ in\ L}{number\ of\ terms\ of\ L} \tag{4}$$

The precision evaluates the number of correctly extracted terms, the recall the rate of correct extracted terms (vice versa the rate of correct terms which have not been extracted). Other measures could be important to compute but are not related to the efficiency of the systems: the number of good candidates which are lexicalised (*unithood* [33]), the choice of the pilot term for a term and its variants, the new terms, the non compositional semantics of the candidates, etc.

4.2 ACABIT Evaluation

To prototype ACABIT, several statistical scores have been evaluated through the sorts they assigned to candidate terms [17]. This evaluation allows us to retain the best measure for a terminology acquisition task; it is an intermediary evaluation which could be compared to the evaluation by [9] of the quality of the linguistic analysis of their systems.

Terminology Mining. For French, ACABIT was evaluated in the ARC A3 project [4] in the field of Education. The test corpus was composed of articles from the SPIRALE journal (423 texts, 23 numbers). The evaluation was carried on one issue of the journal containing 13 articles (79 000 word forms). The results of the term extraction systems were made available to the human experts who had to come to a decision concerning the relevance of the lists of terms. Each human expert is assigned to one system only. ACABIT obtained a precision of 67 % and proposed only 29 % of not relevant terms. As a matter of comparison, the second system obtained a precision of 40 % with 50 % of non relevant terms. ACABIT was only evaluated for its first functionality, i.e. to propose a list of ranked terms. However, the experts noticed that the morphological variations detected would be useful for the indexers and the terminologists (also even for the translators).

For English, ACABIT was evaluated by [49] in the field of computer sciences, in the sub-domain of computer architecture. The corpus consisted of texts of the *IBM Journal of Research and Development* (280 000 forms). ACABIT obtained 67 % of precision. These results show that English is easier to treat than French for this kind of application. Indeed, the English module is less advanced that for French: morphological variants are not treated and the lemmatiser used during the pre-processing is a simple projection of a lexical database which does not make predictions on word suffixes and thus does not lemmatise numerous words.

The recall of ACABIT in these two evaluations was not computed.

Free Indexing. Through the ARC A3 project, no evaluation was made for indexing. However, ACABIT's evaluator found relevant the candidate terms and more precise than the descriptors proposed by the French Education Ministry's thesaurus.

The ILIAD linguistic engineering program [53] is an intelligent workstation prototype designed to assist librarians in indexing documents. It includes different modules which organise a set of documents and associated terms: module for automatic linguistic analysis of documents and for the acquisition of terminological knowledge. The modules for free and controlled indexing were submitted to expert-based evaluation through a precise protocol [20]. ACABIT obtained 79 % of precision and 67,5 % of recall. These scores, higher than those obtained for terminology extraction, could be explained either by the fact that the candidate terms were filtered for text and not for a set of texts, or contrary to ARC A3, the corpus was built with bibliographic records which contained only titles and abstracts.

5   Conclusion

We presented a method for terminology mining which is based on linguistic criteria and implemented several computational methods. By terminology mining, references are made to the acquisition of complex candidate terms, the discovery of new terms but also the linguistic structuring of the acquired candidate terms. Linguistic criteria cover lexicality, the well-formed syntactic structures of base terms and their variations, and lexicalisation, the automatic identification of clues denoting a naming character. These linguistic criteria stress the crucial part of handling term variations for building a linguistic structuring, for detecting advanced lexicalisation and obtaining an optimised representativity of the candidate terms occurrences. The computational methods implemented cover: shallow parsing, morphological analysis, morphological rule learning, and lexical statistics. These linguistic criteria and computational methods are conflated in a system that identifies and structures base terms and their variations, ACABIT (Automatic Corpus-Based Acquisition of Binary Terms) which has been evaluated for different terminology tasks: extraction of terminology and free indexing. Even if the methodology of term extraction evaluation is still to be improved, ACABIT obtained encouraging results that prove the validity of the adopted method. A further step to be developed will consist of a advanced semantic structuring between candidate terms.

References

[1] Steven Abney. Parsing By Chunks. In Robert Berwick and Carol Tenny, editors, *Principle-Based Parsing*, volume 44, pages 257–278. Kluwer Academic Publishers, 1991.

[2] Steven Abney. Part-of-Speech Tagging and Partial Parsing. In Steve Young and Gerrit Bloothooft, editors, *Corpus-Based Methods in Language and Speech Processing*, volume 2, chapter 4. Kluwer Academic Publishers, 1997.

[3] G. Adda, G. Mariani, J. Paroubek, M. Rajman, and J. Lecomte. L'action GRACE d'évaluation de l'assignation des parties du discours pour le français. In *Langues*, volume 2, pages 119–129. 1999.

[4] Muriel Amar, Annette Béguin, Marcilio de Brito, Sophie David, Marie-Claude L'Homme, Widad Mustafa El Hadi, and Patrick Paroubek. Rapport final auf arc a3 : évaluation d'outils d'aide à la construction automatique de terminologie et de relations sémantiques entre termes à partir de corpus. Technical report, Université Charles-de-Gaulle, Lille-III, 2001.

[5] Shlomo Argamon, Ido Dagan, and Yuval Krymolowski. A Memory-Based Approach to Learning Shallow Natural Language Patterns. In *Proceedings, 17th International Conference on Computational Linguistics (COLING'98)*, Montreal, Canada, Août 1998.

[6] G. Berry-Rogghe. The computation of collocations and their relevance in lexical studies. *The computer and the literary studies*, pages 102–112, 1973.

[7] Didier Bourigault. Surface grammatical analysis for the extraction of terminological noun phrases. In *Proceedings, 14th International Conference on Computational Linguistics (COLING'92)*, pages 977–981, Nantes, France, 1992.

[8] Didier Bourigault and Cécile Fabre. Approche linguistique pour l'analyse syntaxique en corpus. *Cahiers de Grammaire*, 25:131–152, 2000.

[9] Didier Bourigault and Benoît Habert. Evaluation of terminology extractors: Principles and experiments. In *Proceedings of the First International Conference on Language Resdources and Evaluation (LREC'98)*, pages 299–305, Granada, Spain, 1998. ELRA.

[10] G. Burnage. *CELEX: A Guide for Users*. Center for Lexical Information, University of Nijmegen, 1990. http://www.kun.nl/celex/.

[11] Lee-Freng Chien and Chun-Liang Chen. Incremental extraction of domain-specific terms from online text resources. In Didier Bourigault, Christian Jacquemin, and Marie-Claude L'Homme, editors, *Recent Advances in Computational Terminology*, volume 2 of *Natural Language Processing*, pages 89–109. John Benjamins, 2001.

[12] Kenneth Ward Church and Patrick Hanks. Word association norms, mutual information, and lexicography. *Computational Linguistics*, 16(1):22–29, 1990.

[13] Danielle Corbin. *Morphologie dérivationnelle et structuration du lexique*. Tübingen, Niemeyer, 1987.

[14] Danielle Corbin. Hypothèses sur les frontières de la composition nominale. *Cahiers de grammaire*, 17:26–55, 1992.

[15] Béatrice Daille. Qualitative terminology extraction. In Didier Bourigault, Christian Jacquemin, and Marie-Claude L'Homme, editors, *Recent Advances in Computational Terminology*, volume 2 of *Natural Language Processing*, pages 149–166. John Benjamins, 2001.

[16] Béatrice Daille. Morphological rule induction for terminology acquisition. In *The 18th International Conference on Computational Linguistics (COLING 2000)*, pages 215–221, Sarrbrucken, Germany, August 2000.

[17] Béatrice Daille, Gaussier Éric, and Jean-Marc Langé. An evaluation of statistical scores for word association. In Jonathan Ginzburg, Zurab Khasidashvili, Carl Vogel, Jean-Jacques Lévy, and Vallduví Entic, editors, *The Tbilisi Symposium on Logic, Language and Computation: Selected Papers*, pages 177–188. CSLI Publications and FoLLI, 1998.

[18] Béatrice Daille, Benoît Habert, Christian Jacquemin, and Jean Royauté. Empirical observation of term variations and principles for their description. *Terminology*, 3(2):197–257, 1996.

[19] Béatrice Daille and Christian Jacquemin. Lexical database and information access: A fruitful association. In ELRA, editor, *Proceedings, First International Conference on Language Resources and Evaluation (LREC'98)*, pages 669–673, Granada, June 1998.

[20] Béatrice Daille, Jean Royauté, and Xavier Polanco. Evaluation d'une plate-forme d'indexation de termes complexes. *Traitement automatique des langues (TAL)*, 41(2):395–422, 2000.

[21] Ted Dunning. Accurate methods for the statistics of surprise and coincidence. *Computational Linguistics*, 19(1):61–74, 1993.

[22] C. Enguehard. Supple equality of terms. In H.R. Arabnia, editor, *Proceedings of the International Conference on Artificial Intelligence, IC-AI'2000*, pages 1239–1245, Las Vegas, Nevada, USA, June 2000.

[23] B. S. Everitt. *The Analysis of Contingency Tables*. Chapman & Hall, second edition, 1992.

[24] Éric Gaussier. Unsupervised learning of derivational morphology from inflectional lexicons. In *Proceedings, Workshop on Unsupervised methods for NLP, 37th Annual Meeting of the Association for Computational Linguistics (ACL'99)*, 1999.

[25] John Goldsmith. Unsupervised Learning of the Morphology of a Natural Language. *Computatinal Linguistics*, 27(2):153–198, 2001.

[26] Gaston Gross. Degré de figement des noms composés. *Langages*, 90, 1988. Larousse, Paris.

[27] Louis Guilbert. Terminologie et linguistique. In V. I. Siforov, editor, *Textes choisis de terminologie*, GISTERM, pages 199–219. Université de Laval, Québec, 1981.

[28] Thierry Hamon and Adeline Nazarenko. Detection of synonymy link between terms: Experiment and results. In Didier Bourigault, Christian Jacquemin, and Marie-Claude L'Homme, editors, *Recent Advances in Computational Terminology*, volume 2 of *Natural Language Processing*, pages 185–208. John Benjamins, 2001.

[29] Zelig S. Harris. *Mathematical Structures of Language*. Wiley, New York, 1968.

[30] C. Jacquemin. Guessing Morphology from Terms and Corpora. In *Proceedongs, 20th annual international ACM SIGIR Conference on Research and Development in Information Retrieval (SIGIR'97)*, Philadelphia, PA, USA, 1997.

[31] Karen Sparck Jones. What is the role of NLP in Text Retrieval? In Tomek Strzalkowski, editor, *Natural Language Information Retrieval*, pages 1–24. Kluwer Academic Publishers, Boston, MA, 1999.

[32] Kyo Kageura. The dynamics of terminology: A theoretico-descriptive study of term formation and terminological growth. Non published, 2001.

[33] Kyo Kageura and Bin Umino. Methods of automatic term recognition: a review. *Terminology*, 3(2):259–289, 1996.

[34] Kyo Kageura, Masaharu Yoshioka, Koichi Takeuchi, Keruo Koyama, Keita Tsuji, and Fuyuki Yoshikane. Recent advances in automatic term recognition: Experiences from the NTCIR workshop on information retrieval and term recognition. *Terminology*, 6(2):151–173, 2000.

[35] Kyo Kageura, Masaharu Yoshioka, Keita Tsuji, Fuyuki Yoshikane, Koichi Takeuchi, and Keruo Koyama. Evaluation of the term recognition task. In *NTCIR Workshop 1: Proceedings of the First NTCIR Workshop on Research in Japanese Text Retrieval and Term Recognition*, pages 417–434. Tokyo: NACSIS, 1999.

[36] Alexandra Kinyon. A language-independant shallow-parser compiler. In *Proceedings, 39th Annual Meeting of the Association for Computational Linguistics and 10th Conference of the European Chapter of the Association for Computational Linguistics (ACL-EACL 2001)*, pages 322–329, 2001.

[37] Georges Kleiber. Dénomination et relation dénominatives. *Langages*, 76:77–94, 1984.

[38] V. I. Levenshtein. Binary codes capable of correcting deletations, insertions and reversals. *Sov. Phys.-Dokl*, 10(8):707–710, 1966.

[39] Diana Maynard and Sophia Ananiadou. Term extraction using a similarity-based approach. In Didier Bourigault, Christian Jacquemin, and Marie-Claude L'Homme, editors, *Recent Advances in Computational Terminology*, volume 2 of *Natural Language Processing*, pages 261–279. John Benjamins, 2001.

[40] Anne Monceaux. *La formation des noms composés de structure NOM ADJECTIF*. Phd thesis in linguistics, Université de Marne la Vallée, 1993.

[41] Emmanuel Morin. Des patrons lexico-syntaxiques pour aider au dépouillement terminologique. *Traitement Automatique des Langues*, 40(1):143–166, 1999.

[42] Emmanuel Morin. *Extraction de liens sémantiques entre termes à partir de corpus de textes techniques*. PhD Thesis in Computer Sciences, Université de Nantes, 1999.

[43] Patrick Paroubek and Martin Rajman. Étiquetage morpho-syntaxique. In Jean-Marie Pierrel, editor, *Ingénierie des langues*, pages 131–150. Hermès, 2000.

[44] Jennifer Pearson. *Terms in Context*. John Benjamins, 1998.

[45] Marie-Paule Péry-Woodley. Quels corpus pour quels traitements automatiques. *Traitement automatique des langues (TAL)*, 36(1-2):213–232, 1995.

[46] Lance Ramshaw and Mitchell Marcus. Text chunking transformation-based learning. In *3rd Workshop on Very Large Corpora*, pages 82–94, 1995.

[47] G. Salton and M. J. McGill. *Introduction to Modern Information Retrieval*. Computer Science Series. McGraw Hill, 1983.

[48] Gerard Salton. *Automatic Text Processing*. Addison-Wesley Publishing Company, 1989.

[49] Agata Savary. *Recensement et description des mots composés - méthodes et applications*. Phd thesis in computer science, Université de Marne-la-Vallée, 2000.

[50] Frank Smadja. Retrieving collocations from text: Xtract. *Computational Linguistics*, 19(1):143–177, 1993.

[51] Jean-David Sta. Comportement statistique des termes et acquisition terminologique à partir de corpus. *Traitement automatique des langues (TAL)*, 36(1-2):119–132, 1995.

[52] Annie Tartier. Méthodes d'analyse automatique de l'évolution terminologique au travers des variations repérées dans les corpus diachroniques. In *Actes, Quatrième rencontre Terminologie et Intelligence Artificielle (TIA 2001)*, pages 191–200, 2001.

[53] Yannick Toussaint, Fiametta Namer, Béatrice Daille, Christian Jacquemin, Jean Royauté, and Nabil Hathout. Une approche linguistique et statistique pour l'analyse de l'information en corpus. In *Actes, Cinquième Conférence Nationale sur le Traitement Automatique des Langues Naturelles (TALN'98)*, pages 182–191, Paris, 1998.

[54] A. Voutilainen. NPTool, a detector of English noun phrases. In *Proceedings of the Workshop of Very Large Corpora*, pages 48–57, 1993.

[55] R.A. Wagner and M.J. Fisher. The string-to-string correction problem. *Journal of the Association for Computing Machinery*, 21(1):168–173, 1974.

[56] Pierre Zweigenbaum and Natalia Grabar. A contribution of Medical Terminology to Medical Processing Resources: Experiments in Morphology Knowledge Acquisition from Thesauri. In *Proceedings, Conference on NLP and Medical Concept*, pages 155–167, 1999.

Measuring Term Representativeness

Toru Hisamitsu[1] and Jun-ichi Tsujii [2]

[1] Central Research Laboratory, Hitachi, Ltd.
1-280, Higashi-koigakubo, Kokubunji, Tokyo 185-8601, Japan
`hisamitu@harl.hitachi.co.jp`
[2] Graduate School of Science, the University of Tokyo
and CREST (Japan Science and Technology Corporation)
7-3-1 Hongo, Bunkyo-ku, Tokyo 113-8654, Japan
`tsujii@is.s.u-tokyo.ac.jp`

Abstract. This report introduces several measures of term representativeness and a scheme called the *baseline method* for defining the measures. The representativeness of a term T is measured by a normalized characteristic value which indicates the bias of the distribution of words in $D(T)$, the set of all documents that contain the term. $Dist(D(T))$, the distance between the distribution of words in $D(T)$ and in a whole corpus was, after normalization, found to be effective as a characteristic value for the bias of the distribution of words in $D(T)$. Experiments showed that the measure based on the normalized value of $Dist(D(\bullet))$ strongly outperforms existing measures in evaluating the representativeness of terms in newspaper articles. The measure was also effective, in combination with term frequency, as a means for automatically extracting terms from abstracts of papers on artificial intelligence.

1 Background and Motivation

With the recent dramatic increase of importance of electronic communication and data sharing over the Internet, there is an increasingly growing demand of organizing information scattered in texts to access them effectively. While the recent proposal of Semantic Web is to promote the meta-data approach to data sharing in which authors of texts provide clues of the content, there always remain demands for bottom-up methods that automatically identify key terms or phrases to characterize texts and to link them with other texts and knowledge sources.

This is the main reason of the renewed interests in automatic term recognition, since terms are the linguistic units that are related with concepts in extra-linguistic information domain and play the central roles in characterizing the contents of texts and thereby relating them with other information sources. Although conventional methods based on *tf-idf*[34] and its variants used intensively in IR systems have also been used to identify terms in texts in network, the empirical nature of such measures has prevented us from using them in far more dynamic and heterogeneous situations we are now in the network era.

M.T. Pazienza (Ed.): SCIE 2002, LNAI 2700, pp. 45–76, 2003.
© Springer-Verlag Berlin Heidelberg 2003

Unlike conventional IR systems, we have to deal with much diverse text types with varied lengths and subject fields, and we can no more rely on carefully calibrated parameters that performances of these empirical measures are highly dependent on.

In order to understand why some empirical measures work well in certain application but perform rather poorly in other application environments, we first have to disentangle the integrated nature of these measures and identify a set of new measures whose mathematical properties can be understood well. Since the termhood comprises several different dimensions, each dimension should be understood in terms of their mathematical properties, and then different measures that represent different aspects of termhood can be combined to accomplish goals specific to given application environments.

In this paper, we focus on the aspect of terms' being "representative" and give a mathematically sound formulation of the concept.

While the *idf* part in *tf-idf* method captures the specificity or representativeness of terms, the *tf* part tends to have stronger influence on the measure and *tf-idf* tends to be biased favorably towards words or phrases with high frequency. We may be able to introduce parameters in combining these two measures and adjust them so that the *idf* part has a proper share of influence. However, there is no systematic way of adjusting such parameters. This is a typical defect of empirically determined measures. Our method of assessing representativeness of a term, called the baseline method, is defined by a characteristic value $M(D(T))$ for the distribution of words in $D(T)$, the set of all documents in which the term T occurs. As we see later, the characteristic value M can be any measure as long as it reflects the distribution of words in the document set $D(T)$. Our method is based on the assumption that, if a term characterizes a meaningful set of documents that share certain interesting properties in common such as topics, subject fields, etc., the set of documents, $D(T)$, in which the term occurs show peculiar distributional properties, "peculiar" properties in the sense that a set of randomly chosen documents do not show them.

We call our method "baseline method", because the value of $M(D(T))$ is normalized by the estimated characteristic value of a randomly chosen document set of the same size. Because of normalization and the clear mathematical nature of the method, we can compare the values assigned to term candidates with different total frequency and sort them according to their values. We can use a single threshold value, which can be obtained systematically, to choose terms among candidates with different frequency.

The method is being used effectively in our commercial IR system, *Dual-NAVI*[30][39] which chooses a set of informative terms in a set of retrieved documents and shows them to the user in an interactive manner. The experience of *DualNAVI* shows that our method can effectively filter out non-representative terms. Our experiments also show that our method outperforms existing measures in judging representativeness of terms in newspaper articles. Being combined with term frequency, it is shown to be very effective in choosing indexing terms for scientific papers as well.

In section 2, we give a brief survey of the existing measures. In section 3, we introduce the basic idea of the baseline method and several measures using different characteristic values of M, developed on the basis of this method. Experimental results on the selecting and discarding representative and non-representative from newspaper articles and on the automatic extraction of terms from abstracts of papers in AI domain are given in section 4. In the final section, we outline open problems and future directions.

2 Related Work

Various measures of assigning weights to words and sequence of words that indicate their significance inside texts have been proposed in the fields of IR and other applications of natural language processing such as IE (information extraction), QA, etc. While techniques developed for IR have mainly focused on the degree of informativeness or domain specificity of a word that is similar to the concept of representativeness in this paper, the techniques in IE, QA, etc. have been concerned with identifying units of terms by using co-occurrences of words within sequences. The units thus identified are supposed to correspond to concepts in subject domains.

While the main topic of this paper is "representativeness", recognition of units of expressions is inherently intertwined with the topic. In the following, we give a brief review of measures that have been proposed to assess the termhood and unithood of expressions, essentially following the schema of a survey paper by Kageura et al. [18] with reference to papers in a journal's special issue on Automatic Term Recognition [41].

The standard and widely accepted definition of a term is "a lexical unit consisting of one or more than one word which represents a concept inside a domain" [2]. As this definition shows, the concepts of unithood and termhood are inseparably related. The unithood is "the degree of strength or stability of syntagmatic combinations or collocations", and termhood is "the degree to which a linguistic unit is related to (or more straightforwardly, represents) domain-specific concepts". In the following, we use representativeness and termhood interchangeably since the two concepts are closely related and somewhat orthogonal to the unithood.

2.1 Studies in the IR Domain

The main concern of IR has been to choose appropriate indexing words. While they have been interested in measures of significance of words in characterizing texts, researchers have not been so much interested in units that are related to domain specific concepts. This is because most current IR systems use single-word terms as index terms. This is now changing since they are also interested in using domain ontology or thesauri to make their system more intelligent.

The simplest weighting measures only concern the existence or nonexistence of a word in a document. The most straightforward measure of this type is given as follows:

$$I_{ij} = g_{ij},\qquad(1)$$

where I_{ij} is the weight of a word w_i in a document d_j, and g_{ij} gives 1 when $w_i \in d_j$ and 0 when $w_i \notin d_j$. Luhn proposed a normalized version of this measure [24]:

$$I_{ij} = \frac{g_{ij}}{\sum_k g_{ik}}.\qquad(2)$$

Another straightforward measure is f_{ij}, the frequency with a word w_i appears in a document d_j:

$$I_{ij} = f_{ij}.\qquad(3)$$

This measure is also normalized by taking the total number of word occurrences in a document into account [31][38]:

$$I_{ij} = \frac{f_{ij}}{\sum_k f_{ik}}.\qquad(4)$$

More elaborate measures of *termhood* combine the frequency of a word within a document with the number of occurrences of the word over the whole of a corpus. For instance, the last measure is modified to take the occurrences of the focal word over the whole of a corpus into account [31][38]:

$$I_{ij} = \frac{f_{ij}}{\sum_k f_{kj} \times \sum_l f_{il}}.\qquad(5)$$

Several measures are based on similar ideas; the most commonly used of these is called *tf-idf*, which was originally defined as:

$$I_{ij} = f_{ij} \times \log(\frac{N_{total}}{N_i}),\qquad(6)$$

where N_i is the number of documents that contain a word w_i and N_{total} is the total number of documents [34]. Although there are several variants of this measure (for example, [32][36][37]), their basic and common feature is that a word which appears more frequently in fewer documents is assigned a higher value.

If documents have been categorized beforehand, we can use more sophisticated measures that take the cross-category distribution of a word into account. For instance, Nagao et al. have proposed a measure which is based on the result of the χ^2 test of the hypothesis that the occurrences of the focal word are independent of category [27]:

$$I_i = \chi_i^2 = \sum_j \frac{(c_{ij} - m_{ij})^2}{m_{ij}},$$

$$m_{ij} = \frac{\sum_k c_{ik}}{\sum_l \sum_m c_{lm}} \times \sum_n c_{nj},\qquad(7)$$

where I_i is the weight of a word w_i in the whole corpus and c_{ij} is the frequency of w_i in the documents of category c_j.

Note that this measure aims to pick out indexing terms by observing distributions of candidates of indexing terms in the whole corpus, rather than in individual documents. The measures of this type are most relevant to our work, while certain measures of the other type can be used as weights for choosing indexing terms. For example, we use a modified version of *tf-idf* being combined with our measures (see section 4).

2.2 Studies in the ATR Domain

When one is interested in explicit relationship between linguistic expressions and domain specific concepts, one has to deal with the whole consequence of the definition of a term. That is, one has to take both the unithood and the termhood into account. Most of automatic term recognition (ATR) systems start by identifying term candidates (a term candidate is either a single word or a word sequence) on the basis of some criteria for unithood, and then try to assess their semantic properties like their semantic classes, etc.

While the latter, i.e. assessing semantic properties of terms, is beyond this paper, identification of term candidates requires evaluating the termhood as well as the unithood (togetherness of words).

Criteria for unithood can be classified into two groups: one is to use a kind of syntactic knowledge of putting constituent words into a candidate, while the other is to use statistical measures for assessing co-occurrence strength of constituent words. Criteria of the former type are an indispensable basis for any practical ATR system and are, in general, not quantitative. To make this clear, we refer to criteria of the former type as 'grammatical criteria' and to those of the latter type as 'measures of co-occurrence strength' in the remainder of this section.

Many ATR systems select term candidates by using grammatical criteria with measures of co-occurrence strength (for example, [9][10][23]). In this case, the termhood of a term candidate is of implicit concern, being solely represented by the value of co-occurrence strength of the constituent words of the candidate. However, one still has to note that, while the value of co-occurrence strength seems a measure of the unithood, the unithood alone cannot choose term candidates and that single-word terms cannot be treated by unithood alone. We need another type of measures that distinguish units with significance in semantic domains from units without such significance. We introduce representative measures in section 2.2.1.

Some ATR systems, however, use explicit measures of termhood in combination with unithood criteria. Term candidates that satisfy some unithood criterion are assigned termhood values and non-informative (or non-representative) words are filtered out. The measures of termhood are defined in terms of the frequencies of words and of word sequences in the corpus. Some measures are introduced in subsection 2.2.2.

Several ATR systems consider information other than unithood and termhood: some focus on syntactic criteria that are concerned with the dependency structure of constituent words in a term candidate and the degree of the candidate's structural variation from some 'normal form' of the term. A few ATR systems take some pragmatic information into account. Frantzi et al., for example, have introduced the NC-value which is a version of the C-value modified in order to take into consideration the occurrences of specific words (indicators of term existence) in the context of the focal candidate [11][26]. Fukushige et al. took linguistic analysis into account by including the semantic compositionality of the focal term candidate in their formulation (i.e., by checking what Fukushige et al. calls the 'non-synthesis' nature of the semantics of the focal candidate [12]). These syntactic-structure-oriented forms of ATR and measures of termhood that incorporate pragmatic information are important, particularly when extraction is recall-oriented and low-frequency terms must be dealt with. However, these studies are beyond the scope of this section and we limit the remainder of the review to measures which are based on frequency statistics. For detailed information on syntactic-structure-oriented ATR systems, see the cited work by Jacquemin [17].

2.2.1 Measures of Co-occurrence Strength

The most widely used measure of this kind is mutual information (MI), a measure of the adjacent co-occurrence of words which was introduced by Church and Hanks [4] and is defined as follows:

$$I(w_i, w_j) = \log_2 \frac{P(w_i, w_j)}{P(w_i)P(w_j)}, \tag{8}$$

where $P(w_i)$ and $P(w_j)$ are the probabilities that w_i and w_j occur in the whole corpus, respectively, and $P(w_i, w_j)$ is the probability of an occurrence of w_i and w_j as a pair of adjacent words.

Dunning pointed out that the log-likelihood ratio is more appropriate than MI in the treatment of a mixture of high-frequency bigrams and low-frequency bigrams [8]. Cohen applied the LLR in a character-ngram-based ATR system [5]. Daille et al. applied the LLR, in combination with a grammatical criterion, to multiword-term extraction [6]. Their work had a particular focus on the extraction of pairs of two adjacent content words (which they called 'base multiword unit' or simply 'base MWU') because a longer multiword term is formed on the basis of base MWUs and overcomposition (e.g., "[side lobe] regrowth"), modification (e.g., "interfering [earth station]"), or coordination (e.g., "packet assembly/disassembly"). The measure of the co-occurrence of w_i and w_j which they used is defined as follows:

$$I(w_i, w_j) = \log L(p_1, k_1, n_1) + \log L(p_2, k_2, n_2) - \log L(p, k_1, n_1) - \log L(p, k_2, n_2),$$

$$\log L(p, k, n) = k \log L(p) + (n - k)\log(1 - p), \quad p_1 = \frac{k_1}{n_1}, p_2 = \frac{k_2}{n_2}, p = \frac{k_1 + k_2}{n_1 + n_2},$$

$$\tag{9}$$

where k_1 is the frequency with which w_i occurs and is followed by w_j, and n_1 is the frequency of w_j, k_2 is the frequency with which w_i occurs and is followed by words other than w_j, and n_2 is the frequency of words other than w_j.

The C-value proposed by Franzi et al. [10] is concerned with term occurrences in structures of nested terms. A higher value is assigned to a term candidate if it occurs more independently and more frequently according to the following formula [26]:

$$Cvalue(w_1, \cdots, w_k) = \log_2 k \times f(w_1, \cdots, w_k); \text{ if } w_1, ..., w_k \text{ is not nested,}$$

$$Cvalue(w_1,\cdots,w_k) = \log_2 k \times (f(w_1,\cdots,w_k) - \frac{1}{P(T_{w_1,\cdots,w_k})}\sum_{t\in T_{w_1,\cdots,w_k}} f(t))$$

$$\text{; otherwise.} \qquad (10)$$

where $f(w_1,...,w_k)$ is the frequency of $w_1,...,w_k$ in the whole corpus, T_a is the set of extracted term candidates that contain a, $P(T_a)$ is the number of elements in T_a.

Aizawa has introduced a further measure of co-occurrence strength, the FQ-value, which combines frequency and MI to provide a measure that allowed an information theoretical interpretation [1]. For a word sequence $w_1,...,w_k$, the FQ-value of $w_1,...,w_k$ is defined as follows:

$$I(w_1,\cdots,w_k) = P(w_1,\cdots,w_k)\log\frac{P(w_1,\cdots,w_k)}{P(w_1)\times\cdots\times P(w_k)}, \qquad (11)$$

where $P(w_1,...,w_k)$ stands for the probability of the occurrence of $w_1,...,w_k$. $I(w_1,...,w_k)$ is defined as 0 when $k = 1$.

As was stated above, measures with a basis in co-occurrence (in particular, MI and the LLR) may implicitly reflect termhood, but they are intrinsically incapable of evaluating the termhood of a single-word term.

2.2.2 Measures of Termhood

Salton et al. defined a termfood measure to weight complex units [35]. Their system extracts every word bigram w_iw_j and gives it a termhood weight $I(w_i, w_j)$ as follows:

$$I(w_i,w_j) = \frac{f_i \cdot f_j}{2} \times \left(\log_2(N_{total}) - \frac{\log_2 N_i + \log_2 N_j}{2} \right) \qquad (12)$$

where N_{total}, N_i, and N_j are defined in the same way as in equation 6.

Damerau first collects word bigrams by using mutual information, which is a typical measure of unithood, and then gives termhood weights to the collected bigrams. Assuming that w_i and w_j occur independently in the corpus, while $P(w_i, w_j)$, the probability that w_i and w_j occur adjacently, is biased to S, a certain subset of the corpus. Damerau gives weight $I(w_i, w_j, S)$ to w_iw_j as follows [7]:

$$I(w_i,w_j,S) = \log_2\frac{P(w_i,w_j,S)}{P(w_i,w_j)}, \qquad (13)$$

where $P(w_i, w_j, S)$ is the probability that w_i and w_j occur adjacently in the subset S.

Nakagawa et al. attempts to treat termhood by taking statistical information on the words around focal term candidates into account. They considered the term-productivity of a focal term candidate, assuming that a word (sequence) that produces more terms through combination with other words has a corresponding greater termhood [28][29]. This measure is called *Imp* and is defined by using measures called *Pre* and *Post* for a single-word term, which are defined as follows:

Pre(w): the number of distinct nouns that immediately precede *w* to form compound nouns,

Post(w): the number of distinct nouns that immediately succeed *w* to form compound nouns,

where *w* is a single noun that occurs in the focal corpus. Nakagawa used *Pre* and *Post* to define *Imp* in the two ways following:

$$Imp_1(w_1,...,w_k) = (\prod_{i=1}^{k} (Pre(w_i) + 1)(Post(w_i)+1)))^{\frac{1}{k^a}},$$

$$Imp_2(w_1,...,w_k) = \frac{1}{k^a} \sum_{i=1}^{k} (Pre(w_i) +Post(w_i)), \tag{14}$$

where w_i is a constituent noun of a nominal compound, and a ($a \geq 0$) is a parameter whose value is experimentally determined. Imp_1 and Imp_2 are reported to work similarly well in ATR [29].

Note that the value of Imp can be defined for any word (or word sequence) if the definitions of Pre and $Post$ are loosened in the way below:

$Pre(w)$: the number of distinct nouns that immediately precede w,

$Post(w)$: the number of distinct nouns that immediately succeed w.

In this case, high values can be expected for function words, since a function word such as the subject-marker particle "*ga*" (in Japanese) and the preposition 'of' (in English) may succeed or precede any noun in a sentence. Therefore it is difficult to generalize the notion of Imp so that it acts as a measure of termhood of any word.

2.3 Problems with Existing Measures

As we see in the previous sections, most measures proposed so far are for assessing the unithood with only implicit consideration of the termhood. It is also the case that measures of the termhood used in the ATR are mostly concerned with terms in single subject fields and attempt to capture term formation rules specific to a given field. Even when they consider statistical measures, they assume that the measures characterize term formation rules inside a given single field. The measures are local in this sense.

Only exceptions are *idf* and few methods for cross category word distribution like χ^2, which relate distributional properties of terms across documents or fields (categories) with their termhood. However, the statistical foundation of *idf* is dubious, while methods based on cross category word distribution presuppose categorization of corpus in advance that severely restricts their applicability in real application.

In the following section, we propose a method that focuses on the termhood explicitly and relates it with global distributional properties of term candidates, or more precisely the distributional properties of documents in which a candidate term occurs, with the termhood of the candidate. Since the measures our method produces are independent of the unithood and local term formation rules, they can be combined with most of the measures discussed in the previous section.

3 The Baseline Method and Novel Measures of Term Representativeness

This section introduces the baseline method and novel measures that have been developed within the framework [13][14]. Let us first define some basic notations:

T is a term;

D_0 is the set of all documents in a corpus;

$D(T)$ is the set of all documents in D_0 that contain T;

$\#S$ is the number of words (tokens) that appear in a given set of words S; and

M is a measure which characterizes the distribution of words in any set of words.

$\#D(T)$, for example, means the number of word tokens in a set of all documents in which the term T appears, while $M(D(T))$ is the value of the measure M that characterizes the set of documents in which T appears.

3.1 The Basis of the Baseline Method

The basic assumption of our method is that:

For any term T, if the term is representative, the distribution of words in $D(T)$ should be biased according to the distribution of words in D_0.

This assumption is transformed into the following procedure:

Given a measure M and a term T, calculate $M(D(T))$, the value of the measure for $D(T)$. Then compare $M(D(T))$ with $B_M(\#D(T))$, where B_M estimates the value of $M(D)$ when D is the set of randomly chosen documents such that $\#D = \#D(T)$.

This means that, if a term candidate T is really a term, the set of documents in which T occurs shows peculiar distributional properties in terms of M. To choose a specific M means to focus on a certain aspect of the global termhood. We have tried several measures as candidates for M. One was the number of distinct words that appear in a document set (here referred to as *DIFFNUM*). Teramoto et al. conducted experiments with a small corpus [40][1] and reported that *DIFFNUM(D(T))* was useful for selecting important terms under the assumption that fewer different words co-occur with a representative word than with a generic word. This assumption reflects our intuition that the document set in which a term represents is more homogeneous than an arbitrary document set. Therefore, a more general form of *DIFFNUM(D(T))* would be *ENTROPY(D(T))*, where *ENTROPY(D)* is defined as the entropy of the distribution of words in a given set of documents D.

Another measure that we have tested is the distance between the word distribution in $D(T)$ and the word distribution in the whole corpus D_0. The distance between the two distributions can be measured in various ways, and, after comparing four different '*distances*', we chose the log-likelihood ratio (LLR) [13], with *Dist(D(T))* denoting the distance. The LLR is defined as logarithm of the ratio of the maximum

---

[1] With Teramoto's method, eight parameters must be experimentally tuned to normalize *DIFFNUM(D(T))*, but the details of this process were not given.

value of the likelihood function under a hypotheses H_1 to the maximum value of the likelihood function under another hypotheses H_2, where H_1 is the hypotheses to be assumed and H_2 is the alternative hypothesis of H_1.

In our application, H_1 is the hypothesis that the word distribution in $D(T)$ is independent of the word distribution in D_0, and H_2 is the hypothesis that the word distribution in $D(T)$ is the same as the word distribution in D_0. Under the hypothesis H_1, the maximum value of the likelihood function M_1 is given by the following equation:

$$M_1 = \sum_{i=i}^{n} \left(\frac{k_i}{\#D(T)} \right)^{k_i}, \tag{15}$$

$$M_2 = \sum_{i=i}^{n} \left(\frac{K_i}{\#D_0} \right)^{K_i}, \tag{16}$$

where $\{w_1,...,w_n\}$ is the set of all words in D_0 and k_i and K_i are the frequencies of a word w_i in $D(T)$ and D_0, respectively. $Dist(D(T))$, the logarithm of M_1 over M_2, is thus represented as follows:

$$\sum_{i=i}^{n} k_i \log \frac{k_i}{\#D(W)} - \sum_{i=i}^{n} k_i \log \frac{K_i}{\#D_0}, \tag{17}$$

Fig. 1 plots coordinates $(\#D, M(D))$, where M is $DIFFNUM$ or $Dist$, and D varies over sets of documents of varied sizes that have been randomly selected from the articles in the 1996 archive of *Nihon Keizai Shimbun*.

For a measure M, we define $Rep(T, M)$ by normalizing $M(D(T))$ on $B_M(\#D(T))$, and call the result 'the representativeness of T with respect to M', or simply, 'the representativeness of T'. The next subsection describes the construction of B_M and the normalization.

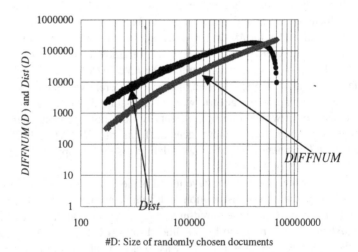

Fig. 1. Values of *DIFFNUM* and *Dist* for the set of randomly chosen documents

3.2   The Baseline Function and Normalization

As we discuss in section 3.1, we can use arbitrary measures for M that reflect certain aspects of distributional properties of D_0 and $D(T)$. In this section, we use $Dist$ as an example of M to illustrate why normalization is necessary and how we construct a baseline function for normalization.

Throughout this and the following sections, we use a set of articles retrieved from D_0, which is now the 1996 archive of *Nihon Keizai Shimbun*, when *"denshi-manee"*(electronic money) is given as a keyword. *Nihon Keizai Shinbun* is a Japanese newspaper similar to *Financial Times* or *Wall Street Journal*.

Fig. 2(a) is a graph of $\{(\#D(T), Dist(D(T)))\}_T$ along with $\{(\#D, Dist(D))\}_D$ in Fig. 1, where T varies over *"angou"*(cipher), *"nenn"*(year), *"getsu"*(month), *"yomi-toru"*(read out), *"ichi"*(one), *"suru"*(do), *"denshi"*(electronic), *"manee"*(money), and *"inntaanetto"*(Internet). These are the words the frequency of which is high in D_0. Since the words of *"nen"*(year) and *"getsu"* (month) always appear in date expressions in Japanese, they should be judged as insignificant expressions that appear frequently across broad rages of subject fields. On the other hand, *"manee"* (money) and *"denshi"* (electronic) should be judged significant, since *"manee"*(money) is a peculiar way of denoting money that appears only in special case such as the translation of 'electronic money' in Japanese.

"suru"(do) is the most frequently used light verb in Japanese and *"ichi"* (one) is part of numerical expressions. Both should be judged insignificant.

Some of our intuitions of termhood of these words are captured in Fig. 2(a). For example, $Dist(D(\text{'do'}))$ is smaller than $Dist(D(\text{'Internet'}))$, while the frequency of 'do' is much higher than that of 'Internet'. That is, the word distribution in the document set in which 'Internet' appears is more peculiar than that of the set in which 'do' appears.

However, $Dist(D(\text{'cipher'}))$ is smaller than $Dist(D(\text{'read out'}))$ and even smaller than $Dist(D(\text{'do'}))$. This contradicts our intuition, and is why values of $Dist$ are not directly used to compare the representativeness of terms. This effect arises because, as Fig.1 and Fig.2(a) show, $Dist(D(T))$ generally increases with $\#D(T)$. In other words, the values of $Dist$ are strongly correlated with the size of a document set, and therefore, we need to normalize them to offset the correlation.

We use a baseline function to normalize the values. In the case of $Dist$, $B_{Dist}(\bullet)$ is designed to approximate the curve in Fig. 2(a). From the definition of $Dist$, it is obvious that $B_{Dist}(0) = B_{Dist}(\#D_0) = 0$. At the limit, when $\#D_0 \to \infty$, $B_{Dist}(\bullet)$ becomes a monotonically increasing function.

A precise approximation of the curve may be attained through logarithmic linear approximation around the document size of 1000 to 30,000 words. The curve is fairly distorted in the far end where the document size is beyond 1,000,000 words. This is because $Dist(D)$ approaches to zero when $\#D$ becomes the same as $\#D_0$.

To make this approximation, up to 300 articles of *Nihon Keizai Shinbun* are randomly sampled at a time (let each randomly chosen document set --- a set of articles --- be denoted by D; the number of sampled articles is increased from one to 300, repeating each number up to five times) Each $(\#D, Dist(D))$ is converted to $(\log(\#D),$

$\log(Dist(D)))$. The curve of fit to the $(\log(\#D), \log(Dist(D)))$ values, which is very close to a straight line, is further divided into multiple parts and is piece-wise approximated by linear functions. For instance, in the interval $I = \{x | 10000 \leq x < 15,000\}$, $\log(Dist(D))$ is approximatable by $1.103 + 1.023 \times \log(\#D)$ to obtain $R^2 = 0.996$.

Thus, when $1,000 \leq \#D(T) < 3,0000$, we define $Rep(T, Dist)$, the representativeness of a given term T, by normalizing $Dist(D(T))$ on $B_{Dist}(\#D(T))$ as follows:

$$Rep(T, Dist) = \frac{\log(Dist(D(T)))}{\log(B_{Dist}(\#D(T)))}. \tag{18}$$

For instance, when we obtained the randomly selected document set D $(1,000 \leq \#D < 3,0000)$ from *Nihon Keizai Shimbun* 1996, the average value for $\log(Dist(D(T))/B_{Dist}(\#D(T)))$, Avr, was 1.011 and the standard deviation, σ, was about 0.0501. Every observed value fell within $Avr \pm 4\sigma$ and 99% of observed values fell within $Avr \pm 3\sigma$. This was the case for all of the corpora we tested (the seven corpora listed in Table 3). Therefore, we can define the threshold of representativeness as, say, $Avr + 4\sigma \approx 1.2$. The values of Avr and σ are very stable over various corpora.

3.3 Treatment of Very Frequent Terms

For normalization of $Dist(D(T))$ of extremely frequent terms such as 'do', we do not use $D(T)$ as they are. To use $D(T)$ is neither desirable nor efficient. As we see in the previous section, the values of $Dist(D(T))$ and $B_{Dist}(\#D(T))$ are extremely skewed when $\#D(T)$ gets closer to $\#D_0$. We therefore estimate the 'bias of word distribution in $D(T)$' by using a randomly sampled, much smaller sub-document set $D^{rand}(T)$ of $Dist(D(T))$ which satisfies $1,000 \leq \#D^{rand}(T) \leq 3,0000$, and define $Rep(T, Dist)$ as $Rep(T, Dist)^{rand}$ which is given as follows:

$$Rep(T, Dist)^{rand} = \frac{\log(Dist(D^{rand}(T)))}{\log(B_{Dist}(\#D^{rand}(T)))}. \tag{19}$$

Estimation based on a smaller set is desirable because we can avoid skewed values, and more importantly, the computation is far more efficient by using a smaller set instead of a set in which, in the case of 'do', more than 10,000,000 words are contained.

In the experiment of *Nihon Keizai Shimbun*, the average number of words per article was around 200 words, so we used a threshold of 150 articles. If $D(T)$ contains more than 150 articles, a randomly sampled subset $D^{rand}(T)$ containing 150 articles was used for computing $R(T, Dist)^{rand}$.

By using the approximation as such, we obtained $Rep(\text{'do'}, Dist) = 0.982$, $Rep(\text{'read out'}, Dist) = 1.381$, and $Rep(\text{'cipher'}, Dist) = 1.809$. These values conform to our intuition that 'do' is very common across broad ranges of topics and 'cipher' is a very peculiar word that appear in very restricted subject domains such as 'electronic commerce', 'electronic money' etc. while 'read out' is between these two extremes. It is also worth noting that 'manee' which means "money" but is only used in restricted contexts, such as in the Japanese translation of the term "electronic money", is located in a position in Fig.2(b) that shows this word is equally peculiar as the technical terms such as "Internet", "read out", etc.

In Fig. 2(b), words are displayed at coordinates of the form $(\#D(T), Rep(T, Dist))$ or $(\#D^{rand}(T), Rep(T, Dist)^{rand})$, where T varies over the set of {'cipher', 'year', 'month', 'read out', 'one', 'do', 'electronic', 'money', 'Internet'}. Note that the random sampling mentioned above was used to calculate $Rep(T, Dist)$ for each T except 'cipher' because elements of the above set other than 'cipher' appear in more than 150 documents.

$Rep(T, M)$ has the following advantages by virtue of its definition:
(1) It provides a way of comparing high-frequency terms with low-frequency terms.
(2) The threshold values of representativeness are systematically definable.
(3) It is applicable to all n-gram terms for any n, and particularly applicable to single-word terms.

4 Experiments

4.1 Topic-Word Selection from Newspaper Articles

One of the authors has been engaged in developing a commercial IR-Navigation system *DualNAVI*[2] [30][39]. Once a set of documents is retrieved by given keywords, the system shows another set of keywords that appear in the document set, together with association strengths among them, in order to facilitate guided navigation in the document space by the user. Fig. 3 is an example of graph that is shown to the user. The user can choose another set of keywords by clicking words on the screen that interest him/her.

To choose or highlight a set of good keywords to show is crucial for the success of such guided navigation, and the methods described in the previous section are being used. In order to assess the effectiveness of our methods in such application environments, we conducted an experiment using 158,000 articles in the 1996 issues of the *Nihon Keizai Shimbun*. In the experiment, we chose a set of randomly selected words and compared the evaluation of their significance based on various measures such as *tf, tf-idf*, $Rep(\bullet, DIFFNUM)$, $Rep(\bullet, ENTROPY)$, and $Rep(\bullet, Dist)$, with human subjective judgments.

---

[2] *DualNAVI* has two navigation windows; one displays a graph of representative words in the retrieved documents and the other displays the titles of retrieved articles. The navigation window gives user some idea of the contents of the retrieved documents. The more frequently a word appears, the higher in the window the word is displayed.

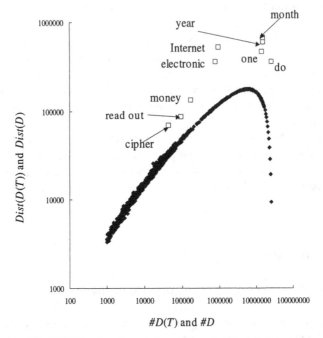

Fig. 2. (a) The baseline curve and sample-word distribution

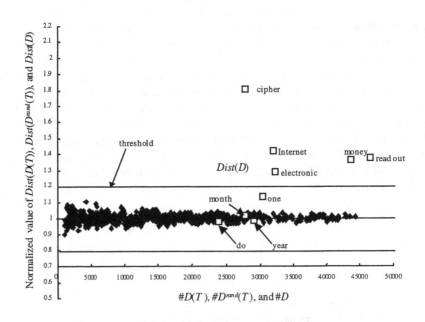

Fig. 2. (b) The effect of normalization

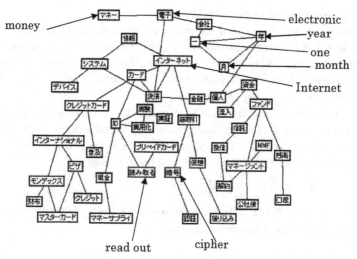

money — electronic — year — one — month — Internet — read out — cipher

Fig. 3. An example of a word-graph in the navigation window for the query "*dennshi-manee*"(electronic money)

4.1.1 Preparation

We randomly chose 20,000 words[3] having document frequencies greater than 2, then randomly chose 2,000 of these for manual classification. The words are classified into three classes:

(1) *Class a* (accepting): words that are useful for the navigation window
(2) *Class d* (discarding): words that are not useful for the navigation window
(3) *Class u* (uncertain): words, whose usefulness in for the navigation window is either neutral or difficult to judge.

In the classification process, a human subject used the words with the *DualNAVI* system to examine their respective degrees of utility. Classifying words as class *d* was done conservatively because the consequence of removing an informative word from the window is more serious than that of allowing a useless word to appear.

Table 1 shows the classifications for a few of the 2,000 words. The words marked "*p*" are proper nouns. In general, the difference between proper nouns in *class a* and proper nouns of the other classes is that the former are well-known. Class "*d*" mainly consists of very common verbs (such as "*suru*" (*do*) and "*motsu*" (*have*)), adverbs, demonstrative pronouns, conjunctions, and numbers. This shows the impossibility of defining a stop-word list by part-of-speech alone, because almost all parts-of-speech appear among words of *class d*.

---

[3] The total number of words having document frequencies greater than 2 was 86,000.

4.1.2 Measures Used in the Experiments

To evaluate the effectiveness of the measures, we compared the utility of the respective measures in terms of gathering and avoiding, respectively, representative and non-representative terms. We randomly sorted the 20,000 words and compared the results with the results of sorting according to the five criteria: *tf*, *tf-idf*, *Rep*(•, *DIFFNUM*), *Rep*(•, *ENTROPY*), and *Rep*(•, *Dist*).

The comparison was done in terms of the cumulative number of words that were marked as being of a specified class and appeared in the first N ($1 \leq N \leq 2,000$) words, with decreasing rank for representativeness in the set of 20,000 words according to each measure. The definition we used for *tf-idf* was

$$tf - idf = \sqrt{TF(T)} \times \log \frac{N_{total}}{N(T)}, \tag{20}$$

where T is a term, $TF(T)$ is the term frequency of T, N_{total} is the total documents, and $N(T)$ is the number of documents that contain T.

4.1.3 Results

Fig. 4 gives a comparison, for all of the sorting criteria, of the cumulative numbers of words marked "*a*". The total number of *class a* words was 911. *Rep*(•, *Dist*) clearly outperformed the other measures. Although *Rep*(•, *DIFFNUM*) outperformed *tf* and *tf-idf* on roughly the first 9,000 words, this result was then reversed. *Rep*(•, *ENTROPY*)'s performance was overall very similar to, but slightly inferior to *Rep*(•, *DIFFNUM*)'s performance. If we use the threshold value of *Rep*(•, *Dist*), the words from the first to the 1,511th word among the chosen 2,000 words are considered significant or representative. In this case, the recall and precision of the 1,511 words against all *class a* words are 85% and 50%, respectively. When using *tf-idf* to sort words and pick up the first 1511 words, the recall and precision of the first 1,511 would be 79% and 47%, respectively (note, however, that there is no clear threshold value for *tf-idf*).

Considering the fact that, when we use this type of comparison based on cumulative totals, it is very difficult for sophisticated measures to outperform even the simple method of using term frequency in automatic term extraction (for example, [3][6]), this performance of *Rep*(•, *Dist*) is impressive and promising.

Fig. 5 gives a comparison of results, for all of the sorting criteria of the cumulative number of words marked as *d* (454 in total). In this case, the fewer the words, the better the result. The difference is far clearer in this case: *Rep*(•, *Dist*) significantly outperforms the other measures. In contrast to this, *tf* and *tf-idf* barely outperformed random sorting. *Rep*(•, *DIFFNUM*) outperformed *tf* and *tf-idf* over roughly the first 3,000 monograms, but under-performed otherwise. *Rep*(•, *ENTROPY*) outperformed *Rep*(•, *DIFFNUM*), *tf*, and *tf-idf* over roughly first 5,000 monograms but slightly under-performed *tf-idf* otherwise.

Fig. 6 gives a comparison of results, for all of the sorting criteria of the cumulative number of words marked as *ap* (acceptable proper nouns, 216 in total). We see that the superiority of *Rep*(•, *Dist*) is again more pronounced than in the result of Fig. 4. Also, *Rep*(•, *DIFFNUM*) outperformed *tf* and *tf-idf* over the entire range, while *tf* and *tf-idf* showed nearly the same or even worse levels of performance than random sorting. *Rep*(•, *ENTROPY*) slightly under-performed *Rep*(•, *DIFFNUM*) overall, and outperformed random, *tf*, and *tf-idf* overall.

In the experiments, proper nouns generally had a high *Rep*-values, with some having particularly high scores: for instance, the names of *sumo* wrestlers and horses. This may be explained that such names repetitively appear in items that have special formats, such as lists of sports results.

We attribute the difference between the performance of *Rep*(•, *Dist*) and *Rep*(•, *DIFFNUM*) to the respective quantities of information used. Obviously, information on the distribution of words in a document is more comprehensive than information on the numbers of distinct words. Other measures of document properties that incorporate even more precise information are thus of interest.

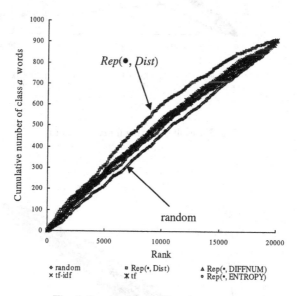

Fig. 4. Result of sorting for *class a* words

Table 1. Examples of the classified words

Class *a*	Class *u*	Class *d*
"*amyuuzumentopaaku*" (amusement park)	"*hinyari*" (chilly)	"83,000,000"
"*kyouhakujoo*" (threatening letter)	"*shoochin*"(depressed)	"*tadai-na*" (greatly)
"*faiaaohru*"(firewall)	"*Ishigami*" (Ishigami) p	"1,146"
"*atoranta*"(Atlanta) p	"*Shigeyuki*" (Shigeyuki) p	"*subete*" (all)
	"*binshoh*" (agility)	"*sukoshimo*" (not…in the least)

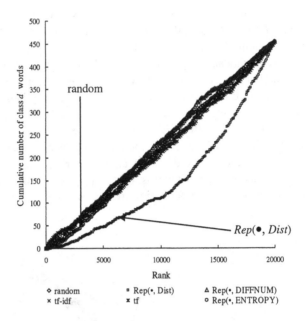

Fig. 5. Result of sorting for *class d* words

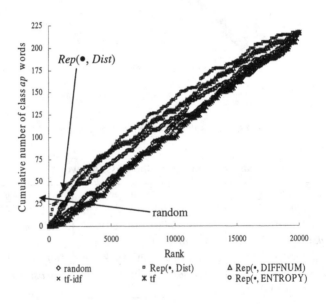

Fig. 6. Result of sorting for *class ap* words

4.1.4 Measure-to-Measure Correlations of Ranking

We investigated the rank-correlations for the results of sorting of the 20,000 terms that had been used in the experiments described above (subsection 4.1.1). Rank correlation was measured by Kendall's method (see the Appendix) for 2,000 terms randomly selected from the 20,000 terms. Table 2 shows the correlation between $Rep(\bullet, Dist)$ and these other measures. It is interesting that ranking by $Rep(\bullet, Dist)$ had a very low correlation with ranking by $Rep(\bullet, DIFFNUM)$; lower, in fact, than the correlations with tf and tf-idf. This indicates that a combination of $Rep(\bullet, Dist)$ and $Rep(\bullet, DIFFNUM)$ should provide a strong discriminative ability in term classification; this possibility deserves further investigation.

Table 2. Kendall's rank correlation between the term-rankings obtained by $Rep(\bullet, Dist)$ and other measures.

	$Rep(\bullet, DIFFNUM)$	$Rep(\bullet, ENTROPY)$	tf-idf	tf
Correlation	-0.0646	0.175	0.161	0.153

4.1.5 Portability of Baseline Functions

We examined the robustness of baseline functions; that is, whether a baseline function drawn from a given corpus is applicable to normalization with a different corpus. This was investigated by using $Rep(\bullet, Dist)$ with seven different corpora. Seven baseline functions were drawn from seven corpora, then applied to normalization in defining $Rep(\bullet, Dist)$ for the corpus used in the experiments described in previous subsections. The performance of the $Rep(\bullet, Dist)$ values defined by using the various baseline functions was compared in the same way as the performance comparisons above. The seven corpora used to construct the baseline functions and statistics on their content words are given in Table 3. Fig. 7 gives a comparison, for all of the baseline functions, the cumulative numbers of words marked "a" (see subsection 4.1). The performance decreased only slightly for the baseline drawn from NC-ALL. In the other cases, the differences were so small that they are almost invisible in the figure. The same results were obtained for *class d* words and *class ap* words.

  We also examined the rank correlations between the rankings produced by measures of the respective representativeness, in the same way as was described in subsection 4.1.4 (see Table 4). These were close to 100%, except for the combination of the Kendall's method and the NACSIS-corpus baseline.

  The results given in this subsection suggest that a baseline function constructed from one corpus may be used to rank terms in a significantly different corpus. This is particularly useful when we are dealing with a corpus that similar to a known corpus but do not know the precise word distribution in the corpus. The same kind of robustness was observed for $Rep(\bullet, DIFFNUM)$ and $Rep(\bullet, ENTROPY)$. This robustness of baseline functions is an important feature of measures that are defined by using the baseline method.

Table 3. Corpora and statistics on their content words

Corpus	Description	Number of total words	Number of different words
NK96-50,000	50,000 articles randomly selected from the NK96 corpus (the 206,803 articles of *Nihon Keizai Shimbun* 1996)	13,498,244	127,852
NK96-100,000	100,000 articles randomly selected from NK96	26,934,068	172,914
NK96-158,000	15,8000 articles from *Nihon Keizai Shimbun* 1996 restricted to exclude such atypical articles as company personnel-affairs notices	42,555,095	210,572
NK96-200,000	200,000 articles randomly selected from NK96	53,816,407	233,668
NK98-158,000	158,000 articles randomly selected from *Nihon Keizai Shimbun* 1998	39,762,127	196,261
NACSIS-J	The 333,003 Japanese-language abstracts in the NACSIS*-NII** test collection (see subection 4.2).	64,806,627	350,991
NACSIS-158,000	158,000 abstracts randomly selected from NC-ALL	30,770,682	231,769

Table 4. Kendall's rank correlation between the measures defined by an NK96-15,8000 baseline functiones and by other baseline functions (%)

	NK96-50,000	NK96-100,000	NK96-200,000	NK98-158,000	NC-158,000	NC-ALL
correlation	0.970	0.956	0.951	0.979	0.789	0.780

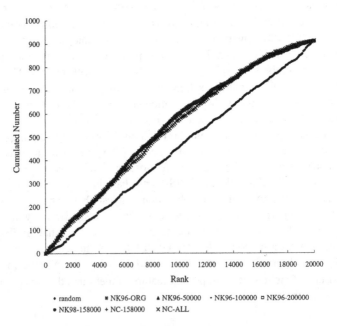

Fig. 7. Results of sorting for *class a* words

4.2 Extracting Technical Terms from Abstracts of Academic Papers

4.2.1 Details of the Task and Source for Term Extraction

The team which developed *DualNAVI* participated in the NTCIR workshop on term extraction (TMREC; [19][20]). The source for term extraction was part of the NACSIS-J corpus described in table 3 [22]: 1,870 Japanese-language abstracts of papers on artificial intelligence (NACSIS-AI). The terms in the abstracts were manually tagged by the TMREC group, the organizing committee of the workshop (we refer to the tagged corpus as NACSIS-AI-Tagged). The participants were instructed to use this tagged corpus as a common test set. Un-tagged NACSIS-AI and the entire NACSIS-J were allowed to use, if they wished.

The task was to identify technical terms from NACSIS-AI, which is very different from keyword extraction in the IR-Navigation system in 4.1. Furthermore, the document type i.e. abstracts of science and technological papers is also significantly different from newspaper articles. Neither a description of the concept of a term nor a training set of terms was given[4], since the aim of the workshop was the exchange of ideas (including the concept of a 'term' in itself) and techniques for ATR and related domains, including index-term extraction for IR. Term weighting was encouraged. The results of extraction were compared against two term sets: manual-candidates (MC, the terms that had been manually selected by the TMREC Group) and index-candidates (IC, the terms that had been found in an AI dictionary)[5]. MC contained 8,834 terms and IC contained 671 terms. A review of the workshop and results of additional experiments were published in the workshop proceedings [19][20] and in a special issue of *Terminology* [41].

As was stated in section 2, ATR systems generally use measures of termhood in combination with some criteria for unithood. Term candidates that satisfy the criteria are assigned termhood values and non-informative (or non-representative) candidates are filtered out. The following subsections summarize the results of two series of experiments.

4.2.2 Experiments I – Extraction of Single- and Double-Word Terms

The team's intention at the TMREC workshop was to see, in as direct a way as possible, the effectiveness of $Rep(\bullet, Dist)$ in capturing the termhood of technical terms. The term candidates were thus limited to word monograms and word bigrams because such terms are the base terms (actually, about 90% of the IC terms are single-word terms and double-word terms) and this limitation almost eliminated the effect of grammatical filters. This round of experiments is summarized below.

---

[4] After all participants had submitted their term candidates, the TMREC group disclosed the set of terms, which had been manually extracted by the group as a 'reference set' rather than a 'golden standard' [19][20].

[5] Terms in MC and those in IC are not exclusive.

Tokens and Initial Term Candidates

The team conducted word-based term extraction and used a Japanese morphological analysis (JMA) program to segment the sentences of NACSIS-AI into words [33]. Every single word and every word bigram which is surrounded by the delimiters of Japanese such as commas and particles in the corpus was extracted from the JMA output as an initial term candidate.

Selection of Term Candidates

For every initial term candidate T, $Rep(T, Dist)$ was calculated; T was then eliminated if $Rep(T, Dist)$ was below a threshold value.

Use of NACSIS-J

The $Rep(\bullet, Dist)$-value was calculated in two ways: in experiment E1, NACSIS-AI was used as the whole corpus; in experiment E2, NACSIS-AI was embedded in NACSIS-J and NACSIS-J was used as the whole corpus.

Evaluation

Six other teams participated and they submitted a total of 10 sets of extracted terms, which were then evaluated by the TMREC Group [19][20]. Table 5 shows the recall and precision rates obtained by the *DualNAVI* team for terms that fully matched some terms in the reference sets, where the numbers in parentheses are the rank of each rate in the 12 (E1, E2, and 10 others) submitted term sets. The team had anticipated fairly low recall rates for the results they submitted because they had limited the term candidates to single- and double-word candidates. This crude criterion was also expected to have affected the precision rate. On the other hand, embedding NACSIS-AI in NACSIS-J was effective, which had also been expected because of the statistical nature of $Rep(\bullet, Dist)$.

Of the results in table 5, the result for E2 vs. IC, is of interest [20]. Far fewer terms (5,275) were extracted than by the other teams (each of which extracted over 10,000 candidates) but the recall and precision rates were relatively higher (note that the only higher precision was the results vs. IC for E1 in table 5(a), where the corresponding recall rate is much lower). This indicates that the team's methods is suitable in picking out 'core terms' (e.g., those that would be adopted as the entries of an AI dictionary) because it eliminated frequently occurring but non-representative terms, while keeping the representative and frequently occurring terms, which are likely to be index terms.

Table 5. Submitted experimental results

(a) Result for E1

Number of ex-tracted terms	Comparison with MC		Comparison with IC	
	recall	precision	Recall	precision
943	4.90% (12)	45.92% (3)	21.01% (12)	14.49% (1)

(b) Result for E2

Number of ex-tracted terms	Comparison with MC		Comparison with IC	
	recall	precision	Recall	precision
5275	26.61% (8)	44.59% (4)	62.30% (3)	7.93% (2) .

4.3 Experiments II – Combination of Two Measures

In Experiments I, the focus had been on single- and double-word terms. The team conducted other experiments in which the order of term weights was considered and multi-word term candidates that contain n words are obtained form NACSIS-AI-Tagged, where n is unlimited. A measure of unithood is here indispensable.

The Measure of Unithood and the Rank of Term Candidates

Simply picking out those word n-grams that have higher values of $Rep(\bullet, Dist)$ to obtain topic words is a natural way of using the measure of representativeness, because in this case we need not worry about whether or not an n-gram thus obtained would be appropriate as, for example, a dictionary entry. In other words, the $Rep(\bullet, Dist)$ value does not, by definition, indicate anything with regard to the unithood of a word n-gram. This explains the low ranking correlation between the $Rep(\bullet, Dist)$ value and term frequency in Table 2.

However, if word n-grams are to be handled with their degrees of naturalness taken into consideration, some measure of unithood is indispensable. The team therefore used term frequency as the measure of *unithood*, since this is the easiest measure to calculate for any word n-gram. More importantly, term frequency provides a natural measure of both unithood and termhood and has been shown in the literature to provide a good baseline [3][6]. The fatal drawback of frequency is that it does not exclude frequently occurring non-representative terms.

On the other hand, low $Rep(\bullet, Dist)$ values (values which are below a threshold) are a natural indicator that subject n-grams are not terms, because terms to be registered as dictionary entries should have relatively high values for representativeness.

Therefore, it is natural to combine frequency with $Rep(\bullet, Dist)$ in term extraction: results for the former indicate unithood and results for the latter indicate representativeness. As for the order of the extracted terms candidates, term candidates are first sorted by frequency; those with $Rep(\bullet, Dist)$ values below a certain threshold are then eliminated. Frequency was used as term weight because an *ad-hoc* combination that has no mathematical foundation (for example, a linear combination of two weights) is not desirable and frequency does not provide a theoretically-based threshold value for the elimination of non-representative term candidates, while $Rep(\bullet, Dist)$ does.

Procedures of Experiments

The initial set of term candidates was the set of single nouns and compound nouns marked as NN or NS in NACSIS-AI-Tagged (17,149 items in total). Two different methods for eliminating terms were tested.

AND-type elimination: Eliminating those terms whose $Rep(\bullet, Dist)$ values are below a threshold (as in Series I).

OR-type elimination: Eliminating those terms where every constituent noun has a $Rep(\bullet, Dist)$ value which is below a threshold.

The effect of using NACSIS-J instead of NACSIS-AI in calculating $Rep(\bullet, Dist)$ values was also tested. Lastly, a simple grammatical filter was used to excluded non-terms of several types, including time expressions.

This gives us four combinations (experiments E3, E4, E5, and E6). A further experiment, E7, was conducted as a reference. In E7, the same initial candidate terms were simply sorted in order of term frequency and no elimination was applied. Table 6 lists these five experiments.

Table 6. Combination of elimination type and use/non-use of NACSIS-J as the superset of NACSIS-AI

	Elimination type	NACSIS-J used
E3	AND	Yes
E4	OR	Yes
E5	AND	No
E6	OR	No
E7	no elimination	No

Evaluation

Fig. 8 and Fig. 9 show the recall and precision of the results for E3 to E7, and table 7 shows the F-values. Fig. 8, 9, and table 7 include the other sets of experimental results that were submitted to the TMREC workshop (experiments "a", "b", …, "n", and "o" [20]). In the following, let us denote terms with highest N weights in the weighted list obtained in experiment E-i as $WL(i, N)$. Each linearly interpolated "curve" in Fig. 8 and Fig. 9 connects points whose coordinates are in the form (recall of $WL(E\text{-}i, N)$ with MC, precision of $WL(E\text{-}i, N)$ with MC), where $i = 3,…,7$ and N was increased in steps of 1,000 from 1,000.

Fig. 8, Fig. 9, and table 7 show that E4, with its combination of OR-type elimination and embedding NACSIS-AI into NACSIS-J outperformed all previously submitted results, E3, E5, and E6 in terms of F-values, where F-values was calculated by taking all output term candidates into account.

One striking fact is that E7, the simple reference experiment, had the best performance in terms of F-measure. This is further evidence that it is hard to outperform the simple use of frequency in term extraction.

However, if the number of output terms is limited to any size up to 5,000, E4 evidently outperforms the other four. From the viewpoint of collecting dictionary entries, selecting 5,000 terms out of 17,149 initial candidates is more reasonable than accepting all of the initial term candidates, as is the case for E7, since the number of the source abstracts is 1,870. The interpretation of the results of a term extraction process depends on the given aim.

The F-values for E3, …, E7 were slightly lower than that for a revised *Imp*-based system [29], but are substantially comparable when we take the grammatical criteria into account, since the criteria applied in the *Imp* system are more elaborate than those applied in E3, …, E7. Moreover, the *Imp* system does not provide a threshold value for termhood. Lastly, the top 2,000 candidates of E4 also turned out to have the best quality among those of E4 and the *Imp*-based system [29], although, as was mentioned above, comparing the performance of different measures of termhood in different ATR systems is very difficult because grammatical criteria differ from system to system.

Table 7. F-values of experiments

Experi-ment	F-value with MC	F-value with IC	Experi-ment	F-value with MC	F-value with IC
a	0.0886	0.175	k	0.4715	0.063
b	0.3333	0.141	l	0.5086	0.042
c	0.0270	0.065	m	0.5240	0.042
d	0.0355	0.068	n	0.4048	0.047
e	0.0509	0.092	o	0.3135	0.041
f	0.1126	0.188	E3	0.4440	0.095
g	0.2034	0.075	E4	0.5480	0.065
h	0.4356	0.047	E5	0.2070	0.147
i	0.4277	0.074	E6	0.5440	0.063
j	0.2555	0.084	E7	0.5500	0.073

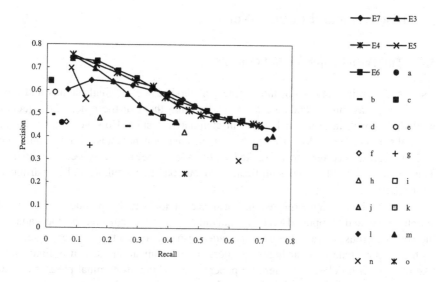

Fig. 8. Recall and precision of full match with manual-candidates

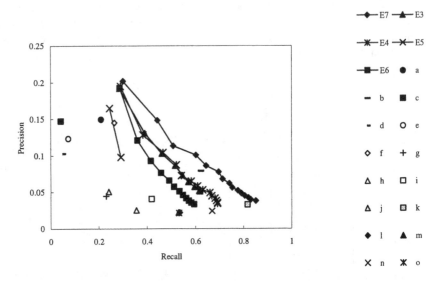

Fig. 9. Recall and precision of full match with index-candidates

5   Discussion and Future Work

5.1   The Term Frequency and Context

As was shown in section 4.3, the simplest method (using all single nouns and compound nouns as initial candidate terms and sorting them in the order of frequency) works fairly well in terms of F-value in cumulative results. However, such a simple method suffers a series drawback in the higher ranks of candidates. That is, candidates with no significance tend to be ranked highly simply because they occur frequently. This drawback is alleviated significantly in our baseline method and in particular, *Rep*(•, *Dist*).

The better-than-expected performance of the simple method that takes all simple nouns and compound nouns as candidates may be explained by the nature of the source corpus, i.e. a collection of academic-paper abstracts. It is very likely that such a corpus contains a far higher proportion of technical terms than ordinary texts like newspaper articles, full scientific papers, etc. Taking all nominal phrases as candidates, even with low frequency, can work well in such a field.

On the other hand, since our method is based on distributional property of $D(T)$, it performs poorly if the frequency of T is very low. We need to combine our method with other types of measures that generalize the contexts in which other terms with high frequency occur and thereby compensate the low frequency of specific candidates. The NC-value seems such an extension of the original C-value[10][11].

5.2   The Unit of Word Co-occurrence

In the experiments in section 4, we used an newspaper article or an abstract of scientific paper as the basic unit of document that actually defines the window size for word co-occurrence. However, when the actual document size increases, taking a document as the basic unit may be too crude. For example, if we deal with single books or even full scientific papers, to take them as basic unit would not work. In such cases, we may have to use a "word window" or a well-defined unit such as a sentence or a paragraph as basic unit.

The baseline method can be generalized by changing '$D(T)$' in the definitions of the measures in section 3 to '$Co(T)$', where $Co(T)$ denotes the set of all words that co-occurs with T in such defined unit.

For example, if we define $Co(T)$ as the set of all words which immediately precede T to form compound nouns, Nakagawa's $Pre(T)$ can be interpreted as $DIFFNUM(Co(T))$ for a single noun T (as for $DIFFNUM$, see section 3). $Post(T)$ can be defined in the same manner by defining $Co(T)$, as the set of all nouns noun which immediately follow T to form a compound noun. Thus $Pre(T)$ and $Post(T)$ can be normalized by the generalized baseline method, respectively. Note that $Pre(T)$ and $Pre(T)$ can be further defined in another way by choosing a different characteristic function on a set of words other than $DIFFNUM$[6], for instance, $ENTROPY$.

5.3   Combination with Other Measures

Section 4 showed that the rank correlation between $Rep(\bullet, Dist)$ and other measures, such as frequency, is very low. This means that $Rep(T, Dist)$ captures a property of T that is somewhat different from those captured by other measures. In general, the combination of low-correlation measures works better than an individual measure. To know actual correlations of ranks given by different measures, and to understand the qualitative properties of individual measures is therefore very important.

We are planning to investigate rank correlations between various measures (including $Rep(\bullet, Dist)$, Imp, C-value, and term frequency) and to further clarify the qualitative properties of the individual measures so as to find effective combinations of these measures for identification of terms.

5.4   Analytical Modeling of Baseline Functions

In the process of normalization, the baseline functions play a crucial role. The approximation of a baseline curve can be done within a few minutes by using a fast word-article association engine which the *DualNAVI* team developed [39]. Moreover,

---

[6] The generalized baseline method is not directly applicable to Imp, since $Imp(T)$ cannot be defined in the form $M(Co(T))$ where M is a characteristic function on a set of words.

we have experimentally clarified the portability of the baseline functions (see subsection 4.1).

However, we have not yet obtained an analytic model of the baseline functions. If the parameters of such a model be easily obtained by statistics that reflect the distribution of words over the whole corpus, immediate normalization on the baseline function would be possible for any given corpus, which would greatly extend the applicability of the baseline method. Therefore, obtaining an analytic model of a baseline function is not only of theoretical interest, but is also of practical importance.

5.5   Stop-Word Extraction

'Automatic term extraction' has been extensively studied in the fields of IR and NLP, as was stated in section 2. However, little attention has been paid to 'automatic *stop-word* extraction', which is a twin task of automatic *term* extraction, in spite of its importance. Since there is no established method for creating a stop-word list, the lists have generally been created by costly human labor with the help of some crude automatic techniques (such as discarding function words and words with 'extremely high' frequencies), or publicly available stop-word lists (for instance, that of the SMART system; [36]) have been used.

However, stop-word lists should be created on a corpus-by-corpus basis, because the notion of 'stop-word' changes according to the corpus. The experimental results shown in section 4 strongly suggest that $Rep(\bullet, Dist)$, in combination with frequency information, is applicable to the creation of stop-word lists. One possible approach is to discard a word w if its frequency is over a threshold (for example, a technique related to Zipf's law may be used to define this threshold; [25]) and, at the same time, its $Rep(\bullet, Dist)$ value is under a threshold value for representativeness.

The automatic creation of stop-word lists is an important topic, while intensive study of the effect of stop-word list on required tasks like IR is also required.

5.6   Further Measure That Characterizes Document Sets

Although $Rep(T, Dist)$ outperforms existing measures, it has still shares one intrinsic drawback with other measures, that is, words which are irrelevant to T and simply happen to occur in $D(T)$ – let us call these words non-typical words – contribute to the calculation of $M(D(T))$. Their contribution accumulates as *background noise* in $M(D(T))$, which is the very part that requires normalization on the baseline function. In other words, if $M(D(T))$ were to exclude the contribution of non-typical words, it would not need to be normalized and would be more precise.

This consideration led us to propose a different approach to measuring the bias of word occurrences: that is, we only take those words with frequencies of occurrences that are *saliently biased* in $D(T)$ into account, and let the number of such words be the degree of bias of word occurrence in $D(T)$. Thus, $SAL(D(T), s)$, the number of words in $D(T)$ that have a saliency above a threshold value s, is expected to be free from the above *background noise* and sensitive to the number of major subtopics in $D(T)$. The essential problem is how to define the *saliency of bias* of word occurrences and the threshold value of saliency. One of the authors found a solution to this problem and clearly demonstrated that $SAL(D(\bullet), s)$ is a more effective measure than $Rep(\bullet, Dist)$ in capturing topic-specific words. This work is to be published elsewhere [16].

6 Summary

We have developed several measures of term representativeness and a scheme called the *baseline method* for defining the measures. The representativeness of a term T is measured by a normalized characteristic value which reflects the bias of the distribution of words in $D(T)$, the set of all documents that contain T. $Dist(D(T))$, the distance between the distribution of words in $D(T)$ and in a whole corpus was, after normalization, found to be effective as a characteristic value which reflects the bias of the distribution of words in $D(T)$. We use $Rep(T, Dist)$ to denote the normalized value of $Dist(D(T))$.

A measure defined by the baseline method offers several advantages over classical measures: (1) its definition is mathematically simple and clear, (2) it can compare representativeness of a high-frequency term with that of a low-frequency term, (3) the threshold value for being representative is systematically definable, and (4) it is applicable to n-gram terms with any n.

Experiments showed that $Rep(T, Dist)$ strongly outperforms existing measures in evaluating the representativeness of terms in newspaper articles. It was particularly effective in discarding frequently occurring but non-informative terms. It was also effective, in combination with term frequency, as a means for automatically extracting terms from abstracts of papers on artificial intelligence.

We plan to apply $Rep(\bullet, Dist)$, in combination with other measures, to several tasks in the IR domain, such as the construction of stop-word lists for use in indexing and term weighting in calculations of document similarity. Theoretical modeling of the baseline functions by using such fundamental parameters as the total number of words in a corpus or the total number of distinct words is another interesting topic for future work.

Acknowledgements. This research was supported in part by the Advanced Software Technology Project under the auspices of the Information-Technology Promotion Agency, Japan and by the Core Research for Evolutional Science and Technology under the auspices of the Japan Science and Technology Corporation.

We would like to express our gratitude to Prof. Sophia Ananiadou of Salford University, Prof. Kyo Kageura of National Institute of Informatics, Dr. Hideki Mima of the University of Tokyo, Dr. Yoshiki Niwa of Hitachi, Ltd., and Prof. Akihiko Takano of National Institute of Informatics, for their insightful comments.

References

1. Aizawa, A.: The Feature Quantity: An Information Theoretic Perspective of Tf-id-like Measure. Proc. of ACM SIGIR2000. (2000) 104–111
2. Bessé, B.: "Terminological Definitions" in Handbook of Terminology Management, (transl. & ed. Sager, J. C.), Amsterdam: John Benjamins (1996) 69–80
3. Caraballo, S. A. and Charniak, E.: Determining the specificity of nouns from text. Proc. of EMNLP'99. (1999) 63–70
4. Church, K. W. and Hanks, P.: Word Association Norms, Mutual Information, and Lexicography. Computational Linguistics, Vol. 6, No. 1. (1990) 22–29
5. Cohen, J. D.: Highlights: Language- and Domain-independent Automatic Indexing Terms for Abstracting. J. of American Society for Information Science, Vol. 46, No. 3. (1995) 162–174
6. Daille, B. and Gaussier, E., and Lange, J.: Towards automatic extraction of monolingual and bilingual terminology. Proc. of COLING'94. (1994) 515–521
7. Damerau, F. J.: Evaluating Domain-oriented Multi-word Terms from Texts. Information Processing and Management, Vol. 29, No. 4. (1993) 433–477
8. Dunning, T.: Accurate Method for the Statistics of Surprise and Coincidence, Computational Linguistics, Vol. 19, No. 1. (1993) 61–74
9. Frantzi, K. T. and Ananiadou, S.: Statistical Measures for Terminological Expression. Proc. of the Third International Conference on Statistical Analysis of Textual Data. Rome: N.p. (1995) 297–308
10. Frantzi, K. T., Ananiadou, S., and Tsujii, J.: Extracting Terminological Expressions. Information Processing Society of Japan, Technical Report of SIGNL, NL112-12. (1996) 83–88
11. Frantzi, K. T., Ananiadou, S., and Tsujii, J.: The C-value/NC-value Method of Automatic Recognition for Multi-Word Terms. Proc. of European Conference on Digital Libraries. (1999) 585–604
12. Fukushige, Y. and Noguchi, N.: Statistical and Linguistics Approaches to automatic term recognition: NTCIR experiments at Matsushita, Terminology, Vol. 6, No. 2. (2000) 257–286
13. Hisamitsu, T., Niwa, Y., Nishioka, S., Sakurai, H., Imaichi, O., Iwayama, M., and Takano, A.: Term Extraction Using A New Measure of Term Representativeness. Proc. of NTCIR Workshop 1. (1999) 475–481
14. Hisamitsu, T., Niwa, Y., and Tsujii, J.: A Method of Measuring Term Representativeness −Baseline Method Using Co-occurrence Distribution−. Proc. of COLING2000. (2000) 320–326
15. Hisamitsu, T., Niwa, Y., Nishioka, S., Sakurai, H., Imaichi, O., Iwayama, M. and Takano, A.: Extracting Terms by a Combination of Term Frequency and a Measure of Term Representativeness. Terminology, Vol. 6, No. 2. (2000) 211–232
16. Hisamitsu, T. and Niwa, Y.: A Measure of Term Representativeness Based on the Number of Co-occurring Salient Words. Proc. of COLING2002. (2002) (to appear)
17. Jacquemin, C.: Spotting and Discovering Terms through NLP. MIT Press, Cambridge MA.(2001)
18. Kageura, K. and Umino, B.: Methods of automatic term recognition: A review. Terminology, Vol. 3, No. 2. (1996) 259–289
19. Kageura, K., Yoshioka, M., Takeuchi, K., Koyama, T., Tsuji,. K., Yoshikane, Y., and Okada, M.: Overview of TMREC Tasks. (1999) Proc. of NTCIR Workshop 1. (1999) 415

20. Kageura, K., Yoshioka, M., Tsuji,. K., Yoshikane, Y., Takeuchi, K., and Koyama, T.: Evaluation of the Term Recognition Task. Proc. of NTCIR Workshop 1. (1999) 417–434

21. Kageura, K., Yoshioka, M., Takeuchi, K., Koyama, T., Tsuji,. K., and Yoshikane, Y.: Recent Advances in automatic term recognition: Experiences from the NTCIR workshop on information retrieval and term recognition. Terminology, Vol. 6, No. 2. (2000) 151–174

22. Kando, N., Kuriyama, K., and Nozue, T.: NACSIS test collection workshop (NTCIR-1). Proc. of the 22nd Annual International ACM SIGIR Conf. on Research and Development in IR. (1999) 299–300

23. Kit, C.: Reduction of Indexing Term Space for Phrase-based Information Retrieval. Internal memo of Computational Linguistics Program. Pittsburgh: Carnegie Mellon University (1994)

24. Luhn, H. P.: A Statistical Approach to Mechanized Encoding and Searching Literary Information. IBM J. of Research and Development, Vol. 2, No. 2. (1957) 159–165

25. Maron, M. E.: Automatic Indexing: An Experimental inquiry. J. of the Association for Computer Machinery, Vol. 8, No. 3. (1961) 404–417

26. Mima, H. and Ananiadou, S.: An application and evaluation of the C/NC value approach for the automatic term recognition of multi-word units in Japanese. Terminology, Vol. 6, No. 2. (2000) 175–194

27. Nagao, M., Mizutani, M., and Ikeda, H.: An Automated Method of the Extraction of Important Words from Japanese Scientific Documents, Trans. of Information Processing Society of Japan, Vol. 17, No. 2. (1976) 110-117 (in Japanese)

28. Nakagawa, H. and Mori, T.: Nested Collocation and Compound Noun For Term Extraction, Proc. of Computerm'98. (1998) 64-70

29. Nakagawa, H: Automatic term recognition based on statistics of compound nouns. Terminology, Vol. 6, No. 2. (2000) 195–210

30. Niwa, Y., Nishioka, S., Iwayama, M., and Takano, A.: Topic graph generation for query navigation: Use of frequency classes for topic extraction. Proc. of NLPRS'97. (1997) 95–100

31. Noreault, T., McGill, M., and Koll, M. B.: A Performance Evaluation of Similarity Measure, Document Term Weighting Schemes and Representation in a Boolean Environment. In Oddey, R. N. (ed.), Information Retrieval Research. London: Butterworths. (1977) 57–76

32. Robertson, S. E., Walker, S., and Beaulieu, M.: Experimentation as a way of life: Okapi at TREC. Information Processing and Management. Vol. 36, No. 1. (2000) 95–108

33. Sakurai, H. and Hisamitsu, T.: A Data Structure for Fast Lookup of Grammatically Connectable Word Pairs in Japanese Morphological Analysis. Proc. of ICCPOL'99. (1999) 467–471

34. Salton, G. and Yang, C. S.: On the Specification of Term Values in Automatic Indexing Journal of Documentation. Vol. 29, No. 4. (1973) 351–372

35. Salton, G., Yang, C. S., and Yu, C. T.: A Theory of Term Importance in Automatic Text Analysis. J. of the American Society for Information Science. Vol. 26, No. 1. (1975) 33–44

36. Salton, G.: Automatic Text Processing. Addison-Wesley. (1988)

37. Singhal, A., Buckley, C., and Cochrane, P. A.: Pivoted Document Length Normalization, Proc. of ACM SIGIR'96. (1996) 126–133

38. Sparck-Jones, K.: Index Term Weighting. Information Storage and Retrieval. Vol. 9, No. 11. (1973) 619–633

39. Takano, A., Niwa, Y., Nishioka, S., Iwayama, M., Hisamitsu, T., Imaichi, O., and Sakurai, H.: Information Access Based on Associative Calculation. Lecture Notes in Computer Science, Vol. 1963. Springer-Verlag, Berlin Heidelberg New York (2000) 187–201

40. Teramoto, Y., Miyahara, Y., and Matsumoto, S. (1999). Word weight calculation for document retrieval by analyzing the distribution of co-occurrence words, Proc. of the 59th Annual Meeting of IPSJ. IP-06. (in Japanese)
41. Terminology, Vol. 6, No. 2. (2000)

Appendix

Kendall's Rank Correlation

Asusume that items $I_1,...,I_N$ are ranked by measures A and B, and that the rank of item I_j assigned by A (by B) is $R_A(j)$ ($R_B(j)$), where $R_A(i) \neq R_A(j)$ ($R_B(i) \neq R_B(j)$) if $i \neq j$. Then, Kendall's rank correlation between the two rankings is given as

$$\frac{1}{{}_N C_2} \times \left(\{ \#\{(i,j) \mid \sigma(R_A(i) - R_A(j)) = \sigma(R_B(i) - R_B(j))\} - \right.$$
$$\left. \#\{(i,j) \mid \sigma(R_A(i) - R_A(j)) = -\sigma(R_B(i) - R_B(j))\} \}\right), \tag{21}$$

where $\sigma(x) = 1$ if $x > 0$, else if $x < 0$, $\sigma(x) = 1$.

Finite-State Approaches to Web Information Extraction

Nicholas Kushmerick

Computer Science Department, University College Dublin; nick@ucd.ie

1 Introduction

Information agents are emerging as an important approach to building next-generation value-added information services. An information agent is a distributed system that receives a goal through its user interface, gathers information relevant to this goal from a variety of sources, processes this content as appropriate, and delivers the results to the users. We focus on the second stage in this generic architecture. We survey a variety of information extraction techniques that enable information agents to automatically gather information from heterogeneous sources.

For example, consider an agent that mediates package-delivery requests. To satisfy such requests, the agent might need to retrieve address information from geographic services, ask an advertising service for freight forwarders that serve the destination, request quotes from the relevant freight forwarders, retrieve duties and legal constraints from government sites, get weather information to estimate transportation delays, etc.

Information extraction (IE) is a form of shallow document processing that involves populating a database with values automatically extracted from documents. Over the past decade, researchers have developed a rich family of generic IE techniques that are suitable for a wide variety of sources, from rigidly formatted documents such as HTML generated automatically from a template, to natural-language documents such as newspaper articles or email messages.

In this chapter, we view information extraction as a core enabling technology for a variety of information agents. We therefore focus specifically on information extraction, rather than tangential (albeit important) issues, such as how agents can discover relevant sources or verify the authenticity of the retrieved content, or caching policies that minimize communication while ensuring freshness.

Before proceeding, we observe that XML alone will not eliminate the need for automatic information extraction. First, there are terabytes of content available from numerous legacy services that will probably never export their data in XML. Second, it is impossible to determine "the" correct annotation scheme, and applications will have their own idiosyncratic needs ("should the unit of currency be included when extracting prices?", "should people's names be split into first and surname?", "should dates such as 'Sun. May 14, 67' be canonicalized to 14/05/1967?"). For these reasons we expect that automatic information extraction will continue to be essential for many years.

M.T. Pazienza (Ed.): SCIE 2002, LNAI 2700, pp. 77–91, 2003.

Scalability is the key challenge to automatic information extraction. There are two relevant dimensions. The first dimension is the ability to rapidly process large document collections. IE systems generally scale well in this regard because they rely on simple shallow extraction rules, rather than sophisticated (and therefore slow) natural language processing.

The second and more problematic dimension is the number of distinct sources. For example, a package-delivery agent might need to request quotes from a thousand different freight forwarders, weather information from dozens of forecast services, etc. IE is challenging in this scenario because each source might format its content differently, and therefore each source could require a customized set of extraction rules.

Machine learning is the only domain-independent approach to scaling along this second dimension. This chapter focuses on the use of machine learning to enable *adaptive information extraction* systems that automatically learn extraction rules from training data in order to scale with the number of sources.

The general idea behind adaptive information extraction is that a human expert annotates a small corpus of training documents with the fragments that should be extracted, and then the learning system generalizes from these examples to produce some form of knowledge or rules that reliably extract "similar" content from other documents. While human-annotated training data can be expensive, the assumption underlying adaptive IE is that it is easier to annotate documents than to write extraction rules, since the latter requires some degree of programming expertise. Furthermore, we will describe techniques aimed at minimizing the amount of training data required for generalization, or even eliminating the need for manual annotation entirely.

The adaptive information extraction research community has developed a wide variety of techniques and approaches, each tailored to particular extraction tasks and document types. Many of these approaches to Web information extraction can be categorized as *finite-state* approaches, in that the learned extraction knowledge structures are formally equivalent to (possibly stochastic) regular grammars or automata. We survey several prominent examples, as well as some additional research that relates to the entire wrapper "life-cycle" beyond the core learning task:

- Section 2 introduces *wrapper induction*, an approach to adaptive IE tailored for highly regular Web documents;
- Section 3 describes a variety of *expressive extensions* to the basic wrapper induction framework;
- Section 4 explores whether finite-state techniques can be used for *natural language* documents;
- Section 5 describes the use of *hidden Markov models* for adaptive IE;
- Section 6 discusses approaches to wrapper *verification and maintenance*, two central issues in the long-term "lifecycle" of adaptive IE systems;
- Section 7 describes a technique for post-processing the extracted fragments into *coherent meaningful objects*; and

- Section 8 explains how *active learning* techniques can be used to minimize
the amount of manually-annotated training data required for accurate generalization.

For the sake of brevity we can not describe these techniques in detail, but see
[15] for more information about some of these ideas.

2   Wrapper Induction

Kushmerick first formalized adaptive Web information extraction with his work
on *wrapper induction* [12,8,10]. Kushmerick identified a family of six wrapper
classes, and demonstrated that the wrappers were both relatively expressive
(they can learn wrappers for numerous real-world Web sites), and also relatively
efficient (only a handful of training examples, and a few CPU seconds per example, are needed for learning).

To illustrate Kushmerick's wrapper induction work, consider the example
Web page shown in Figure 1(a), its HTML encoding (b), and the content to be
extracted (c). This example is clearly extremely simple, but it exhibits all the
features that are salient for our discussion.

Kushmerick's wrappers consist of a sequence of delimiters strings for finding
the desired content. In the simplest case (shown in Figure 1(d–e)), the content is
arranged in a tabular format with K columns, and the wrapper scans for a pair
of delimiters for each column, for a total of $2K$ delimiters. The notation "ℓ_k"
indicates the left-hand delimiter for the k'th column, and "r_k" is the k'th column's right-hand delimiter. In this case of the country-code wrapper ccwrap$_\mathrm{LR}$,
we have $K = 2$.

To execute the wrapper, procedure ccwrap$_\mathrm{LR}$ (Figure 1(d)) scans for the
string ℓ_1 =<B> from the beginning of the document, and then scans ahead until
the next occurrence of r_1 =</B>. The procedure then extracts the text between
these positions as the value of the first column of the first row. The procedure
then scans for ℓ_2 =<I> and then for r_2 =</I>, and extracts the text between
these positions as the value of the second column of the first row. This process then starts over again with ℓ_1; extraction terminates when ℓ_1 is missing
(indicating the end of the document).

Figure 1(e) formalizes these ideas as the *Left-Right* (LR) wrapper class. An
LR wrapper w_LR consists of a set $\{\langle \ell_1, r_1 \rangle, \dots, \langle \ell_K, r_K \rangle\}$ of $2K$ delimiters, one
pair for each column to be extracted, and the "operational semantics" of LR
are provided by the exec$_\mathrm{LR}$ procedure (Figure 1(e)). This procedure scans for
ℓ_1 from the beginning of the document, and then scans ahead until the next
occurrence of r_1. The procedure then extracts the text between these positions
as the value of the first column of the first row. ccwrap$_\mathrm{LR}$ then scans for ℓ_2 and
then for r_2, and extracts the text between these positions as the value of the
second column of the first row. This process is repeated for all K columns. After
searching for r_K, the procedure starts over again with ℓ_1; extraction terminates
when ℓ_1 is missing (indicating the end of the document).

(a)

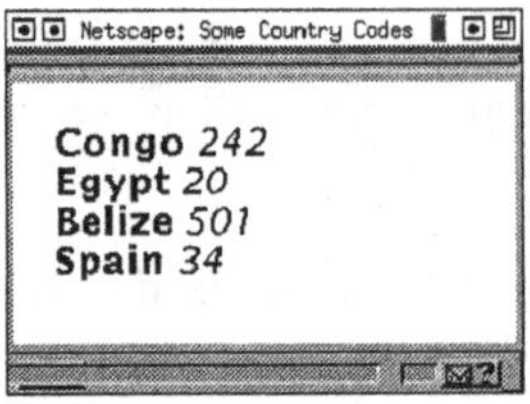

```
Netscape: Some Country Codes

Congo 242
Egypt 20
Belize 501
Spain 34
```

(b)

```
<HTML><TITLE>Some Country Codes</TITLE><BODY>
<B>Congo</B> <I>242</I><BR>
<B>Egypt</B> <I>20</I><BR>
<B>Belize</B> <I>501</I><BR>
<B>Spain</B> <I>34</I><BR>
</BODY></HTML>
```

(c)
$$\left\{ \begin{array}{l} \langle\text{'Congo'}, \text{'242'}\rangle, \\ \langle\text{'Egypt'}, \text{'20'}\rangle, \\ \langle\text{'Belize'}, \text{'501'}\rangle, \\ \langle\text{'Spain'}, \text{'34'}\rangle \end{array} \right\}$$

(d)

procedure $\text{ccwrap}_{\text{LR}}(\text{page } P)$
    while there are more occurrences in P of '<B>'
        for each $\langle\ell_k, r_k\rangle \in \{\langle\text{'<B>'}, \text{'</B>'}\rangle, \langle\text{'<I>'}, \text{'</I>'}\rangle\}$
            scan in P to next occurrence of ℓ_k; save position as start of k'th attribute
            scan in P to next occurrence of r_k; save position as end of k'th attribute
    return extracted $\{\ldots, \langle\text{country}, \text{code}\rangle, \ldots\}$ pairs

(e)

procedure $\text{exec}_{\text{LR}}(\text{wrapper } w_{\text{LR}} = \{\langle\ell_1, r_1\rangle, \ldots, \langle\ell_K, r_K\rangle\}, \text{page } P)$
    $m \leftarrow 0$
    while there are more occurrences in P of ℓ_1
        $m \leftarrow m + 1$
        for each $\langle\ell_k, r_k\rangle \in \{\langle\ell_1, r_1\rangle, \ldots, \langle\ell_K, r_K\rangle\}$
            scan in P to the next occurrence of ℓ_k; save position as $b_{m,k}$
            scan in P to the next occurrence of r_k; save position as $e_{m,k}$
    return label $\{\ldots, \langle\langle b_{m,1}, e_{m,1}\rangle, \ldots, \langle b_{m,K}, e_{m,K}\rangle\rangle, \ldots\}$

Fig. 1. A fictitious Internet site providing information about countries and their telephone country codes: (a) an example Web page; (b) the HTML document corresponding to (a); (c) the content to be extracted; (d) the $\text{ccwrap}_{\text{LR}}$ procedure, which generates (c) from (b); and (e) the exec_{LR} procedure, a generalization of $\text{ccwrap}_{\text{LR}}$.

Given this definition, the LR machine learning task is to automatically construct an LR wrapper, given a set of training documents. LR learning is relatively efficient, because the $2K$ delimiters can all be learned independently. The key insight is that whether a particular candidate is valid for some delimiter has no impact on the other delimiters. Based on this observation, Kushmerick describes a quadratic-time algorithm for learning LR wrappers. The algorithm simply enumerates over potential values for each delimiter, selecting the first that satisfies a constraint that guarantees that the wrapper will work correctly on the training data. Kushmerick demonstrates (both empirically, and theoretically under the PAC model) that this algorithm requires a modest training sample to converge to the correct wrapper.

Of course, just because an efficient learning algorithm exists does not mean that the wrappers are useful! Below, we discuss the limitations of the LR class and show that it can not handle documents with more complicated formatting. However, even the very simple LR class was able to successfully wrap 53% of Web sites, according to a survey. While LR is by no means a definitive solution to Web information extraction, it clearly demonstrates that simple techniques can be remarkably effective.

LR is effective for simple pages, but even minor complications to the formatting can render LR ineffective. For example, consider ℓ_1. The LR class requires a value for ℓ_1 that reliably indicates the beginning of the first attribute. However, there may be no such delimiter. For example, suppose that Figure 1(b) was modified to include a heading `<B>Country code list</B>` at the top of the document. In this case the delimiter $\ell_1 = $`<B>` used by ccwrap$_{LR}$ would not work correctly. Indeed, it is possible to show that there is no legal value for ℓ_1 and hence no LR wrapper for documents modified in this manner.

Kushmerick tackled these issues by extending LR to a family of five additional wrapper classes. First, the *Head-Left-Right-Tail* (HLRT) class uses two additional delimiters to skip over potentially-confusing text in either the head (top) or tail (bottom) of the page. In the example above, a head delimiter h (such as $h = $`list`) could be used to skip over the initial `<B>` at the top of the document, enabling $\ell_1 = $`<B>` to work correctly. Alternatively, the *Open-Close-Left-Right* (OCLR) class uses two additional delimiters to identify an entire tuple in the document, and then uses the regular LR strategy within this mini-document to extract each attribute in turn. These two ideas can be combined in fourth wrapper class, the *Head-Open-Close-Left-Right-Tail* (HOCLRT) class.

Finally, Kushmerick explored two simple wrappers for data that is not formatted in a simple tabular fashion. The *Nested-Left-Right* (NLR) class can be used to extract hierarchically-organized data, such as a book's table of contents. NLR operates like LR except that, after processing r_k, there are $k+1$ possibilities (start at level $k+1$, continue level k, return to level $k-1$, ..., return to level 1) instead of just one (proceed to attribute $k+1$). The *Nested-Head-Left-Right-Tail* (NHLRT) class combines NLR and HLRT.

Kushmerick developed specialized learning algorithms for each of these five classes. He demonstrated, both empirically and using complexity theory, that there is a trade-off between the expressive power of the wrapper classes and the extent to which they can be efficiently learned. For example, even though the six classes can successfully wrap 70% of surveyed sites, the algorithms for learning NLR and NHLRT wrappers take time that grows exponentially in the number of attributes, and a PAC analysis reveals that HOCLRT requires substantially more training examples to converge compared to the other classes.

3   More Expressive Wrapper Classes

Following Kushmerick's initial investigation of the LR family of wrappers, there has been substantial research effort at elaborating various alternative wrapper classes, and deriving more efficient learning algorithms. Even when Kushmerick's various extended wrapper classes are taken into consideration, there are numerous limitations. Muslea et al [16], Hsu and Dung [6], and others have developed various wrapper-learning algorithms that address the following shortcomings:

Missing attributes. Complicated pages may involve missing or null attribute values. If the corresponding delimiters are missing, then a simple wrapper will not process the remainder of the page correctly. For example, a French e-commerce site might only specify the country in addresses outside France.

Multi-valued attributes. The simple wrapper classes discussed so far assume a simple relational model in which each attribute has a single value, but non-relational structures such as multi-valued attributes are natural in many scenarios. For example, a hotel guide might explicitly list the cities served by a particular chain, rather than use a wasteful binary encoding of all possible cities.

Multiple attribute orderings. The wrappers described so far assume that the attributes (and therefore the delimiters) will occur in one fixed ordering, but variant orderings abound in complicated documents. For example, a movie site might list the release date before the title for movies prior to 1999, but after the title for recent movies.

Disjunctive delimiters. The wrappers discussed above assume a single delimiter for each attribute, but complicated sites might use multiple delimiters. For example, an e-commerce site might list prices with a bold face, except that sale prices are rendered in red.

Nonexistent delimiters. The wrappers described earlier assume that some irrelevant background tokens separate the content to be extracted, but this assumption may be violated in some cases. For example, how can the department code be separated from the course number in strings such as "COMP4016" or "GEOL2001". This problem is also relevant for many Asian languages in which words are not tokenized by spaces.

Typographical errors and exceptions. Real-world documents may contain errors, and if these errors occur in the formatting that drives extraction, then a simplistic wrapper may fail on the entire page even if just a small portion is badly formatted.

Sequential delimiters. So far, the wrapper classes above assumed a single delimiter per attribute, but the simplest way to develop an accurate wrapper might be to scan for several delimiters in sequence. For example, to extract the name of a restaurant from a review it might simpler to scan for <B>, then to scan for <BIG> from that position, and finally to scan for <FONT>, rather than to force the wrapper to scan the document for a single delimiter that reliably indicates the extracted content.

Hierarchically organized data. Kushmerick's nested classes are a first step at handling non-tabular data, but his results are largely negative. In complicated scenarios there is a need extraction according to a nested or embedded structure.

Hsu and Dung [6] addresses the problem of learning wrappers that correspond to an expressive class of deterministic finite-state transducers. This formalism handles all but the last two requirements just mentioned. The transducer processes the document to extract a single tuple; after extraction control returns to the start state and the second tuple is extracted, etc. Each extracted attribute is represented as a pair of states: one state to identify the start of the attribute value and the second to identify the end.

Since a general automaton model is used, states can be connected in an arbitrary manner, permitting missing attributes (skipped states), multi-valued attributes (cycles) and multiple attribute orderings (multiple paths from the start to end state). Furthermore, state-transitions are governed by an expressive rule language that allows disjunctive delimiters. A limited form of exception-processing is permitted, allowing the system to recover from formatting errors and exceptions. Crucially, Hsu and Dung describe an algorithm for efficiently learning their wrapper transducers from training data. Empirically, the report that their wrapper classes handles the 30% sites that could not be wrapped by Kushmerick's wrapper classes.

Muslea et al [16] identify a class of wrappers that, unlike Hsu and Dung, tackle the last two issues mentioned above. The main distinguishing feature of Muslea et al's wrappers is the use of multiple delimiters that they call landmarks. Rather than insisting that there exist a single delimiter that exactly identifies the relevant position deep inside some document, landmark-based wrappers use a sequence of delimiters to jump to the appropriate position in a series of simple steps. These simple steps are usually easier to learn, and enable more robust extraction. A second major feature of Muslea et al's work is that their "embedded catalog" formalization of nested data is more expressive than the simple hierarchical approach used by Kushmerick.

4   Extraction from Natural Text

The techniques described so far are aimed at highly regular documents, such as machine-generated HTML emitted by CGI programs. However, most research on information extraction has focused on natural free-text documents, such as email messages, newspaper articles, resumes, etc. Are the "wrapper" results relevant to these less structured domains. Several recent investigations have shown promising results.

Freitag and Kushmerick [4] explore "boosted wrapper induction". They define a class of extraction patterns that is essentially the LR class, for the case when there is exactly $K = 1$ attributes. They then enrich this class by permitting delimiters to contain wild-cards over token types (eg, <Num> rather than specific instances such as 23).

For example, for a corpus of email seminar announcements, the algorithm learns the following rule for extracting the starting time: {([time :],[<Num>]), ([], [- <Num> : <*> <Alpha>])}, which matches a document such as "...Time: <u>2:00</u> - 3:00 pm ...", where the fragment to be extracted has been underlined. This rule basically says "to find the start of the time, look for 'time:' followed by any number; then find the end of the time by looking for a dash, another number, a colon, any token at all, and finally an alphanumeric token".

This simple rule language is by itself not very useful for extraction from free text. Freitag and Kushmerick improve the performance by using boosting (a general technique for improving the accuracy of a weak learning algorithm) to learn many such rules. Each individual rule has high precision, but low recall; when combined, the rule set has both high precision and high recall. The result is an accurate extraction algorithm that is competitive with other state-of-the-art approaches in a variety of free-text domains, and superior in many. For example, boosted wrapper induction performs essentially perfectly at the task of extracting seminar announcement times, and better than most competitors at other attributes such as the speaker name and seminar location.

Soderland [19] describes a related approach to using finite-state techniques for information extraction from free text. Soderland's extraction rules correspond to a restricted class of regular expressions. These regular expressions serve two purposes: they can be both contextual pattern for determining whether a particular fragment should be extracted, or delimiters for determining the precise boundaries of the target fragment. Soderland's language is important because it is designed to work for documents that span the spectrum from unstructured natural text through to highly structured Web pages. Depending on the degree of structure in the training documents, the learning algorithm automatically creates appropriate patterns. For example, if simple delimiter-based extraction is sufficiently accurate then the learning algorithm will not bother to add additional contextual constraints.

For example, consider extracting the price and number of bedrooms from apartment listing documents such as "Capitol Hill- 1 br twnhme. D/W W/D. Pkg incl $675. 3BR upper flr no gar. $995. (206) 999-9999". Soderland's system learns rules such as "* (<Digit>) 'BR' * '$' (<Numb>)", where the parenthesized portions of the regular expression indicate the values to be extracted. This rule would extract the content {(1, 675), (3, 995)} from the example document.

5   Hidden Markov Models

The work of Freitag and Kushmerick [4] and Soderland [19] are two instances of generalizing finite-state approaches from rigidly structured HTML documents to less structured documents such as email and newspaper articles. However, these approaches are still brittle because they do not have any facility for evaluating the strength of the evidence that guides extraction decisions. For example, suppose the phrase will be held in often precedes a seminar location, but a new document contains the typographical error will held in. The techniques described so far make binary decisions and thus have no way to use this uncertain evidence.

Hidden Markov Models are a principled and efficient approach to handling this sort of inherent uncertainty. A Hidden Markov Model (HMM) is a stochastic finite-state automaton. States emit tokens according to a fixed and state-specific distribution, and transitions between states occur according to a fixed distribution. HMMs are an attractive computational device because there are efficient algorithms for both learning the model's distribution parameters, and for inferring the most-likely state sequence given some observed token sequence.

To use HMMs for information extraction, states are associated with the tokens to be extracted. For example, with the email seminar announcement corpus, the HMM would contain a state for the start time tokens, the end time tokens, the speaker name tokens, and the location tokens. Optionally, there may be additional states that generate "background" tokens. To perform extraction, the standard HMM Viterbi decoding algorithm is used to determine the most-likely state-sequence to have generated the observed document, and then the extracted fragments can simply by read off this most-likely path.

Hidden Markov models have been used successfully by numerous researchers in a variety of extraction scenarios (eg, [1,13]). They key challenge is that there is no efficient general-purpose algorithm for determining an appropriate state topology (ie, which state-state distribution probabilities should be forced to be zero and which should be permitted to be positive). Initial work has generally used a hand-crafted topology, in which the states are connected manually in a "reasonable" way after evaluating the training corpus.

More recently, there have been several attempts to automatically learn an appropriate topology. The general approach is to greedily search the space of possible topologies for one that maximizes some objective function. Seymore et al [18] attempt to maximize the probability of the training data given the topology. This approach is reasonably efficient but potentially misguided: the goal of using an HMM is not to model the training data per se, but to perform accurate extraction. Freitag and McCallum [5] therefore use as the objective function the actual accuracy of the proposed topology for extraction from a held-out validation corpus. While this approach is significantly slower it can result in a more compact topology and better generalization.

6 Wrapper Maintenance

All of the wrapper-learning work described earlier ignores an important complication. Information agents generally have no control over the sources from which they receive data. As described above, the agent's wrappers tend to be relatively brittle, as the invariably rely on idiosyncratic formatting details observed during the learning process. Unfortunately, if the source modifies its formatting (for example, to "remodel" its user interface) then the observed regularities will no longer hold and the wrapper will fail. As a concrete example, Figure 2 shows the Altavista search engine, before and after a site redesign.

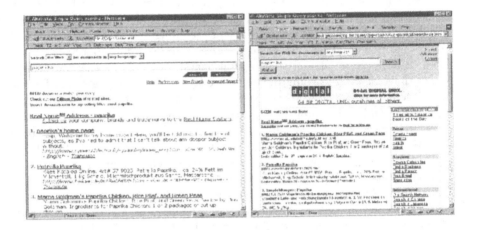

Fig. 2. Two snapshots of the Altavista search engine, before and after a remodeling of the site on 29 May 1998. Note that both the presentation and content have changed.

The two key challenges to wrapper maintenance are *wrapper verification* (determining whether the wrapper is still operating correctly), and *wrapper re-induction* (learning a revised wrapper). The second challenge is considerably more difficult, although even wrapper verification is non-trivial. The difficulty is that at most web sites, either the content to be extracted, or the formatting regularities, or both, may have changed, and the verification algorithm must distinguish the two. For example, suppose that the change in the Microsoft stock price is checked three times at a stock-quote server, and the extracted values are +3.10, -0.61 and <B><IMG src=advert.gif>. Intuitively our verification algorithm should realize that the relatively the first two values are "similar" and do not indicate trouble, but the third value is an outlier and probably indicates a defective wrapper.

Kushmerick [9,11] describes a simple and accurate algorithm for wrapper verification. The algorithm first learns a probabilistic model of the data extracted by the wrapper during a training period when it is known to be operating correctly. This model captures various properties of the training data such as the length or the fraction of numeric characters of the extracted data. To verify the wrapper after the training period, the extracted data is evaluated against the learned model to estimate the probability that wrapper is operating correctly. The algorithm is domain independent and is not tied to any particular wrapper class or learning algorithm, but rather treats the wrapper as a black-box and inspects only its output. The algorithm handles (acyclic) XML data, not just relational data, so it is applicable to all of the wrapper classes described above.

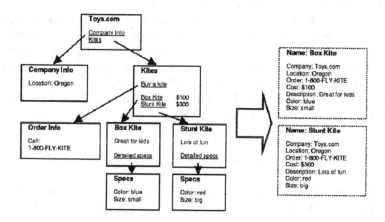

Fig. 3. A complicated extraction task in which attribute values are both distributed across multiple documents, and reused across objects. (Adapted from [7].)

Wrapper re-induction has also received some attention. Lerman et al [14] learn a probabilistic model of the extracted data that is similar to (though substantially more expressive than) that used by Kushmerick. This more sensitive model enables wrapper re-induction as follows. After a wrapper is deemed to be broken, the learned model is used to identify probable target fragments in the (new and unannotated) documents. This training data is then post-processed to (heuristically) remove noise, and the data is given to a wrapper induction algorithm. Lerman et al demonstrate empirically that this semi-supervised approach is highly accurate in many real-world extraction scenarios.

7   Post-processing Extracted Content

The work described so far is highly simplified in that the task is assumed to involve simply processing a given document to extract particular target fragments. However, in many extraction scenarios, the information to be extracted is actually distributed across multiple documents, or an attribute value is given only once on a page but is relevant to several extracted objects. For example, Figure 3 shows a simple scenario in which some attribute values are "re-used" across multiple extracted objects, and other values must be harvested from a collection of hyperlinked documents.

Some of these issues are handled by the wrapper classes defined earlier. For example, Muslea et al's embedded catalog formalism [16] permits an extracted fragment to be "shared" across multiple objects. Furthermore, the information extraction community has long investigated the issue of cross-document references. However, these approaches require considerable linguistic processing and are not applicable to the example shown in Figure 3.

Jensen and Cohen [7] address these problems by proposing a language for specifying how the extracted data should be post-processed. Rules express how the raw extracted data should be grouped into larger composite objects. Jensen and Cohen argue that their language is sufficiently expressive to handle the data extracted from 500 web sites exporting job and product advertisements. Furthermore, they suggest (though do not implement) an algorithm for automatically learning such rules from examples of grouped data.

8   Beyond Supervision

The key bottleneck with adaptive information extraction is obtaining the labeled training data. The use of machine learning is motivated by the fact that the cost of labeling documents is usually considerably less than the cost of writing the wrapper's extraction rules by hand. Nevertheless, labeling documents can require considerable domain expertise, and is generally tedious and error-prone. The approaches described so far simply assumes that an adequate training corpus exists, but considerable research effort has investigated so-called "active learning" methods for minimizing the amount of training data required to achieve a satisfactory level of generalization.

The basic idea of active learning is to start with a small amount of training data, run the learning algorithm, and then used the learned wrapper to predict which of the remaining unlabeled documents is most informative, in the sense of helping the learning system generalize most with the one additional training document. As a trivial example, if the corpus contains duplicate documents, then the learner should not suggest that the same document be annotated twice.

As one example of the use of active learning in the context of wrapper induction, consider Muslea et al [17]. The basic idea of this approach is that every information extraction task has a "dual", and correlations between the original task and its dual can help the system identify useful unlabeled documents.

Recall that Muslea et al's wrapper learning algorithm learns a sequence of landmarks for scanning from the beginning of the document to the start of a fragment to be extracted. An alternative way of finding the same position is to scan backwards from the end of the document for a (different!) set of landmarks. Muslea's active-learning extensions solves both learning tasks in parallel on the available training data. The two resulting wrappers are then applied to all the unlabeled documents. The system then asks the user to label one of the documents for which the two wrappers give different answers. Intuitively, if the two wrappers agree for a given unlabeled document, then the document is unlikely to be useful for subsequent learning.

Muslea et al demonstrate that the active-learning version of their algorithm requires significantly less training data to obtain the same level of generalization. For example, averaged across a variety of challenging extraction tasks, the error of the learned wrapper is about 50% less when the user annotates ten training documents chosen in this intelligent manner, compared to ten documents chosen randomly.

Brin [2] explores a different sort of extraction task, in which the user gives the system examples of some concept. For example, to learn to extract book title/author pairs, the user would supply a small sample of pairs, such as {(Isaac Asimov, The Robots of Dawn), (Charles Dickens, Great Expectations), ... }. The job of the extraction system is then to flesh out this list with as many additional instances as possible.

Brin's algorithm iteratively searches the Web for the seed pairs. When it finds a document that contains a pair, it learns an information extraction pattern for that particular pair, and then applies this pattern to the remainder of the page. The resulting extracted pairs are added to the seeds and the process iterates. There is no guarantee that this process will converge or even that the extracted pairs are correct. Nevertheless, preliminary experiments demonstrated promising results.

Finally, Crescenzi et al [3] focus on an even bigger challenge: wrapper learning without any supervision (labeled training data) at all. Consider the pages from some online bookstore that would be returned by two queries, for Dickens and for Asimov. In most cases, these pages would be formatted the same way, with the only difference being the content to be extracted. The intuition behind Crescenzi et al's approach is that a wrapper can be learned by comparing these two pages and finding similarities and differences. The similarities correspond to common formatting and structural elements; the differences correspond to data to be extracted. By repeatedly replacing the differences with wild-cards and noting repetitive structures, their algorithm can learn a wrapper that corresponds to a regular grammar, without the need for any manually labeled training data. Crescenzi et al report that their algorithm works well in a variety of real-world domains.

9 Summary

Information extraction is a core enabling technology for a wide variety of information-gathering and -management agents. The central challenge to information extraction is the ability to scale with the number and variety of information sources. We have described a variety of adaptive information extraction approaches that use machine learning techniques to automatically learn extraction rules or knowledge from training data.

Due to the highly practical nature of the IE task, all of the approaches described in this chapter have been tested on various real world examples. That means the gap between pure research and practical usage in agent systems is smaller than it might seem at first glance.

We have focused on one particular sub-field of adaptive information extraction: *finite state* techniques that learn extraction knowledge corresponding to regular grammars or automata. In addition to the core adaptive IE techniques, we also briefly discussed several issues related to the entire information extraction "lifecycle".

Perhaps the most fundamental open issue in adaptive information extraction is a method for determining which technique is best suited to any particular extraction task. Today, this complicated judgment requires considerable expertise and experimentation. Ultimately, we foresee a semi-automated methodology in which the heterogeneity of the documents could be measured in various dimensions, in order to predict the simplest approach that will deliver satisfactory performance.

Acknowledgments. I thank Bernd Thomas for helpful discussions. This research was supported by grant N00014-00-1-0021 from the US Office of Naval Research, and grant SFI/01/F.1/C015 from Science Foundation Ireland.

References

1. D. Bikel, S. Miller, R. Schwartz, and R. Weischedel. Nymble: A high-performqance learning name-finder. In *Proc. Conf. on Applied Natural Language Processing*, 1997.
2. S. Brin. Extracting patterns and relations from the World Wide Web. In *Proc. SIGMOD Workshop on Databases and the Web*, 1998.
3. V. Crescenzi, G. Mecca, and P. Merialdo. Roadrunner: Towards automatic data extraction from large web sites. In *The VLDB Journal*, pages 109–118, 2001.
4. D. Freitag and N. Kushmerick. Boosted Wrapper Induction. In *Proceedings of the Seventh National Conference on Artificial*, pages 577–583, July 30 - August 3 2000. Austin, Texas.
5. D. Freitag and A. McCallum. Information Extraction with HMM structures learned by stochastic optimization. In *Proceedings of the Seventh National Conference on Artificial*, July 30 - August 3 2000. Austin, Texas.
6. C. Hsu and M. Dung. Generating finite-state transducers for semistructured data extraction from the web. *J. Information Systems*, 23(8):521–538, 1998.
7. L. Jensen and W. Cohen. Grouping extracted fields. In *Proc. IJCAI-01 Workshop on Adaptive Text Extraction and Mining*, 2001.
8. N. Kushmerick. *Wrapper Induction for Information Extraction*. PhD thesis, University of Washington, 1997.
9. N. Kushmerick. Regression testing for wrapper maintenance. In *Proc. National Conference on Artificial Intelligence*, pages 74–79, 1999.
10. N. Kushmerick. Wrapper induction: Efficiency and expressiveness. *Artificial Intelligence*, 118(1–2):15–68, 2000.
11. N. Kushmerick. Wrapper verification. *World Wide Web Journal*, 3(2):79–94, 2000.
12. N. Kushmerick, D. S. Weld, and R. Doorenbos. Wrapper Induction for Information Extraction. In M. E. Pollack, editor, *Fifteenth International Joint Conference on Artificial Intelligence*, volume 1, pages 729–735, August 1997. Japan.
13. T. Leek. Information extraction using hidden Markov models. Master's thesis, University of California, San Diego, 1997.
14. K. Lerman and S. Minton. Learning the common structure of data. In *Proc. National Conference on Artificial Intelligence*, 2000.

15. I. Muslea. Extraction patterns for information extraction tasks: A survey. In *Proc. AAAI-99 Workshop on Machine Learning for Information Extraction*, 1999.
16. I. Muslea, S. Minton, and C. Knoblock. A hierarchical approach to wrapper induction. In *Proc. Third International Conference on Autonomous Agents*, pages 190–197, 1999.
17. I. Muslea, S. Minton, and C. Knoblock. Selective sampling with redundant views. In *Proc. National Conference on Artificial Intelligence*, 2000.
18. K. Seymore, A. McCallum, and R. Rosenfeld. Learning hidden Markov model structure for information extraction. In *Proc. AAAI-99 Workshop on Machine Learning for Information Extraction*, 1999.
19. S. Soderland. Learning information extraction rules for semi-structured and free text. *Machine Learning*, 34(1-3):233–272, 1999.

Agents Based Ontological Mediation in IE Systems[1]

Maria Teresa Pazienza and Michele Vindigni

Department of Computer Science, Systems and Production
University of Roma "Tor Vergata"
{pazienza,vindigni}@info.uniroma2.it

Abstract. Building more adaptive SW applications is a crucial issue to scale up IE technology to the Web, where information is organized following different underlying knowledge and/or presentation models. Information agents are more and more being adopted to support extraction of relevant information from semi-structured web sources. To efficiently manage heterogeneous information sources they must be able to cooperate, to share their knowledge, and to agree upon appropriate terminology to be used during interaction. Being the internal knowledge representation possibly different for each participant, it reveals to be unfeasible to directly communicate concepts, while agents autonomy promotes abstraction from details about the internal structure of other agents. We will argue on main topics involved in adapting natural language to achieve semantic agreement in communication, and we will introduce a novel architecture based on a pool of intelligent agents. It will be done by defining a communication model that foresees a strong separation between terms and concepts, (being this difference often undervalued in the literature, where terms play the ambiguous roles of both concept labels and communication lexicon). For agents communicating through the language, lexical information embodies the possibility to "express" the underlying conceptualizations thus agreeing to a shared representation. To make the resulting architecture adaptive to the application domain three different agents typologies have been defined: resource agents, owning the target knowledge; service agents, providing basic skills to support complex activities and control agents, supplying the structural knowledge of the task, with coordination and control capabilities. We will focus on two dedicated service agents: a mediator, that will care about understanding the information an agent wants to express as well as the way to present it to others, and a translator, dealing with lexical misalignment due to different languages. The resulting agent community dynamically assumes the most appropriate configuration, in a transparent way with respect to the involved participants.

1 Introduction

The continuous growth of web systems and information sources with different/independent technologies and knowledge representation models motivated the definition of a new dynamic scenario involving innovative methodologies to manage

---

[1] This work has been partially founded under the CROSSMARC project (IST 2000-25366) of the Information Society Technologies Programme of the European Union

such a "chaos". The goal of a complete "interoperability" suddenly revealed difficult to pursue due to the continue innovations in the market of tools and applications. Nevertheless a strong interest exists in operating in such an environment. Agent-orientation is emerging as a new paradigm in developing web information systems aiming to inherit concepts and techniques from agent theory that offers an high level of abstraction and suitable mechanisms to address conceptual modeling of complex issues as Knowledge representation and reasoning, communication, coordination and cooperation among heterogeneous and autonomous parties.

Agent theory goes in the direction of developing entities (agents) with an adequate amount of abilities and knowledge to autonomously interact with their similar for task completion purposes. Multi-agents societies (MAS) [Gustavsonn, 1997] constitute the most advanced model for a dynamic and unstructured framework in which specialized (both in functionalities and in knowledge) agents could interact and communicate through messages.

A few standards have been introduced for supporting communication (KQML [Finin e Weiderhold, 1991], FIPA-ACL [Dale et al., 2001]) among intelligent agents willing to support humans in accessing the higher and higher volume of data accessible on the Web. It should be useful to introduce specific intelligent agents that could work jointly and interact with systems for document management fulfilling the final goal of finding, extracting and presenting relevant information where and when required. This pushes for heterogeneous agents able to share a language, domain related ontologies (conceptual structures) and cooperating to task solution. Several problems have to be approached; among others: terminology mediation, ontology sharing, context disambiguation, etc.

In traditional software semantics subsumed in interactions is well coded in programs since the design and, in any case, involved entities share communication language and knowledge representation model. In a general framework in which heterogeneous systems interact with unforeseen partners, it is very important to adopt formalisms supporting content description and knowledge sharing.

In such a framework we have to face both the enormous complexity of the task and the need to focus on problems related to modeling specific aspects of sharing knowledge. Generally for different entities interacting on the web it is impossible to guarantee they share content meaning either in an early design phase or during implementation. This is a major issue for sharing documents content, where recognition of texts and identification of values base heavily on a shared/common knowledge model. Such an aspect of agents communication is still neglected due to the difficulty in defining "a priori" the quality and quantity of needed background (i.e. commonly agreed) knowledge. Nevertheless, as the ability to access (autonomously and dynamically changing time by time) any kind document currently on the Net is vital for an agent society, we have to consider this matter in details.

Different components should be considered when dealing with documents content. In fact different levels of problems arise related to the two existing communication layers: lexical and conceptual. A group of interacting agents could be seen as a small cooperative society requiring a shared language and communication channels in order to circulate ideas, knowledge and background assumptions. General abilities for language processing may be considered as part of the agent knowledge: differences in formal representation may be overcome by means of transposition – conversion mechanisms.

As document content is supported by specific linguistic expressions (surface representation and underlying content structuring), these must be covered when leaving to agents authority in searching and extracting content in the context of document retrieval and information extraction activities. Such a specificity is not related to a general knowledge of the language, but requires information onto sub languages and domain related knowledge repositories.

A high level competence on language understanding is required as well as the ability to abstract concepts by their lexicalizations. In the context of knowledge sharing we can refer to ontology as the means for specifying a conceptualization. That is an ontology may be a description of concepts and relationships that can exist for an agent community for the purpose of enabling knowledge sharing and reuse, thus supporting ontological commitments (e.g. an agreement to use a vocabulary to put queries and make assertions in a way that is consistent – but not complete – with respect to the underlying theory). In ontologies, definitions associate the names of entities in the universe of discourse with human-readable text describing what the names mean, while formal axioms constrain both the interpretation and the well-formed use of these terms. A common ontology defines the vocabulary with which queries and assertions are exchanged among agents; conversely agents sharing a vocabulary need not to share a knowledge base; each one knows things the other does not, and an agent that commits to an ontology is not required to answer all queries that can be formulated in the shared vocabulary. A commitment to a common ontology is a guarantee of consistency, but not completeness, with respect to queries and assertions by using the vocabulary defined in the ontology. Ontologies are seen as a means for "real" semantic integration, but current approaches do not consider linguistic insights to an appropriate extent.

In case of a common knowledge representation (both at conceptual and lexical levels), agent communication should be totally effective, as reference to any concept could be realized by direct linking to related node in the ontology without misunderstanding or mistakes. This kind of agent could communicate with others in its internal language, being its knowledge base exactly the same of all the others.

In real world applications, this is often unfeasible as agents have a "local" world representation, on which they base their goals and their assumptions; for instance, a seller and a buyer could have very different views of a marketplace, perceiving the same reality with respect to their objectives: an income for the seller becomes a cost for the buyer and although being both situated in the same environment/domain, their knowledge models could greatly differ as reflecting their different behaviors; then, to communicate, they must agree upon some sort of a shared (i.e. conventional) representation to be transmitted to other partners. Without a complete "a priori" agreement, natural language is the only representation tool to be used to carry semantics. Linguistic communication, both in human and agent society, supports a common representation level and enables a synthetic transmission of the information: discourse participants use mutually understandable terms to build phrases in order to communicate propositions.

A problem arises: "What guarantees that a language term is associated with the right semantics?"

A known word denotes a concept for an agent. This concept is thus related to other concepts in taxonomy, ontology, semantic network, or other structured representations for the set of concepts known by the agent. We commonly assume for word meaning its position in the ontology, by means of the relations it has with the rest of the ontology. Nevertheless, the difference between word and concept has been often underestimated until now, as usually terms play both roles of concept labels and communication vocabulary. As a consequence, all agents willing to communicate need much more than to share the same vocabulary. Making explicit the semiotic separation among terms, concepts and domain referents could allow for a better modeling of the communication process.

Agents act on behalf of humans, interacting with other agents. The new perspective of computing is re-centering on processes rather than on tasks, and in examining the nature of information more closely. It will be required to understand what kind of information needs to be represented in order to be used in computing, communication and so on.

The real innovation of the web will be realized when agents could collect content from diverse sources, process the information and exchange the results with other agents. Consumer and producer agents can reach a common understanding by sharing concepts from their ontologies, which provide the vocabulary needed for a wide spectrum communication. The structure and semantics of ontologies should make it easier to share, among an agents community, the document content meaning.

Web resources are accessible to agents surfing the web for performing useful tasks such as improved search and resources discovery, information brokering and information filtering.

The goal of Semantic Web is to have data defined on the web and linked in a way that such its meaning is explicitly interpretable by autonomous agents (rather than just being implicitly interpretable by humans). Ontologies may be considered as the way "to cut" reality in order to understand and process it. Reasoning with terms from deployed ontologies is important for the Semantic Web, but reasoning support is also extremely valuable at the ontology design phase, where it can be used to detect logically inconsistent classes and to discover implicit subclass relations.

Ontology use for the Semantic Web requires rules governing proper interpretation of the structure, as formal representations and constraints (semantics or meanings), and content, as ontology ground terms.

However, what in the reality exists is a multitude of specific ontologies managed by local authorities. Several questions have still to be addressed.

Who could be made responsible for their integration? Who could provide knowledge support for such an operation?

Who could maintain consistency across several lexicalizations of a unique conceptualization?

Who could be responsible of it during application life cycle?

There are several different approaches to the problem of how to define a mapping among concepts belonging to different knowledge bases. Proposed solutions could be grouped under three main clusters:

- **Manual Mapping:** the research is focused on concept representation; this kind of approach is usually followed by data base researchers, that emphasize the ontology role as a scheme for the application knowledge base, where concepts are considered as data types; among others, we remember here the use of conditional rules [Chang and Garcia-Molina, 1998], functions [Chawathe, 1994; Baldonado et al. 1997], first order logics [Guha and Lenat, 1994], declarative representations [Park et al. 1998], where mappings themselves are organized in an ontology. Unfortunately, the manual specification of mappings is an expensive and not error prone task for real scale problems. Moreover, this approach requires one to define a mapping for each couple of involved ontologies, thus determining a sudden grow up of mappings when the number of involved ontologies increases; as an alternative to define a mapping between local ontologies and a general one [Hull, 1997], but this require to agree upon a common general purpose knowledge layer.

- **Adoption of a Formal Theory** as a shared and coherent description layer. In this way, instead of building mappings in a bottom-up fashion (by integrating "local" resources), the resources themselves are built accordingly to common assumption that guarantees the overall consistency. This approach is followed by a number of systems aimed to help human experts during the integration of DB schemes [Bayardo et al., 1997; Knoblock and Ambite, 1997; Benjamins and Fensel, 1998].

- **Automatic Mapping:** this is driven by the assumption that equivalent concepts in different ontologies must show similar observable properties; in this area, classical ML techniques have been adopted, to provide similarity measures with respect to a few relevant attributes, for instance:

  - by identifying similar attributes, through the use of neural networks [Li, 1995]
  - by using relationships defined in a thesaurus and a measure of "semantic distance" [Bright et al., 1994] based on path length;
  - by activating an heuristic search on the candidate mappings among value tuples [Cohen and Hirsh, 1994]

Although several works discuss different qualities of ontological mappings, they focus the analysis on the mapping itself. Among the others, we mention here [Kashyap and Sheth, 1996], where the semantic distance of two concepts is defined by a tuple of their contexts, the values they assume over a domain, their relations, and the data base states. Their analysis produces a hierarchy of semantic nearness, ranging over equivalence, correlation, relevance, similarity and incompatibility; in [Lehmann and Cohn, 1994], authors claim the need for more specialized definitions for prototypical concept instances, and distinguish the set relation over two different definitions in equivalence, inclusion, overlap and disjunction. They show how different configurations of overlapping concepts could exist, and order them by reliability value.

The previously cited approaches could be resumed in two distinct trends with respect to the problem of knowledge sharing:

- all parts willing to interact must adhere to the same ontology. In such a framework, they could refer to shared concepts, being implicit a common semantics for the exchanged information. This solution provides a strict coupling for the system components, and doesn't ask for specific inferential capabilities to the involved participants; it becomes unfeasible for really open architectures, where a common sharing of the conceptual model for the environment could not be forced at design time, and thus it could not be adopted in highly dynamic scenarios, as the Web is, where the information model is inherently heterogeneous.

- A set of correspondences across each involved ontology is defined either manually or automatically. The resulting mappings are used during the communication process by a third part when semantic translation is required: this kind of interaction foresees that an exhaustive analysis over the involved ontologies has been carried on before the interaction starts.

Thus, most of the analyzed approaches require either:

- shared instances, or
- shared concepts, or
- shared relations among ontologies or schemas, manually defined or derivable by the use of a shared formalism.

This kind of assumptions strongly reduces the applicability of these methods in an open environment. To let autonomous agents working in a dynamic environment to interact in order to cooperate, a more free approach is needed, with the less possible "a priori" constraints, able to derive them at run time according to the situation emerging from the interaction.

2 A Model for the Communication

Agents willing to cooperate need "to be able" to communicate. A group of agents working together could be considered as a small cooperative society, in which a shared language and communication channels are needed in order to circulate ideas, knowledge and culture.

In case of agents with an "ideal" (that is, consistent and complete) knowledge of the world on which they are situated, successful communication among agents, even if necessary, could be an "easy" task. In fact, when agents base on the same knowledge model, the transmission of an information will be realized by directly "pointing" to concepts, with no mistake or misunderstanding. This sort of "telepathic" agent could communicate with others in its internal language, being its knowledge base totally coincident/overlapping those of the other agents.

In real world applications, agents have indeed a "local" world representation; then for communication purposes, interacting partners have to "agree" upon some sort of shared (i.e. conventional) representation of concepts to be transmitted.

Such an "agreement" is totally inconceivable in most agent applications. On the Web, interaction happens on asynchronous bases while needed information may be found on unknown unexpected sites. In such a framework, to avoid a complete failure, we can do a working hypothesis: agents (as humans do in new unknown environments) will base their interaction on the language.

Without a stronger "a priori" agreement, the use of the natural language could represent the only tool to carry on semantics in communication processes. Linguistic communication, in humans as well as in agents, brings in a common representation level and enables a synthetic transmission of the information: discourse participants use mutually understandable terms to build phrases in order to communicate propositions.

Also in very degraded frameworks (low level in language comprehension) communication could be successful at a certain extent. For example, as in human interactions, also in case of partners adopting different jargons, comprehension could happen at least at terminological level as well as at proper names level. Sharing this kind of linguistic knowledge will be enough for both comprehension of discourse topic and related levels of interest. Similar considerations could be done in an agent framework. Neverthles, the adoption of natural language as representation support will introduce further levels of complexity in reasoning mechanisms. In fact all language-processing difficulties (from syntactic to semantic disambiguation, adoption of different ontologies and lexicals, etc) could make more complex communication mechanisms. Nevertheless, a part the case of lack in any other kind of shared knowledge in which our linguistic choice becomes mandatory, our approach supports agents communication and reasoning on a wide number of not strictly predefined interactions.

2.1 Terms and Concepts Relationship

A known word denotes a concept for a linguistic agent. This concept is generally related to other concepts in any taxonomy, ontology, semantic network, or other structured representation for the set of concepts known by the agent. We commonly associate the meaning of a word to a specific concept, in a specific position in the ontology, by means of the relations it has with the rest of the ontology.

The difference between words and concepts has been often undervalued in several previously described approaches, where terms play the ambiguous roles of concept labels and of communication vocabulary. As a consequence, most systems require that all agents willing to communicate share the same vocabulary, while making explicit the semiotic separation (firstly introduced by [Peirce, 1932]) among terms, concepts and domain referents allows for a better modeling of the communication process. People could conceptualize something even without knowing how to name it, and a concept could be made accessible even without referring explicitly to it, by evocating other concepts. Being aware of this separation, in language based communication we have to manage linguistic autonomous behavior in agents.

2.2 What Expresses the Meaning of a Concept?

Concept semantics could not be captured only through its structural representations [Sheth et al., 1993]. Knowledge Engineering has devoted great efforts to propose semantic descriptions flexible enough to represent partial knowledge and at the same time multiple descriptions of different aspects of the same entity [Bobrow and Winograd, 1985]. Several descriptive representations have been proposed as alternatives to the classic symbolic approach; nevertheless we don't want discuss here this problem. As [Sowa, 2000] describes, whichever the formalism to represent knowledge, "...the primary connections are not in the bits and bytes that encode the signs, but in the minds of the people who interpret them. The goal of various metadata proposals is to make those mental connections explicit by tagging the data with more signs. Those metalevel signs by themselves have further interconnections, which can be tagged with metametalevel signs. But meaningless data cannot acquire meaning by being tagged with meaningless metadata. The ultimate source of meaning is the physical world and the agents who use signs to represent entities in the world and their intentions concerning them".

According to this statement, we could suppose a concept be completely specified only by an "interpretation function" that maps it to those real world entities it refers to, that is:

Given two concepts C_1 e C_2, we will say that they are *ideally equivalent*   (1)
iff they conceptualize the same real world entities.

Thus two concepts could be considered as ideally equivalent iff they conceptualize the same world entities. We call "ideal" this kind of equivalence as such an interpretation function is never available to software agents. An ontology approximates the domain conceptualization in the designer mind, and thus a concept equivalence could not be formally verified inside the model, but only externally postulated. The entire ontology by itself represents the maximal degree of description an agent could provide for a concept: which relations are involved in, among which concepts, and so on. We will call the set of all these information the *ontological context* of a concept. In a real open framework we assume that different agents could adopt different ontologies, while sharing their linguistic knowledge (if any). The lexicon becomes the main support to express concept semantics. Possible mappings between concepts in different ontologies are thus implicitly constrained to be linguistically plausible (that is, represented in a coherent way by shared terms) and to adopt lexical descriptions of ontological structural constraints. The most these descriptions will be similar, the greater will be the confidence in the similarity of the expressed concepts. Then we can reformulate the equivalence definition:

Given two concepts C_1 and C_2, belonging respectively to two agents A_1 and A_2,   (2)
C_1 and C_2 are *equivalent wrt A_1 and A_2*, when the lexical descriptions of their ontological contexts are the same.

This is the same that happens with people: if a speaker wants to communicate a concept to an hearer that doesn't know it, he will try to make it known in terms of other concepts, making the underlying assumption that lexical mismatches are localized, that is, that the probability of a misalignment between lexicon and ontology will decrease by increasing the number of words in the description. In many cases it is assumed that, if both participants know a term, both of the them use it to denote the same concept, that is:

If T is a term that denotes C_1 for agent A_1 and C_2 for agent A_2, then C_1 and C_2 (3)
are supposed to be *equivalent for A_1 and A_2*.

This is driven by the so called "one sense per domain" hypothesis, (i.e., in case of agents linguistically interacting on the same domain, used terms could unambiguously express concepts). There are two kinds problems with this approach:

1. ontologies built for specific tasks couldn't have so much shared terms, or employ morphological variations of the same word

2. either the involved agents could adopt broader ontologies, or the two domains could not totally overlap. This is the case, for instance, of agents devoted to information retrieval on the web, that will adopt a "general purpose" reference ontology, where a broad knowledge is expressed with unknown granularity

In these cases, the above assumption (3) doesn't hold, and we need a more restrictive rule to keep into account the new situation (that is the ambiguity of the lexical information). This suggests a new equivalence definition:

Given $T_1..T_n$ terms in both A_1 and A_2 agents lexicons, if $T_1..T_n$ denote *univo-*   (4)
cally concept C_1 for A_1 and C_2 for A_2, then C_1 and C_2 are supposed to be equivalent for A_1 and A_2

In other words, if we cant suppose a biunivocal correspondence between term and concept, it will be identified by a set of terms (synonyms). In case there is a subset of synonyms that univocally identifies a concept both for the speaker and the hearer in their own ontologies, then we can suppose they are equivalent for the two agents. This rule implies the previous one, as if there is no polysemy, a single term will denote univocally a concept in both the ontologies. It is emerging the role ontologies assume in agents communication. Let us discuss a little bit more on them.

3 Agent Ontologies

Let us define an agent ontology O as the tuple $<C,T,\Re,L>$ where C is a set of concepts, T a set of terms (in a language), $\Re$ a set of relationships $<R_1..R_n>$ among concepts and L: C x T the correspondence relation between terms and concepts.

$\Re$ relations have a structural meaning. Different kinds of semantic relationships could share the same structural meaning, as *IS-A*, *Ownership*, *Part-of*, *Reference*, etc: the correspondence between these relation types and the used relationships depends from the different domains. To be able to rebuild portions of an ontological context of an agent concept, it is necessary that semantics of the involved relations is made explicit and agreed. In an ontology there are different kinds of relationships and while they all participate to structurally define a concept, their contribution could be different. For instance, *Part-of* relationship that explains the structural formation of concepts (a brick is *part-of* an house, a wheel is *part-of* a car, etc,) has a denotational contribute greater than the generic *Related-to*, that doesn't clarify the correlation meaning. Unfortunately, the kind of relationships active in an ontology depends strongly on structure's production objective. As stressed in [Campbell, 1999], from a study of 38 different ontologies derived from the shared Ontolingua Frame ontology [Gruber, 1992], postulating the existence of 85 different relationships, only 58% of them is used at least one time in any ontology, and of these latter, less than the 20% is used more than 10 times (and none in all the ontologies).

It is worth noticing how the preference for several relationships is often biased by the formalism of the adopted implementation framework: the relation *Subclass-of* is used more often than *Superclass-of* (that is not in the first twenty). Adding a new class to the ontology is easier in a top down than in a bottom up fashion, as new concepts are usually related to pre-existing relations by inheritance, and in most of the ontology editing tools this relation is implemented by a meta attribute in the child concept pointing to the parent class.

The lack of a standardized representation makes impossible to assume relations as shared features for a structural definition of the ontological context of a concept. This analysis shows as set of closed theories exist, that are not meant to be compared or expressed in an automatic way.

The only broadly shared relation type (even if sometime implicitly expressed in the ontology, or implemented by using different relationships), is taxonomic description. In most of the ontologies, a taxonomic hierarchy is structured as a tree, where any concept could have at least a single concept as its generalization. However, there are ontologies where multiple inheritances are allowed.

Table 1. Top twenty relationships in the Frame Ontology, their occurrences in the analysed ontologies, and the number of ontologies where they are presented (from [Campbell, 1999])

RELATION	DEF. IN	OCCURS	ONTOS
Instance-of	FRAME-ONTO	1144	27
Sublcass-of	FRAME-ONTO	217	17
Domain	FRAME-ONTO	90	11
=<	KIF-NUMBERS	118	8
Member	KIF-SETS	73	12
Range	FRAME-ONTO	87	10
Documentation	FRAME-ONTO	65	8
Slot-Value-Type	FRAME-ONTO	313	1
>=	KIF-NUMBERS	59	5
Holds	KIF-RELS	48	6
<	KIF-NUMBERS	36	8
Defined	KIF-EXTENT	35	7
>	KIF_NUMBERS	40	3
Subclass-Partition	FRAME-ONTO	14	7
Same-Values	FRAME-ONTO	27	3
Item	KIF_LISTS	13	5
Value-Type	FRAME-ONTO	14	4
Domain-Of	FRAME-ONTO	10	5
Nth-Domain	FRAME-ONTO	10	4
Exhaus.-Subclass-Part	FRAME-ONTO	6	6

Luckily, taxonomy brings a strong definition for concepts. It is the case of dictionaries, where a concept is defined in terms of *genus* and *differentia*, that are respectively its direct super class, and the features that discriminate it from others belonging to the same genus. The existence of a shared taxonomy makes it possible to compare concepts by their positions in hierarchies: more these are similar, less will be the uncertainty on their equivalence.

3.1 Ontological Similarity Evaluation

A communication act could be seen as the activity of sending some information from a sender to a receiver (being this encoded as a message through a communication language) and decoded when received. Several components contribute at different degree in this process. The communication context of two agents (S in the role of a speaker/sender and H in the role of a hearer/receiver) could be sketched as being composed in a number of dimensions orthogonal to the communication flow: these are, the sender conceptual plane O(S), the sender lexical plane V(S), the receiver lexical plane V(H) and the receiver conceptual plane O(H).

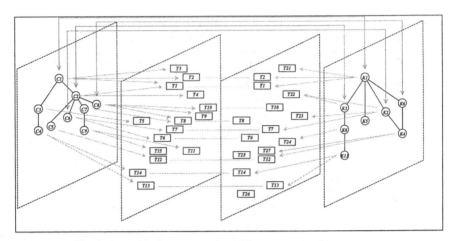

Fig. 1. A graphical representation of the communication context

Conceptual planes O(S) and O(H) contain concepts C and involved relationships $\Re$: they are the "interior" component of agent minds, that is the result of domain conceptualizations made by designers, expressed in some logic formalism.

Lexical planes V(S) and V(H) contain the set of words of T agent lexicons. For (natural language) speaking agents, information in their lexicons represents the possibility to "express" underlying conceptualizations, and thus a (weak) agreement of their minds to a shared formalism.

Relation L among concepts and terms in the language correlates what the agent could represent in its mind with what it could express. This is represented in figure by light arrows, going from the conceptual plane to the lexical one. The mapping between lexicons V(S) and V(H) is shown by dashed lines, declaring the linguistic equivalence relation between the two agents terms: in case S and H speak the same language, these lines represent the (partial) identity relation between symbols in V(S) and V(H); the lines in the upper part of the figure point to the "true" mapping among agent concepts that in our hypothesis are unavailable to the communication.

Agent S, willing to transmit a concept C to agent H, must go by first from its conceptual plane O(S) through its lexical plane V(S), then send some information to the hearer H that will map it to its lexical plane V(H), and finally project it to its conceptual plane O(H).

This makes the communication complex, as in general, there is no one-to-one relationship between different planes, so that each step could go far from the right solution. As a consequence , it is often unfeasible a direct approach where an agent willing to communicate a concept chooses a word in its lexicon as the message content; there is no guarantee that the receiving agent will be able to invert the encoding process to catch the right concept in its own ontology.

In the following paragraph we will use this model to make it clear the role different components play in the communication process, willing to provide an accurate analysis of each of them.

3.2 The Conceptual Planes O(S) and O(H)

To better emphasize the role of conceptual planes, let us suppose that agents could communicate without using their lexicons. In this case, the similarity among the conceptual planes becomes essential for the communication. More they are dissimilar, less it will be plausible to find an equivalent concept for that under analysis. (In next section we shall restore lexicalization as a working hypothesis).

As previously stated, ontologies realize domain conceptualizations and this reflects in their structure. Topological differences could reveal deep differences in conceptualizations (and then in concept meaning, see Fig. 2). Of course not all ontological misalignments imply conceptual misalignments (even if the opposite holds: different conceptualizations will have different models). Unfortunately, conceptual misalignments could not be directly derived in communication as direct mapping is unfeasible by hypothesis; anyway, it is useful for our analysis, to characterize the different typologies that could emerge when comparing concepts in two ontologies.

Given two equivalent concepts C_S in O(S) and C_H in O(H), each of them is involved, more or less directly, in a few relationships with other concepts inside its own ontology. For sake of simplicity, let us consider only the subsumption relation class-subclass (IS-A) and let us call IS-A* its transitive closure. If we collect all relations involving C_S and C_H and compare them, a number of cases could happen:

- Equivalence: $\exists\, C'_H \in O(H) \mid C'_H \cong C'_S \wedge C_H\; IS\text{-}A^*\; C'_H$, that is, there is a concept in O(H) that is equivalent to C'_S and in the same relation with C_H. For instance, in both the ontologies there is a <dog> concept and an <animal> concept and an (extended) relation <dog> IS-A* <animal> (as in case of Fig. 2-1)

- Contradiction: $\exists\, C'_H \in O(H) \mid C'_H \cong C'_S \wedge \neg(C_H\; IS\text{-}A^*\; C'_H)$, that is, the concept in O(H) equivalent to C'_S is not reachable through the relation IS-A* from C_H. For instance, both the ontologies have a concept for <circle> and <polygon>, but one of them declares that <circle> IS-A* <polygon>, whilst the other one does not. This reflects a deep difference in their conceptualization (as in case of Fig. 2-2).

- Indetermination: $\forall\, C'_H \in O(H)\; C'_H \neq C'_S$ that is, there is no concept in O(H) equivalent to C'_S. In this case ontologies are not in contradiction, simply O(H) represents a different conceptualization that O(S). For instance, both ontologies have <dog> concept, but only one of them get the concept <mammal> and the relation <dog> IS-A* <mammal>; in this case there are two possibilities:

  - Compatibility: O(H) could admit the missing concept, that is the misalignment is at the aggregation level: concepts are represented with different granularity. With respect to the previous example, one of the ontologies contains the concept of <mammal> as an intermediate level among <dog> and <animal>, while the other one not (see Fig. 2-3a).

  - Incompatibility: O(H) description could not admit the missing concept, as it uses a different categorization for its concepts. This usually reflects differences in the properties considered to be salient for the agglomeration. For instance, having two different ontologies for animals, one organized around classes as mammal, bird, etc. and the other on their behavior as carnivore, herbivore, etc (as in Fig. 2-3b).

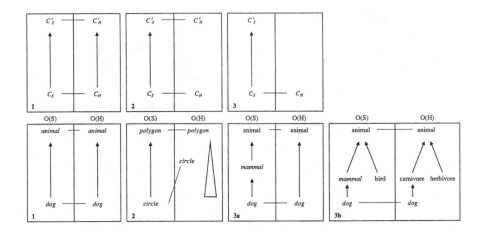

Fig. 2. Comparison against agent conceptual planes: 1 – Equivalence; 2 – Contradiction; 3a – Compatibility; 3b - Incompatibility

Semantic similarity measures based on evaluation of taxonomic links usually use distance metrics between compared concepts, with respect to nodes known as equivalent: shorter is the path between two nodes, greater is their similarity. Such an approach often assumes that taxonomic relations have uniform distances, while it doesn't hold in the general case. In real world taxonomies, the "distance" covered by direct taxonomic relationships is roughly variable, as a few sub-taxonomies, for instance, tend to be more dense than others.

As the *IS-A* relationship induces a partial ordering in concepts, a measure of the topologic similarity of *ontological contexts* could be obtained by counting shared constraints (as positive evidences), the contradicting constraints (as negative evidences) and indeterminate constraints over the two ontologies.

3.3   The Lexical Planes V(S) and V(H)

Let us now reconsider lexical role in communication process. In fact dealing with real events to rightly transmit the information between speaker and hearer, it is necessary that a shared vocabulary exists and is adopted. Greater is the difference between speaker's and hearer's dictionaries, greater is the probability of term known to one agent and unknown to the other one (success in the communication tends to be zero).

A simple measure of similarity could be obtained as the average mutual coverage with respect to the number of words in each dictionary.

The set coverage is defined as a number ranging from 0 to 1. Two identical sets will have maximal coverage, which is 1, while disjoint sets will measure 0; in other cases coverage quantifies the set overlap. We define the coverage as:

given a non-empty set X and a subset $Y \subseteq X$, the coverage of Y over X is the quotient of their cardinality, that is $|Y|/|X|$.

The common coverage of two non-empty sets will be then the average of the coverage of their intersection with respect to each of them. In our case, if V(S) and V(IH) are the speaker's and hearer's dictionaries, then:

$$\sigma(V(S),V(H)) = \frac{1}{2}\frac{|V(S) \cap V(H)|}{|V(S)|} + \frac{1}{2}\frac{|V(S) \cap V(H)|}{|V(H)|} \quad \text{where} \tag{5}$$

$$\sigma(V(S),V(H)) = 0 \; \text{se} \; |V(S)| = 0 \; \text{o} \; |V(H)| = 0 \tag{6}$$

3.4 The Lexical-Semantic Mapping

A strong similarity in conceptual and lexical planes by itself cannot assert complete successful communication. In fact by definition agents do not have an a priori knowledge of characteristics of interacting agent's ontology as they don't know each other. As a consequence they will not use common internal representation language whilst they could. They will pass through the lexical level for communication purposes. The activation of this procedure could generate a failure. Let us do an exemplification; let us suppose that both the agents' ontologies and their lexicons are exactly the same, but that they could use a single word only to express any concept (very poor lexical expressivity). We represent this paradox in Fig. 3.

The agent S will use the unique word it gets ("ngu") as lexicalization for communicating any concept. Even if H knows "ngu" it can't disambiguate what it hears, as this extremely poor lexical espressivity does not allow to focus the right concept among all possible ones in its mind.

The correct mapping between lexical and conceptual planes is fundamental for agents using lexicons for knowledge transmission. This motivates the adoption of a one-to-one correspondence between these planes realized in the majority of ontologies. For exemplification purposes in real application, it is generally considered concepts are represented in an ontology by only one lexicalisations.

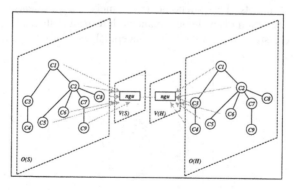

Fig. 3. An extremely hard communicative framework

Lexical redundancy could be seen as a magnifying factor for the lexical plane with respect to the concept plane (see Fig. 4): words are the magnifying glass for concepts. Thus each concept will occupy on the lexical plane a greater surface than in the "concept plane". More this "lens" broaden a concept, more probable will be an intersection among speaker and hearer lexical planes.

In the net framework a communication could be activated between any couple of agents, independently by the amount (if any) of ontology overlapping. In case of partial knowledge/dictionary sharing, several concepts will be cut-off as they could receive different lexicalisations. A richer set of lexicals increases the probability of concept comprehension by the receiver.

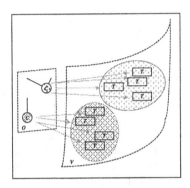

Fig. 4. Dilatation effect on the lexical plane by synonymy

Unfortunately it is not ever possible to extend the number of unambiguous lexicalizations for a concept; as argued in [Clark, 1983], no words are true synonyms of a sense. From a cognitive perspective, the creation of a new word is strictly related to the intention to explicitly specify a concept. However, distinct lexicalizations could denote the same concept in an ontology, if the underlying domain conceptualization makes no difference among referents they have in the real world.

Lexical variety implies an implicit drawback : often a word could denote even totally different concepts. This phenomenon (namely, the *polysemy*) could be seen as the opposite contraction of the lexical plane with respect to the concept plane (see Fig. 5); in this case distinct concepts in the conceptual plane could partially overlapp on the lexical one.

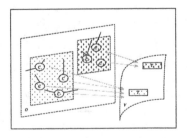

Fig. 5. Contraction effect on the lexical plane by polysemy

Generally, these two phenomena are together present: lexical richness implies greater ambiguity. The resulting situation could be seen as a distortion of the lexical plane (as shown in Fig. 6).

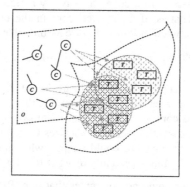

Fig. 6. Complex distortion of the lexical plane resulting from combined effect of synonymy and polysemy

A measure for "linguistic espressivity" for an agent A lexicon is obtained by assigning each word w a *weight P*, inversely proportional to its ambiguity:

$$P_A(w \in T_A) = \frac{1}{|Sense_A(w)|} \quad con \; Sense_A(w) = \{c \mid L_A(c,w) = true\} \tag{7}$$

where $Sense_A(w)$ represents the set of (agent A) concepts associated to word w, (i.e. its different senses).

We then define the *espressivity Expr* of a concept c as the sum of the weights of each word that could express it, that is:

$$Expr(c \in C_A) = \sum_{w \in Words_A(c)} P_A(w) \quad con \; Words_A(c) = \{w \mid L_A(w,c) = true\} \tag{8}$$

being $Words_A(c)$ the set of words that could express c. Low values of $Expr(c)$ denote poorly represented concepts in the lexicon, while high scores stand for richly expressed concepts.

Over the whole ontology of the agent A, we can define the espressivity of the lexicon T_A as the average espressivity of its concepts, that is:

$$\overline{Expr(T_A)} = \frac{\sum_{c \in C_A} Expr(c)}{|C_A|} \tag{9}$$

Note that the espressivity could vary over the range $(0, +\infty)$, where an higher value stands for a wider convexity for the lexical plane with respect to the conceptual one.

3.5 Lexical-Semantic Coherence

Basic assumption for the communication is the lexical-semantic coherence: source and destination use lexicons in a coherent way, by assigning words to concepts in a consistent approach. That is, if C_s is a concept in the conceptual plane O(S) of a speaker agent S and w a word in $Words(C_s)$ we assume that the following rule holds:

$$(\exists\, C_H \in O(H) \mid C_s \cong C_H) \wedge w \in V(H) \rightarrow C_H \in Sense_H(w) \tag{10}$$

that is: if there is a concept C_H in the H hearer's ontology equivalent to C_s and H knows the word w the speaker uses to represent C_s, than H too represents C_H through w. This means that if a concept C exists that is known by both S and H, then each word in their common vocabulary either expresses C for both of them, or doesn't express C at all. Lexical mismatches could happen when the hearer doesn't know the word w or the concept C_H (thus eventually using w to refer to other concepts).

In real frameworks we could not guarantee that rule (9) globally holds. Exceptions to this rule represent situations in which agents use their vocabularies in an inconsistent way. In case of frequent inconsistencies, it becomes very difficult information exchanging between the two agents.

In Fig. 7 several different aspects of these mismatching are shown:[2]
- In the first case (A) both agents know the concept "tassa" as well as the concept "persiana". They both use the word "imposta" (among others) to denote the two concepts
- In case (B) agent H does not know the concept "tassa": it uses the word "imposta" to express the other concept
- In case (C), H simply ignores the word "imposta" (without other assumptions on the concepts it could know)
- In case (D) that represent the only exception to the rule (9), S could use "imposta" to denote "tassa" while agent H adopts it to denote "persiana"; it also knows "tassa", but does not use this lexical form to express it.

This last situation is very dangerous: when S says "imposta" to express the concept "tassa", H will understand "persiana" as in (B). But, in case (B), communication fails, as agent conceptual planes don't overlap on this concept, while in (D) communication fails at a semantic level as they make an incoherent use of the language. If we think this exception to the rule (9) could usually hold, than the equivalence relation between the lexical planes must be considered as an accidental equivalence among strings belonging to two different languages. In this case the shared vocabulary could not convey any information.

---

[2] In Italian language both the words "persiana" and "imposta" indicate the outer part of the window used to avoid light enters into the room while letting air circulate. The two words "tassa" and "imposta", while designing two slightly different kinds of taxations, are generally used as synonyms in current language. In such a framework, a real Italian conversation could incur in a severe mistake for the two senses the word "imposta" assumes.

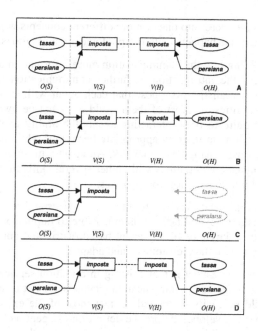

Fig. 7. Different mismatches due to semantic ambiguity of a word

The different factors we analyzed represent the natural dimensions along which the communication flows. We could distinguish between:

- Endogenous factors, i.e. intrinsic conditions, that could be evaluated for each agent and represent its disposition towards the communication based on its cognitive model, that is its *lexical espressivity*
- Exogenous factors, i.e. contextual conditions, defined at communication time between participants, and embedded in the *conceptual plane distance*, the *lexical distance* and the *lexical-semantic coherence*; they represent properties emerging from the interaction much more than individual qualities

4   Linguistic Agent Society

After a deep analysis of linguistic communication model it emerges that, even when supposing participants agree on a communication language (at least for what concerns grammar and protocol), it is possible that direct communication fails at content level. This could happen in the following cases:

1. Hearer dictionary does not include the word used by the speaker; this could happen either in case the hearer adopts another word to express the same concept, or when speaker and hearer use different languages.

2. Hearer does not know a concept the other is speaking about, that is H knowledge does not contain a (unique) lexical representation for this concept;

3. Hearer maps the word into one or more different concepts while only one is known by the speaker; this happens with morphologically ambiguous words.

The need to bring into the communication more information to express the concept meaning requires the introduction of further communication capabilities. In a real framework it is unrealistic to suppose that each agent willing to communicate could have these capabilities, as most of them could even not be aware of such issues. In fact it would require to both interacting agents the ability to manage several kinds knowledge as well as to infer an appropriate behaviour while being in a heterogeneous and continuously changing framework. An agent with inferential abilities needed to deal with language ambiguities will gather several skills that will greatly increase both design and implementation complexities.

Real applications need to access to different services and resources asynchronously while accomplishing several tasks: it is unfeasible to duplicate competences for each agent. Moreover, a key idea of any agent based distributed approach is to keep they simple and easy to maintain, customise, and adapt.

Another important aspect is that existing information services, (whose implementation, query language and communication channels are out of the control of user applications) could be easily integrated. In fact most of the existing Web information sources have been developed before the definition of agent technologies. As a consequence it is more feasible to realize wrapper agents over these resources than directly to update them: this kind of agents simply interface information sources and consumers, providing uniform data access and view.

4.1 Agent Taxonomy

To fulfil all previous problems, we have defined an agents society with different specific competences and in terms of the different functionalities they offer for the communication task. Among others, our main objective from an architectural point of view is to keep the resulting architecture independent from the application domain; three different agent "typologies" have been devised as sufficient for supporting language communication:

1. resource agents, representing the ends of the communication channel. They own the knowledge target of the communication;

2. service agents, owning the single functionalities to support complex linguistic activities (mainly represented by a mediator and a translator);

3. control agents, that supply the structural knowledge of each task, and have coordination and control capabilities.

Whilst they all share the same structural paradigm, each of them exhibit specific design choices oriented to the task it is devoted to. In detail, splitting competences between service and control agents realises a separation between tactical problem-solving skills, highly specialised, and strategic knowledge on how to combine them to achieve a complex goal. In such a way, it is possible to dynamically recombine existing components to solve new problems, and dually, to upgrade single functionalities without having to redesign the entire system.

Let us hereafter provide a preliminary description of this agent society, in which two different hierarchies have been identified: owned knowledge (from resource to control agent) versus processing capabilities (from control to resource agents).

Main functionalities, a _control agent_ has, relate to the ability:
- to identify resource agents involved in the communication act,
- to identify service agents to support communication,
- to manage the information flow among them.

From the application point of view the separation between functionalities and the consequent need to interact with a single agent hide the underlying complexity of the information retrieval activities and communication tasks: these are conceived to be the most frequent application environments to be met.

A _service agent_ has task specific capabilities. It will:
- be delegated by the control agent for the resolution of a specific task that will become its goal
- identify precise sub goals requiring information from resource agents
- delegate to the control agent the task to effectively retrieve the needed information

A _resource agent_ will:
- support a transparent access to the underlying resource
- reply to system queries following agreed communication language and protocol

To realize these functionalities, agents have been endowed with appropriate knowledge and processing capabilities to manage it. Thus a control agent should at least embody the knowledge of the physical model of both resource agent and service agent distribution in the system, a model for the services involved in the communication task through the different situations (i.e. involved agents may have or not the same ontology, or the same language) and a communication protocol to interact with resource and service agents; a service agent will knows at least how to reach its goal, what additional information is needed and a communication protocol to interact with the control agent.

Being at the lowest cognitive level, any resource agent will know only the model of the data it owns, the procedures to reply to specific queries on its knowledge, and the communication protocol to interact with control agents.

In this context we focus on the issues related to the use of the natural language in the communication activity. Although the described architecture is meant to deal with a more general class of problems, we here refer only to the needs of a communication scenario. The reasoning skills could broadly vary in this framework: for instance, every resource could be represented as an agent with a basic set of skills, able at least to receive specific requests, to act in order to satisfy them, while service agents (as described below) expose higher cognitive levels. These roles, according to the chosen organization, could be even implemented by a single agent: the proposed categorization holds for modelling purposes only. In fact it helps in the framework of an overall agents society in which roles have to be clearly defined and taken over.

The simplest agent organization foresees five different agents: two resource agents, (a speaker and a hearer, willing to interact, i.e. communicate), two service agents (a mediator and a translator agent providing the specific services required), and a control agent, the communication coordinator, that will supervise all the different activities.

Resource Agents. As resource agents, Speaker and Hearer are responsible for the management and the presentation of domain knowledge in the resources they encapsulate. They assume the role of Sender and Receiver while information flow is managed by a control agent with which they interact. Nevertheless, domain knowledge and language knowledge are intrinsically different: though they use a communication language, agents are not necessarily aware of the language structure, neither they must be able to learn new words. Language could be seen as an unconscious phenomenon, as it is for people. Of course, people could in some measure reason about language, as their conscious knowledge includes some linguistic skill, but this does not apply for systems. They can't negotiate terminology or autonomously resolve communication failures, as this requires a shift in the discourse domain, from the content to the language level. An hearer agent knows how to reply to the queries it receives. When it does not understand the query, as for instance in case of ambiguous terms, a deeper linguistic knowledge is required. If this knowledge could be successfully factorised externally from each single agent, this will greatly reduce the linguistic skills they must possess. More in detail, we suppose that their knowledge of the underlying language model makes them able to reply to simple queries about:

- the lexical relation L between terms and concepts

- conceptual relations $\mathfrak{R}$ among concepts

with no further assumptions on inference capabilities to correlate concepts in their ontologies.

Service Agents. We will provide details hereafter for the two different instances of this class: the mediator and the translator agents.

The Mediator Agent. The Mediator agent carries on a mediation activity between dialoguing actors, being able to understand the information the speaker wants to express as well as the way to present it to the hearer. He will narrow the gap existing between the information content of each lexicalisation and its joint use, thus providing inferential contribution to the agents communication. The mediation activity overlaps in a transparent fashion the agent interaction. The mediator agent is designed to act independently from a specific domain. We assume that he has no prior knowledge about the dialog topics , while it is focused on understanding which relationships exist between concepts involved in the communication as well as terms used to express them, without any assumption on the adopted internal knowledge representation formalisms. This working modality has been chosen for making the mediator agent universally valid in any application domain. Its role consists in being able to activate the mediation process and manage it until successful completion.

Due to the fact the mediation activity is developed out of the speaking agents, the mediator needs to work on a restricted view of the ontologies. He builds a partial image of the involved parts, by querying agents about specific knowledge on terms and concepts, and dynamically compares the results in order to find a mapping for the target concept.

Let us provide an example: two agents, say John and Mary, are talking together: during the dialog, John uses the word "tassazione" that Mary does not know. The Mediator could come in hand in finding a word known by Mary with the same meaning of "tassazione". To accomplish this task, the mediator must have some specific skills with respect to the reasoning: at least it must be able to judge if two concepts are or not equivalent for the two involved agents. The mediator will learn what John means by "taxation", asking him further terms representing the same concept. In case John could provide synonyms of the sense it is using, the mediator could try to query Mary with these. In case she can identify a corresponding concept (for instance she knows the synonym "imposta"), then the mediation will succeed. But if, for instance, "imposta" is ambiguous for Mary, than the mediator should learn more features of the concept John is expressing. John could explain to the mediator that for him "tassazione" is a "somma di denaro" (money amount). Mediator will ask them Mary if she knows meaning of "somma di denaro", and so on. Conversation will go on until information from two participants will be enough to let the mediator decide, with some "degree of confidence", a mapping among what John is speaking about and what Mary knows. By "degree of confidence" we mean that the mediator offers its service to solve problems tied to the communication, not to the possible inconsistencies of the conceptualisations.

What Mary could infer from speaking with John depends from a number of other factors (for instance, her background knowledge) that, at the moment, are left out from this research.

The mediation function is inspired by human behaviour: if an hearer does not understand the meaning of a word, he asks for more details, firing a sub-dialogue, based on a sequence of query-answer, aimed to identify the target concept, or its position in the ontology: in this activity he will base also on the clues provided by synonyms, relations with other concepts, and so on.

One positive aspect of this kind of mediation is that the analysis is framed into a local search space, as in real world ontologies, big differences in the taxonomic structure already appear in the upper levels, making impossible a large-scale mapping between misaligned structures. Seeing the mediation activity as a terminological problem helps in understanding the analogies existing on the underlying models.

This view of the ontological mediation is based on minimal assumptions on the knowledge model the involved agent has: by adding more restrictive hypotheses on their introspection capabilities, it is possible to include in the same framework other more sophisticated techniques. Reasoning about concept properties, attribute similarity and relations requires a deeper semantic agreement among participants that is out of the scope of this research. We stress here that, in absence of such agreements, what agents could expose about their ontologies is the lexical component, and thus we focus the mediation activity on this.

The Translator Agent. In case the interacting agents speak different languages, lexical misalignment are no more a local problem, but have to be dealt introducing a new entity, able to determine a mapping between terms in the two languages by an intelligent management of an extensive resource: the dictionary. For this reason, a translator agent is foreseen in such a situation.

By "intelligent management" we mean that the translator agent is expected to provide more than simple word-level translation according to the dictionary, trying to find the best "semantic" translation with respect to the sense under analysis, as a human usually does when translating something. Note that the problem of finding a translation in ontological mediation although quite similar to the classical machine-translation problem, exhibit some peculiarities due to the nature of the task: in fact, while machine translation approaches usually take into account the word context represented by the phrase the term is in, in our case the dialog participants have clear intentions to transmit specific senses, and thus could provide additional information on the ontological context of the word under analysis. This means for instance that the translator agent could exploit the useful information provided by a set of synonyms in order to find the most appropriate translation or, depending on the underlying resource, try to match different senses in the dictionary against the ones the agent has.

We choose to localise the mediation and translation tasks in different entities to separate the reasoning mechanism of the mediation activity, that is essentially based on labelled graphs matching, and the translation, that is strictly tied to the amount and modalities of the information stored in the resource.

Control/Coordination Agent. Due to the high level of independence and autonomy that agents exhibit, a further role of coordination is required. Still attention is on functionality much more than in domain knowledge.

In real environment the communicative needs emerging in the dialog are unforeseen, then it is necessary to add a third agent typology, aiming to coordinate the operations carried on by the service agents. A coordinator agent will take in charge determining which interaction flow is necessary to communicate an information, activating for each single task the required service agents and supervising their activities. With respect to the Facilitator agent, proposed in [Widerhold and Genesereth, 1997], a coordinator agent could exhibit a number of extra capabilities, being responsible not only on the information/services routing (as the other does), but making its own plans on the way the information should be combined in the system and on which agents (capabilities) be involved in the process. This usefully decouples the local strategies, adopted by each single service agent to solve its goals from the knowledge on how to combine its results with other parts in the system.

Given this framework, the communication scenario becomes the following: two agents willing to communicate will contact a coordinator, declaring their own languages and ontologies, asking him to organize a meeting and to arbitrate the dialog. The coordinator accepts the task and, if necessary, contacts another agent to support needed knowledge for completing the communication task. If the communication succeeds, the coordinator will continue in its role of "message router"; in case during the meeting a misunderstanding happens, the coordinator will involve one or more mediators, by asking them to solve it. From the two interacting agents points of view, the coordinator is performing all the activities. Task delegation to mediators and translators is thus hidden to the users, that will even ignore the need for these supplementary services.

5   Agents Communication Flow

After identification of agent classes (typologies), their functionalities and roles, it is now important to analyse in details how interactions may occur at a physical layer.

The previously described architecture [Pazienza and Vindigni, 2002b] could be defined as a pool of cooperating agents that interact following two different modalities:

- an event-driven asynchronous communication based on a request/reply protocol
- a demand-driven synchronous communication based on direct queries.

Agents could adopt a message based communication language that is a simplified version of KQML [Finin e Weiderhold, 1991] implementing only the most common performatives (ask-one, ask-all, tell, etc.). In this architecture, software agents owning information sources could freely communicate, through the interaction with a coordinator agent, independently from their physical collocation on the network. Coordinator agents are responsible for finding suitable support agents to process a message, to forward requests to them, to translate responses for dialog participants and to transmit information needed for message building. Depending on the typology of message, the coordinator agent will obtain a direct response or will activate the procedures required to process it. The overall system is information oriented and implements several different functionalities.

The agent architecture is structured in a number of layers that implement the different procedures needed for the communication, the reasoning and the internal knowledge storage and maintenance. The different interfaces among agents and the OS are built over TCP/IP, that represents the basic layer needed to connect and speak with software agents through the underlying network and different OSs. The delivery and monitoring message components along with the agent connection listeners, are wrapped in. These listeners are owned by the coordinator, that is responsible for a coherent activation of service agent requests. Its knowledge base contains information on capabilities, languages and ontologies of each single agent: it dynamically decides upon the involved connections based on all these information.

The coordinator uses its KB to serve requests, that will involve one or more of the following actions:
1. Identification of an agent that could process the request
2. Request translation to be comprehensible for the receiving agent
3. Request decomposition into one or more simpler ones, that are delegated to service agents
4. Results combination in a response for the requesting agent

To compel with these requests, the coordinator continually scans the network operations, waiting for a new agent connection, or an existing agent disconnection. Whenever it receives any one among: a new connection, a disconnection request, a message, it will activate the appropriate procedure. In the following, we briefly sketch the principal procedures involved either in the connection elaboration or in a request.

5.1 Processing Agent Connections

A connection request is sent from an agent to the coordinator agent, a communication channel will be setup between the two agents. Due to the communication protocol, the coordinator waits for a registration message with agents personal data, to which an answer will be sent accordingly. Purpose of this message is to provide to the system an explicit characterization for connecting agents . A newcomer must inform the coordinator with both its category (providing a nickname to let all other agents in the system to logically address it in their messages), and the services it will expose to the community. To be more explicit, the role each agent has in the system is defined on connection basis: this approach makes it possible for the same agent to assume time by time more than one role (for instance, a mediator could be later a translator, or a resource agent). For each role, the agent has to register to the coordinator by declaring what kind services it will provide, thus allowing to build a dedicated communication channel for each specific role. The coordinator records the link among name, role, connection and physical agents in a sort of directory service in its knowledge base, to be used later for message routing.

Depending on the role, further information will be necessary: for instance, the co-ordinator will be informed upon ontology and language the resource agent will adopt, while a translator will specify for which languages could be useful. These additional information is used both to decide run-time the dynamic information path, and to plan adequate support activities to be delegated to service agents.

5.2   Processing Agent Requests

Due to the fact all agents are connected through the coordinator, it is needed to guarantee a coherent information flow through the system. The coordinator behaviour becomes complex and structured related to the knowledge required for the communication task. Let us try to list its actions by decomposing, step by step, its behaviour in a specific task.

For instance, let us suppose an agent A be registered in the system, with a "speaker" (information sender) role. At a certain time, A will send a request to communicate a concept to agent B. At that moment, the coordinator must assume a number of decisions: by accessing its knowledge base, it will check all pre-conditions that should be verified for making communication feasible. First of all, it will verify B is known to the system. While B is available, the coordinator will match the information provided by A versus B to determine one of the following situations:

a)   both A and B use the same ontology: the A message will be directly transmitted to B (see Fig. 8-1);

b)   A and B refer to different ontologies while using the same language (see Fig. 8-2): the coordinator will verify the presence of a mediator agent and if unavailable, A will be notified with an appropriate message; otherwise the coordinator will build a suitable request for mediation, enriched with information on the concept under investigation plus A and B logical names. To make transparent its activity, the coordinator will behave, time by time, as speaker and as hearer, directly replying to the mediator queries if caching the required information, otherwise redirecting them to the appropriate agent. When the mediation activity ends, the coordinator will collect replies from the mediator, will update its knowledge base: in case of success of the mediation, it will send back the appropriate information to the hearer, finally notifying to the speakers the success of information delivery;

c)   both involved parts adopt either different ontologies or languages (see Fig. 8-3): the coordinator will interleave the actions performed in b) with appropriate queries to a translator agent. In fact, the mediation activity happens at symbol level, and further translations will be needed to present to the mediator the requested information in a uniform language. For instance, if the mediator uses language B, then each information flowing through A would first be translated by the translator agent. Depending on the intelligence of the coordinator, some information could also be cached before querying for the translator (for example, to maximize the translation accuracy, waiting for all the synonyms identifying a concept to be collected before querying a translation), thus improving the overall performance.

In case the needed information in each of previous a), b) or c) cases is already available in the coordinator knowledge base, it could directly reply without involving further actions. This knowledge acquisition process is extremely important as, runtime, it could result in new linguistic resources "emerging" from the overall communication process, and eventually, to new resource agents (it could be considered as a positive follow up). In a resource extraction context, we could adopt the same architectural framework by just specializing this process. It is feasible the coordinator releases periodically the acquired knowledge in form of a new resource agent, to maintain distinct as most as possible the identified functional roles in the communication system.

To better explicit the message exchange phase during system activities, in the following the typical dynamics emerging in a generic communication process are described.

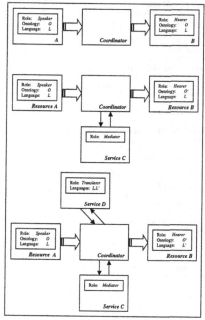

Fig. 8. Different communication configurations: 1 – direct, 2 – mediated and 3 – translated communication

Let us suppose that at a certain time, six agents enter in the system; four resource agents, let's say, agent1, agent2, agent3 e agent4, and two service agents mediator1 and translator1. agent1 declares his speaker role, to work with an ontology ontology1 and to have a lexicon for the italian language, while agent2, agent3 and agent4 declare the hearer role with respectively the ontolgies ontology1, ontology3 and ontology4, being italian the first two and english the third one; mediator1 is a mediator and translator1 is a translator between english and italian languages. The registration phase of the agents will set the following messages (in a pseudo KQML code for an easier readers comprehension) :

```
(package  :content (hello(agent1,speaker(ontology1,italian))))
                   :sender agent1
                   :receiver Coordinator
                   :reply-with id123)

(package  :content (hello(Coordinator,superuser))
                   :sender Coordinator
                   :receiver agent1
                   :in-reply-to id123)

(package  :content (hello(agent2,hearer(ontology1,italian))))
                   :sender agent2
                   :receiver Coordinator
                   :reply-with id125)

(package  :content (hello(Coordinator,superuser))
                   :sender Coordinator
                   :receiver agent2
                   :in-reply-to id125)

(package  :content (hello(mediator1,mediator))
                   :sender mediator1
                   :receiver Coordinator
                   :reply-with id241)

(package  :content (hello(Coordinator,superuser))
                   :sender Coordinator
                   :receiver mediator1
                   :in-reply-to id241)

(package  :content (hello(translator1,translator(english,italian))
                   :sender translator1
                   :receiver Coordinator
                   :reply-with id242)

(package  :content (hello(Coordinator,superuser))
                   :sender Coordinator
                   :receiver translator1
                   :in-reply-to id242)

(package  :content (hello(agent3,hearer(ontology3,italian))))
                   :sender agent3
                   :receiver Coordinator
                   :reply-with id134)

(package  :content (hello(Coordinator,superuser))
                   :sender Coordinator
                   :receiver agent3
                   :in-reply-to id134)

(package  :content (hello(agent4,hearer(ontology4,english))))
                   :sender agent4
                   :receiver Coordinator
                   :reply-with id170)

(package  :content (hello(Coordinatore,superuser))
                   :sender Coordinator
                   :receiver agent4
                   :in-reply-to id70)
```

In a successive instant time, agents communication is required. For istance at a certain time, agent1 says to Coordinator that he wants to comunicate to agent2 the concept concept1. As agent1 and agent2 have the same ontology, Coordinator will only:

1. semantically translate the agent1 speech act in a form understandable by agent2 (see fig. 9),
2. transmit the information to agent2
3. give his acknowledge
4. forward it to agent1.

```
(package  :content (say(agent2,concept1))
                   :sender agent1
                   :receiver Coordinator
```

```
                        :reply-with id128)
(package   :content (hear(agent1,concept1))
                        :sender Coordinator
                        :receiver agent2
                        :reply-with id129)
(package   :content (done)
                        :sender agent2
                        :receiver Coordinator
                        :in-reply-to id129)
(package   :content (done)
                        :sender Coordinator
                        :receiver agent1
                        :in-reply-to id128)
```

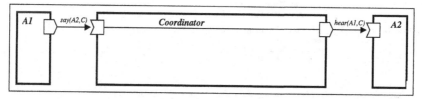

Fig. 9. Communication acts in case of direct connection among transmitter and sender

At another instant time, `agent1` declares to `Coordinator` its intention to comunicate to `agent3` the previous concept. This time, as `agent1` and `agent3` are based upon different ontologies, `Coordinator` must delegate the task of finding the most appropriate ontological translation for `agent3` by asking support to mediator1 (see fig. 10). This one, starting the mediation process, will ask later to `Coordinator` which words use `agent1` to define the concept `concept1`. As `Coordinator` does not know this information, he will reformulate the query to `agent1`. The received reply is then sent to `mediator1` in an appropriate format.

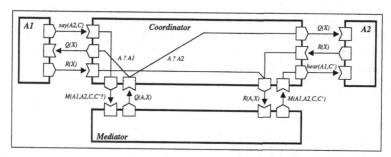

Fig. 10. Communication acts for mediated communication

Mediation continues until `mediator1` determines a mapping between source and target concepts. Such a result will finally be comunicated to `Coordinator`, that will provide to transmit the corrensponding speech act, as in the previous case, to `agent2` sending back the response to the original sender.

```
(package   :content (say(agent3,concept1))
                        :sender agent1
                        :receiver Coordinator
                        :reply-with id512)
```

```
(package  :content  (ask(mediate(agent1,agent3,concept1,?Y)))
                    :sender Coordinator
                    :receiver mediator1
                    :reply-with id111)

(package  :content  (ask(lexicals(agent1,concept1,?X)))
                    :sender mediator1
                    :receiver Coordinator
                    :reply-with id131)

(package  :content  (ask(lexicals(concept1,?X)))
                    :sender Coordinator
                    :receiver agent1
                    :reply-with id139)

(package  :content  (tell(lexicals(concept1,(word1,word2))))
                    :sender agent1
                    :receiver Coordinator
                    :in-reply-to id139)

(package  :content  (tell(lexicals(agent1,concept1,(word1,word2))))
                    :sender Coordinator
                    :receiver mediator1
                    :in-reply-to id131)

...

(package  :content  (tell(mediate(agent1,agent3,concept1,concept4)))
                    :sender mediator1
                    :receiver Coordinator
                    :in-reply-to id111)

(package  :content  (hear(agent1,concept4))
                    :sender Coordinator
                    :receiver agent3
                    :reply-with id115)

(package  :content  (done)
                    :sender agent3
                    :receiver Coordinator
                    :in-reply-to id115)

(package  :content  (done)
                    :sender Coordinator
                    :receiver agent1
                    :in-reply-to id512)
```

For speeding up the process, in case of a successive need for communication of the same concept between agents 1 and 3, Coordinator could remember previously found ontological translation (concept4 in the example) and directly proceed to the last step, thus avoiding a new request for the mediation service.

```
(package  :content  (say(agent3,concept1))
                    :sender agent1
                    :receiver Coordinator
                    :reply-with id721)

(package  :content  (hear(agent1,concept4))
                    :sender Coordinator
                    :receiver agent3
                    :reply-with id798)

(package  :content  (done)
                    :sender agent3
                    :receiver Coordinator
                    :in-reply-to id798)

(package  :content  (done)
                    :sender Coordinator
                    :receiver agent1
                    :in-reply-to id721)
```

The interaction between agent1 and agent4 is more complex, as they use lexicons from different languages. When agent1 expresses to Coordinator its intention to communicate to agent4 the concept concept2, as in the previous case,

Coordinator delegates the task to find the correct ontological translation with a request to mediator1 (see fig. 11). In reformulating the support queries from mediator1 it could emerge the need to involve the translation agent translator1. In the following example, in the dialog excerpt when mediator1 asks to agent1 which terms he uses to denote concept2 as the query has no linguistic information, it could be directly forwarded as in the previous cases. However, when agent1 replies, the translation agent is activated to present the results to mediator1 in the same language as agent4 (assuming that Coordinator decided to use the language of this one for the mediation). Moreover, when mediator1 determines the concept mapping, he will comunicate it to Coordinator, that will transmit the corresponding speech act, as usual, to agent4.

```
(package :content (say(agent4,concept2))
                  :sender agent1
                  :receiver Coordinator
                  :reply-with id532)

(package :content (ask(mediate(agent1,agent4,concept2,?Y)))
                  :sender Coordinator
                  :receiver mediator1
                  :reply-with id131)

(package :content (ask(lexicals(agent1,concept2,?X)))
                  :sender mediator1
                  :receiver Coordinator
                  :reply-with id151)

(package :content (ask(lexicals(concept3,?X)))
                  :sender Coordinator
                  :receiver agent1
                  :reply-with id159)

(package :content (tell(lexicals(concept1,(word3,word8))))
                  :sender agent1
                  :receiver Coordinator
                  :in-reply-to id159)

(package :content (ask(translate((word3,word8),?Z)))
                  :sender Coordinator
                  :receiver translator1
                  :reply-with id183)

(package :content (tell(translate((word3,word8),(word6))))
                  :sender translator1
                  :receiver Coordinator
                  :in-reply-to id183)

(package :content (tell(lexicals(agent1,concept1,(word6))))
                  :sender Coordinator
                  :receiver mediator1
                  :in-reply-to id151)

...

(package :content (tell(mediate(agent1,agent4,concept1,concept9)))
                  :sender mediator1
                  :receiver Coordinator
                  :in-reply-to id131)

(package :content (hear(agent1,concept9))
                  :sender Coordinator
                  :receiver agent4
                  :reply-with id135)

(package :content (done)
                  :sender agent4
                  :receiver Coordinator
                  :in-reply-to id135)

(package :content (done)
```

```
:sender Coordinator
:receiver agent1
:in-reply-to id532)
```

We will underline that the `Coordinator` activities in multilingual ontological mediation requires an higher reasoning ability with respect to the simple interactions between the mediation and the linguistic components. It becomes evident when the `mediator1` query processing requires some caching of the obteined intermediated results. For instance, during the previous case of mediation, if `mediator1` queries `agent1` on admissible senses for word `word5`, also in the hypotesis the mediation be carried on in `agent4` language, it will be necessary to translate the term in the `agent1` language. As translating a single word, `translator1` will probably provide multiple solutions (roughly corresponding to the different senses that `word5` could have in `agent1` language); `Coordinator` will issue on these multiple queries to `agent1`, temporally preserving the responses that will be finally combined (for instance, by making a set union) before being sent back as single reply to `mediator1`. It is evident in this case the inferential capability of `Coordinator`, that by using a specific operator (for instance the union) must "know" semantics of the interaction existing among different service levels (i.e. the mediation vs. the translation).

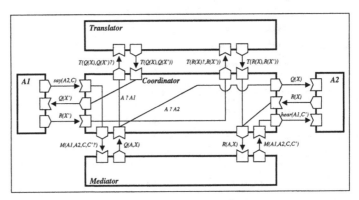

Fig. 11. Communication acts for mediated and translated communication

...

```
(package  :content (ask(senses(agent1,word5,?S)))
                    :sender mediator1
                    :receiver Coordinator
                    :reply-with id181)

(package  :content (ask(translate(?Z,(word5))))
                    :sender Coordinator
                    :receiver translator1
                    :reply-with id184)

(package  :content (tell(translate((word2,word7),(word5))))
                    :sender translator1
                    :receiver Coordinator
                    :in-reply-to id184)

(package  :content (ask(senses(word2,?X1)))
                    :sender Coordinator
                    :receiver agent1
                    :reply-with id189)

(package  :content (tell(senses(word2,(concept1,concept12))))
```

```
                     :sender agent1
                     :receiver Coordinator
                     :in-reply-to id189)
(package   :content  (ask(senses(word9,?X2)))
                     :sender Coordinator
                     :receiver agent1
                     :reply-with id190)
(package   :content  (tell(senses(word9,(concept4,concept12))))
                     :sender agent1
                     :receiver Coordinator
                     :in-reply-to id190)
(package   :content  (tell(senses(agent1,word5,(concept1,concept4,concept12))))
                     :sender Coordinator
                     :receiver mediator1
                     :in-reply-to id181)
```

6 Final Remarks

The increasing demand for intelligent systems able to cooperate in managing heterogeneous information pushes towards the design of flexible communication mechanisms. While several formalisms for expressing at some extent information contents
exist, none is 1) expressive, 2) shared, 3) synthetic as the natural language. Formal
languages, as XML, for document content representation are limited by the lack of an
universal agreement on which categories should be assumed as a shared model and at
what extent. Different domain conceptualisations are hardly compatible as different
aspects emerging from knowledge bases strongly depend on the application tasks they
have been written for. As argued in [Sowa,2000bis] "Many of the ontologies for web
objects ignore physical objects, processes, people, and their intentions. A typical example is SHOE (Simple HTML Ontology Extensions) [Heflin et al. 1999], which has
only four basic categories: String, Number, Date, and Truth. Those four categories,
which are needed to describe the syntax of web data, cannot by themselves describe
the semantics. Strings contain characters that represent statements that describe the
world; numbers count and measure things; dates are time units tied to the rotation of
the earth; and truth is a meta language term about the correspondence between a
statement and the world. Those categories can only be defined in terms of the world,
the people in the world, and the languages people use to talk about the world."

Linguistic communication becomes the only solution in all situations where there
is no explicit agreement among parts to coherently use a formal language, that is
when the ontological agreement is missing.

However, the expressive power on natural language poses a number of issues in
adopting a direct approach to the interpretation of meaning. Polysemy, morphological
variants and synonymy require a linguistic expertise to deal with: even if almost natural for humans, they could seriously deceive computer systems.

The proposed communication model will substantiate the respective contributions
of the different components involved in the communication process by introducing a
novel communication scheme; adopting an explicit separation between the concept
level where contents are organized and the lexical level where they are expressed by
terms in a language helps in incrementally affording the communication problem: to
encode a concept in a set of terms that will express the structural relationships among
concepts in speaker mind, to find mappings among linguistic expressions in partici-

pant languages, to decode the linguistic information in the mind representation of the receiver.

For both information extraction and communication purposes two different aspects need to be tightly integrated converging in a framework in which different autonomous systems could cooperate, while needed, for knowledge exchange.

An intelligent agent based approach could be a suitable solution: definition of an agent society (to which members with different properties and abilities belong) would perform the task of knowledge communication (exchange of information on both a specific matter and the world) with a collective and individual gain. This could happen when the set of related "speech acts" are shared (at least in their meaning) in the agent society.

We can summarize what acts are the most relevant in IE environment for exchanging information:
-    informing partners about the part of involved world in a proactive way (a sort of declaration of proprietary knowledge)
-    querying other agents about specific aspects of the world
-    answering specific questions
-    acknowledging requests and offers
-    sharing results and experiences

What is missing in previous list is the planning of speech acts sequence, that is to define when, what and why to activate. It is a sort of coordination speech act to govern information flow.

It will deal not with a deterministic problem as the sequence will be substantiated by the communication context both in physical and logical organization.

Starting from possible ambiguous input (and in any case unpredictable) the coordination speech act will work forward and backward to decide cognitive models of both extremes of the communication. Moreover, much more than on the general properties of the communication models, we have to focus on the way language is inside specific communication environment. Management of ontologies emerges to be mandatory in such a framework!

In fact, due to the fact we cannot assume agents share the same internal representation language, we need a formal language for knowledge representation purposes. In any case it makes sense to use language for the communication purposes of the following cases:
-    involved agents understand a common language
-    involved agents share a somewhat rational behaviour

We based on these assumptions for defining our linguistic agents society that proved to be successful to support knowledge exchange in a large extent of situations ranging from an homogeneous and compatible to an only partially overlapping world model.

References

[Agirre e Rigau, 1996] E. Agirre and G. Rigau: *Word sense disambiguation using conceptual density*. In Proceedings of COLING'96, Copenhageñ, Danmark, 1996.
[Babylon, 1999] Babylon Translator, avilable at http://www.babylon.com.

[Baldonado et al., 1997] M. Baldonado, C.-C. K. Chang, L. Gravano, and A. Paepcke. *Metadata for digital libraries: Architecture and design rationale*. Technical Report SIDL-WP-1997-0055, Stanford University, 1997.

[Bateman et al., 1990] J.A. Bateman, R.T. Kasper, J.D. Moor and R.A. Whitney: *A general organisation of knowledge for natural language processing: The penman upper model*. Technical report, USC/Information Sciences Institute, 1990.

[Batini et al. 1986] C. Batini, M. Lenzerini & S. B. Navathe: *A comparative analysis of methodologies for database schema integration*. ACM Computing Surveys 18, 1986.

[Bayardo et al., 1997] R. Bayardo, W. Bohrer, R. Brice, A. Cichocki, G. Fowler, A. Helal, V. Kashyap, T. Ksiezyk, G. Martin, M. Nodine, M. Rashid, M. Rusinkiewicz, R. Shea, C. Unnikrishnan, A. Unruh and D. Woelk: *Infosleuth: Semantic Integration of Information in Open and Dynamic Environments*, Proceedings ACM SIGMOD'97 Conference, 1997.

[Benjamins e Fensel, 1998] R. Benjamins and D. Fensel: *Community is Knowledge! in (KA) 2*. In Proceedings of the 11th Banff Knowledge Acquisition for Knowledge-Based System Workshop (KAW98), Banff, Canada, 1998.

[Bobrow e Winograd, 1985] D. Bobrow and T. Winograd: *An overview of KRL, a Knowledge Representation Language*. In Readings in Knowledge Representation. Morgan Kaufmann, 1985.

[Bray et al., 1998] *XML Extensible Markup Language (XML) 1.0*, eds. Tim Bray, Jean Paoli, and C. M. Sperberg-McQueen. 10 February 1998. Available at http://www.w3.org/TR/REC-xml.

[Bright et al., 1994] M.W. Bright, A.R. Hurson, S. Pakzad: *Automated Resolution of Semantic Heterogeneity in Multidatabases*, ACM Transactions on Database Systems, Vol.19, No.2, 1994.

[Campbell e Shapiro, 1995] A.E. Campbell, and S. C. Shapiro: *Ontologic Mediation: An Overview*. IJCAI95 Workshop on Basic Ontological Issues in Knowledge Sharing, Montreal, 1995.

[Campbell, 1999] A. E. Campbell: *Ontological Mediation: Finding Translations Across Dialects by Asking questions*, Phd. Dissertation submitted to the University of New York, Buffalo, 1999.

[Campbell, 1996] A. E. Campbell: *Resolution of the Dialect Problem in Communication through Ontological Mediation*, Proceedings of the AAAI-96 Workshop on Detecting, Preventing, and Repairing Human-Machine Miscommunication, Portland, OR, 1996.

[Catarci e Lenzerini, 1993] T. Catarci and M. Lenzerini. *Representing and using interschema knowledge in cooperative information systems*. Journal of Intelligent and Cooperative Information Systems, 2(4), 1993.

[Chang e Garcia-Molina, 1998] C.-C. K. Chang and H. Garcia-Molina. *Conjunctive constraint mapping for data translation*. In Proc. of the Third ACM Intl. Conf. on Digital Libraries, Pittsburgh, Pa., 1998.

[Chawathe et al., 1994] S. Chawathe, H. Garcia-Molina, J. Hammer, K. Ireland, Y. Papakonstantinou, J. Ullman, and J. Widom. *The TSIMMIS Project: Integration of Heterogeneous Information Sources*. In Proc. of IPSJ Conference, 1994.

[Clark, 1983] E.V. Clark. *Meanings and concepts*. In P. Mussen (Ed.), Manual of child psychology (vol. 3, pp. 787-840). New York: Wiley, 1983.

[Cohen e Hirsh, 1994] W.W.Cohen, H.Hirsh: *The learnability of description logics with equality constraints*, Machine Learning, 17, 1994.

[Cohen e Levesque, 1995] P. R. Cohen and H. J. Levesque: *Communicative actions for artificial agents*. In Proceedings of the First International Conference on Multi-Agent Systems (ICMAS-95), Menlo Park, California, 1995.

[Cohen e Levesque, 1990] P. R. Cohen and H. J. Levesque: *Rational interaction as the basis for communication*. In P. R. Cohen, J. Morgan, and M. E. Pollack, editors, Intentions in Communication. The MIT Press: Cambridge, MA, 1990.

[Collins e Quillian, 1969] A. M. Collins and M. R. Quillian: *Retrieval time for semantic memory*. Journal of Verbal Learning and Verbal Behaviour, 8, 1969.

[Dale et al., 2001] J. Dale and E. Mamdani. *Open Standards for Interoperating Agent-Based Systems*. Software Focus, 1(2), 2001.

[Decker et al., 1996] K. Decker, M. Williamson, and K. Sycara: *Modeling information agents: Advertisements, organizational roles, and dynamic behavior*. In Proceedings of the AAAI-96 Workshop on Agent Modeling, 1996.

[Drogoul e Ferber, 1994] A. Drogoul and J. Ferber: *Multi-agent simulation as a tool for studying emergent processes in societies*. In Doran, J., and Gilbert, G.N., eds. "Simulating Societies: the Computer Simulation of Social Phenomena", ULCP, London, 1994.

[Ferber, 1999] J. Ferber: *Multi-Agent Systems: An Introduction to Distributed Artificial Intelligence*. Addison-Wesley, 1999.

[Fikes et al., 1991] R. Fikes, M. Cutkosky, T. Gruber, and J. V. Baalen: *Knowledge Sharing Technology Project Overview*. Technical Report KSL-91-71, Knowledge Systems Laboratory, Stanford University, 1991.

[Finin e Weiderhold, 1991] T. Finin and G. Weiderhold: *An Overview of KQML: A Knowledge Query and Manipulation Language*, available through the Stanford University Computer Science Department, 1991.

[Franklin e Graesser, 1996] S. Franklin and A. Graesser: *Is it an Agent, or just a Program?: A Taxonomy for Autonomous Agents*, Proc. of the Third International Workshop on Agent Theories, Architectures and Languages, 1996.

[Gruber, 1992] T.R. Gruber: *ONTOLINGUA: A Mechanism to Support Portable Ontologies*, technical report, Knowledge Systems Laboratory, Stanford University, Stanford, United States, 1992.

[Guarino, 1998] N. Guarino: *Formal Ontology and Information Systems*. In N. Guarino, editor, Proceedings of the 1st International Conference on Formal Ontologies in Information Systems, FOIS'98, Trento, Italy. IOS Press, 1998.

[Guha e Lenat, 1990] R. V. Guha and D. B. Lenat. *Building Large Knowledge-Based Systems: Representation and Inference in the CYC Project*. Addison-Wesley, 1990.

[Guha e Lenat, 1994] R. V. Guha and D. B. Lenat. *Enabling agents to work together*. Communications of the ACM, 37(7), 1994.

[Gustavsson, 1997] R. Gustavsson: *Multi Agent Systems as Open Societies*, Intelligent Agents - Theories, Architectures, and Languages (ATAL'97), Springer Verlag, 1997.

[Haas e Hendrix, 1983] N. Haas, and G. Hendrix: *Learning by being told: Acquiring knowledge for information management*. In Michalski, R., Carbonell, J., & Mitchell, T. (Eds.), Machine Learning: An Artificial Intelligence Approach, Vol. I, chap. 13. Morgan Kaufmann Publishers, Inc., 1983

[Heflin et al. 1999] J. Heflin, Hendler, J., and Luke, S. SHOE: A Knowledge Representation Language for Internet Applications. Technical Report CS-TR-4078 (UMIACS TR-99-71), Dept. of Computer Science, University of Maryland at College Park. 1999.

[Hull, 1997] R. Hull: *Managing semantic heterogeneity in databases: A theoretical perspective*. In Proc. ACM Symposium on Principles of Databases, 1997.

[Jones e Paton, 1998] D.M. Jones, and R.C. Paton: *Some Problems in the Formal Representation of Hierarchical Relationships*, in Proc. Conference on Formal Ontology in Information Systems – FOIS'98, June 6-8 , Trento, Italy, IOS Press, 1998.

[Kashyap e Sheth, 1996] V. Kashyap and A. Sheth: *Semantic and Schematic Similarities between Database Objects: A Context-based Approach.*VLDB Journal, 5(4), 1996.

[Khedro e Genesereth, 1994] T. Khedro and M. Genesereth: *The federation architecture for interoperable agent-based concurrent engineering systems*. International Journal on Concurrent Engineering, Research and Applications, 2, 1994.

[Khedro e Genesereth, 1995] T. Khedro and M. Genesereth: *Facilitators: A networked computing infrastructure for distributed software interoperation*. In Working Notes of the IJCAI-95 Workshop on Artificial Intelligence in Distributed Information Networks, 1995.

[Kim e Seo, 1991] W. Kim and J. Seo. *Classifying schematic and data heterogeneity in multi-database systems*. IEEE Computer 24(12), 1991.

[Knight e Luk, 1994] K. Knight and S.K. Luk: *Building a Large-Scale Knowledge Base for Machine Translation.* Proceedings of the AAAI-94, 1994.

[Knoblock e Ambite, 1997] C. A. Knoblock and Jose-Luis Ambite: *Agents for information gathering.* In J. Bradshaw, editor, Software Agents. AAAI/MIT Press, Menlo Park, CA, 1997.

[Kuhn, 1993] N. Kuhn, H.J. Müller and J.P. Müller: *Task Decomposition in Dynamic Agent Societies.* In Proceedings of the Fifth European Workshop on Modelling Autonomous Agents and Multi-Agent Worlds (MAAMAW-93), Neuchatel, Switzerland, 1993.

[Lehmann e Cohn, 1994] F. Lehmann and A. G. Cohn: *The EGG/YOLK reliability hierarchy: Semantic data integrationusing sorts with prototypes.* In Proc. Conf. on Information Knowledge Management, ACM Press, 1994.

[Levy et al., 1996] A. Levy, A. Rajaraman, and J. Ordille: *Query answering algorithms for information agents.* Proceedings of the 13th National Conference on Artificial Intelligence, 1996.

[Li, 1995] W.-S. Li: *Knowledge gathering and matching in heterogeneous databases.* In Working Notes of the AAAI Spring Symposium on Information Gathering from Heterogeneous, Distributed Environments, 1995.

[Martin et al., 1999] G.L. Martin, A. Unruh, and S.D. Urban: *An Agent Infrastructure for Knowledge Discovery and Event Detection.* Available at http://www.mcc.com/projects/infosleuth/publications/ , 1999.

[Miller et al., 1993] G. Miller, R. Beckwith, C. Fellbaum, D. Gross, D. and K. Miller. *Introduction to WordNet: An on-line lexical database.* In Proceedings of the Fifteenth International Joint Conference on Artificial Intelligence, 1993.

[Miller, 1985] G. Miller: *WORDNET: A Dictionary Browser.* In Proceedings of the First International Conference on Information in Data, University of Waterloo Centre for the New OED, Waterloo, Ontario, 1985

[Moore, 1990] R.C. Moore,: *A formal theory of knowledge and action.* In Allen, J. F., Hendler, J., and Tate, A., editors, Readings in Planning, Morgan Kaufmann Publishers: San Mateo, CA, 1990.

[Park et al., 1998] J.Y. Park, J.H. Gennari and M.A. Musen: *Mappings for Reuse in Knowledge-based Systems.* 11th Workshop on Knowledge Acquisition, Modelling and Management KAW 98. Banff, Canada, 1998.

[Pazienza, 2002] M.T.Pazienza, *Intelligent-Agents need ontologies: Why, What, Where, When, Who,* Proceedings of the workshop OMAS Ontologies for Multi-Agent Systems, Siguenza (Spain) 30 sept. 2002

[Pazienza and Vindigni, 2002a] M.T.Pazienza, M. Vindigni, *Mining linguistic information into an e-retail system,* Proceedings of the DATA MINING 2002 Conference, Bologna 23–25 sept. 2002

[Pazienza and Vindigni, 2002b] M.T.Pazienza, M. Vindigni, Language-based agent communication, Proceedings of the EKAW 02 Conference, workshop OMAS Ontologies for Multi-Agent Systems, Siguenza (Spain) 30 sept. 2002

[Peirce, 1932] C.S. Peirce : *Elements of logic.* In C. Hartshorne and P. Weiss, editors, Collected Papers of Charles Sanders Peirce, volume 2. Harvard University Press, Cambridge, MA, 1932.

[Ramesh e Ram, 1997] V. Ramesh and S. Ram: *Integrity Constraint Integration in Heterogeneous Databases: An Enhanced Methodology for Schema Integration.* Information Systems, 22, 8, 1997.

[Sheth et al., 1993] A. P. Sheth, S. K. Gala, and S. B. Navathe: *On automatic reasoning for schema integration.* International Journal of Intelligent and Cooperative Information Systems, 2(1), 1993.

[Sowa, 2000] J. F. Sowa: *Knowledge Representation: Logical, Philosophical, and Computational Foundations,* Brooks Cole Publishing Co., Pacific Grove, CA, 2000.

[Sowa,2000bis] J.F. Sowa *Ontology, Metadata, and Semiotics* in *Conceptual Structures: Logical, Linguistic, and Computational Issues*, Lecture Notes in AI #1867, Springer-Verlag, Berlin, 2000, pp. 55–81.

[Sycara et al., 1998] K. Sycara, J. Lu, and M. Klusch: *Interoperability among Heterogeneous Software Agents on the Internet.* Carnegie Mellon University, PA (USA), Technical Report CMU-RI-TR-98-22, 1998.

[Takeda et al., 1995] H. Takeda, K. Iino, and T. Nishida: *Agent organisation with multiple ontologies.* International Journal of Cooperative Information Systems, 4 (4), 1995.

[Visser et al., 1997] P.R.S.Visser, D.M. Jones, T.J.M. Bench-Capon, and M.J.R. Shave, M.J.R.: *An Analysis of Ontology Mismatches: Heterogeneity versus Interoperability"*, presented at AAAI 1997 Spring Symposium on Ontological Engineering, Stanford University, CA, 1997.

[Widerhold and Genesereth, 1997] G. Wiederhold and M. Genesereth. The conceptual basis for mediation services. IEEE Intelligent Systems, pages 38--47, September/October 1997

[Weinstein e Birmingham, 1998] P. C. Weinstein and W. P. Birmingham: *Creating Ontological Metadata for Digital Library Content and Services.* International Journal on Digital Libraries 2(1), 1998.

[Woolridge e Jennings, 1995] M. Woolridge and N.R. Jennings: *Agent Theories, Architectures and Languages : A Survey.* In Proc. of the ECAI-94 Workshop on Agent Theories, Architectures and Languages (Eds.: Woolridge, M. J.; Jennings, N. R.); Berlin; SpringerVerlag; 1995.

On the Role of Information Retrieval and Information Extraction in Question Answering Systems

Dan Moldovan[1] and Mihai Surdeanu[2]

[1] Human Language Technology Research Institute, University of Texas at Dallas
moldovan@seas.smu.edu
[2] Language Computer Corporation, Dallas, Texas
mihai@languagecomputer.com

Abstract. Question Answering, the process of extracting answers to natural language questions is profoundly different from Information Retrieval (IR) or Information Extraction (IE). IR systems allow us to locate relevant documents that relate to a query, but do not specify exactly where the answers are. In IR, the documents of interest are fetched by matching query keywords to the index of the document collection. By contrast, IE systems extrat the information of interest provided the domain of extraction is well defined. In IE systems, the information of interest is in the form of slot fillers of some predefined templates.

The QA technology takes both IR and IE a step further, and provides specific and brief answers to open domain questions formulated naturally. This paper presents the major modules used to build IR, IE and QA systems and Shows similarities, differences and possible trade-offs between the three technologies.

1 Information Retrieval

The three main technologies used to extract information from large collections of documents are Information Retrieval (IR), Information Extraction (IE), and Question Answering (QA). In this paper we first review briefly the state-of-the-art in each field, compare the similarities and differences between the main building modules, and then explore possible ways of combining the three technologies and performing trade-offs for various application domains.

The goal of Information Retrieval (IR) systems is to extract documents that best match a query. The two main tasks in IR are document indexing and searching. Indexing is the task of representing a document by its key features for the purpose of speeding up its finding when a query is invoked. There were many indexing schemes explored, but the most commonly used are based on word stemming and its enhancements. Term weighting is an indexing technique that gives a degree of importance to a word in a description. Word proximity, especially adjacency, is frequently used to Capture some of the linguistic relations between words. Some advanced indexing methods take into consideration

M.T. Pazienza (Ed.): SCIE 2002, LNAI 2700, pp. 129–147, 2003.

compound terms and phrases, that is groups of words that collectively have a syntactic role. These are detected with shallow syntactic parsing and semantic analysis.

The goal of searching is to locate the most relevant documents and to rank them in Order of decreasing match with a query. Thus, a similarity measure needs to be introduced for this. Similarity algorithms are usually based on term weighting which is by far the most important feature that controls the IR precision. There are two types of weights, initial weights and relevance weights. The first are used when a searcher presents a query to the system, while the later is used after the documents are retrieved for the purpose of ordering them. The most common type of initial weighting is inverse document frequency (idf) which assigns weights to the terms in a query such that the weights are in inverse Proportion to the frequency of occurrence of these terms in the document collection, namely, low frequency terms are likely to point to a relevant document. An improved method is $tf.idf$ weighting, which multiplies the term frequency weights by the collection frequency weight.

Relevance feedback is the name given to methods that try to modify queries automatically, that is to re-weight queries by adding or deleting keywords, or expanding keywords. Conceptual indexing has been studied by [Woods 1997, Mihalcea 2001]. The idea is to index documents based on concepts not words. This involves word sense disambiguation, a Problem that has not been solved yet for open text.

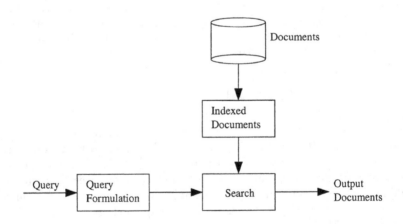

Fig. 1. A generic IR System Architecture

Figure 1 shows a high level block diagram of a generic IR architecture. Search is done by using an inverted file, which contains a dictionary file and postings file. The dictionary file contains lists of keywords, classification terms, journal titles that can be used as keywords. A count is associated with each entry in the dictionary file, it specifies how frequently a key occurs. The postings file contains a series of lists one for each of the entries in the dictionary file. Each such list contains the identifiers of all documents that contain a given term. This enables the IR system to search only those documents that contain query terms. The posting file also stores the term location which facilitates proximity search.

Inverted files provide rapid access to large document collections, but they require large storage overhead; index file may be twice as large as the document file.

Once the initial query terms are submitted they are looked up in the dictionary file to determine whether they have been used to index any of the documents in the collection. If they have, their frequency of occurrence in the database is extracted. Each entry in the dictionary file has a pointer to the corresponding list in the posting file. These lists are further processed to check operators such as AND, OR, NEAR and others. After the logic operations have been performed, a new list that contains the identifiers of all relevant documents is formed. Usually several iterations are necessary to return an appropriate size output file. The user has now access to the documents and if not satisfied another query is formulated.

2   Information Extraction

Information Extraction systems attempt to pull out information from documents by filling out predefined templates. The information typically consists of entities and relations between entities like who did what to whom, where, when and how. IE got a boost with the MUC (Message Understanding Conference) in late 1980's and early 1990's. The MUC IE systems focused on one domain at a time; for example joint ventures, terrorism in Latin America, management successions, and others. Users of such systems had to specify their information need in the form of a template with Slots that the system had to fill automatically.

Figure 2 shows templates filled by the CICERO information extraction on the MUC-6 management succession domain [Harabagiu and Surdeanu 2002]. A template can store information directly extracted from the document, e.g. organization names such as "Fox Inc." and most importantly can store information about the inter-template relations. As shown in Figure 2 each SUCCESSION_EVENT template stores one or more links to IN_AND_OUT templates, which describes the actual succession event: who seized/acquired the management position, with further links to PERSON and ORGANIZATION templates.

A typical IE system architecture is a cascade of modules, like those in Figure 3. A preferred method of implementation for these modules is finite state automata [Hobbs et al. 1996, Harabagiu and Surdeanu 2002]. The *tokenizer* is the first module of the IE system. The task of the tokenizer is to break the document into lexical entities (tokens). Generally, a token is a word or a punctuation sign, but in some cases it may be a word fragment. For example, the word "U.S.A." is broken into six tokens: "U", ".", "S", ".", "A", and ".". It is the task of the next module to identify the above sequence as a complex word representing an abbreviation of "United States of America".

The *Lexicon* module identifies words and complex words that have lexical and semantic meaning. This is done by inspecting both dictionaries and gazetteers. Dictionaries contain open-domain lexico-semantic information, e.g. "house" is an artifact, or to a lesser extent domain-specific information, e.g. "mail bomb" is a kind of bomb. Gazetteers typically store well-known entity names, such as locations, e.g. "Dallas" is a city in the state of "Texas" part of the country "United States of America".

```
<TEMPLATE-9301190125-1> :=
       DOC_NR:     "9301190125"
       CONTENT:    <SUCCESSION_EVENT-9301190125-1>
                   <SUCCESSION_EVENT-9301190125-2>
                   <SUCCESSION_EVENT-9301190125-3>
                   <SUCCESSION_EVENT-9301190125-4>
                   <SUCCESSION_EVENT-9301190125-5>
                   <SUCCESSION_EVENT-9301190125-6>
                   <SUCCESSION_EVENT-9301190125-7>
<SUCCESSION_EVENT-9301190125-1> :=
       SUCCESSION_ORG: <ORGANIZATION-9301190125-1>
       POST:           "chief executive officer"
       IN_AND_OUT:     <IN_AND_OUT-9301190125-1>
                       <IN_AND_OUT-9301190125-2>
       VACANCY_REASON: REASSIGNMENT
       COMMENT:        "Joseph M. Segel OUT, Barry Diller IN as
                       chief executive officer of QVC Network Inc."
<IN_AND_OUT-9301190125-2> :=
       IO_PERSON:      <PERSON-9301190125-1>
       NEW_STATUS:     IN
       ON_THE_JOB:     UNCLEAR
       OTHER_ORG:      <ORGANIZATION-9301190125-2>
       REL_OTHER_ORG:  OUTSIDE_ORG
       COMMENT:        "Barry Diller IN"
...
<ORGANIZATION-9301190125-2> :=
       ORG_NAME:       "Fox Inc."
       ORG_TYPE:       COMPANY
<ORGANIZATION-9301190125-1> :=
       ORG_NAME:       "QVC Network Inc."
       ORG_TYPE:       COMPANY
<PERSON-9301190125-1> :=
       PER_NAME:       "Barry Diller"
       PER_ALIAS:      "Diller"
       PER_TITLE:      "Mr."
<PERSON-9301190125-3> :=
       PER_NAME:       "Joseph M. Segel"
       PER_ALIAS:      "Segel"
       PER_TITLE:      "Mr."
...
```

Fig. 2. Sample templates for the MUC-6 management succession domain

The *Preprocessor* identifies simple lexical entries that are not stored in lexicon or gazetteers. Some of the items identified by the preprocessor are: phone numbers "1-(800) 88-7777", money "$4.75", dates "December 25", times "8:30am", measures such as "10kg", "one hundred degrees", and others.

The *Name Entity Recognizer* is one of the most important modules in IE. It assigns lexical features to words or groups of words such as locations, organizations, persons, addresses, and others. Proper names are particularly useful for extraction systems since they point to objects about which we need to identify properties, relations, events. The technique is to use capitalization if available.

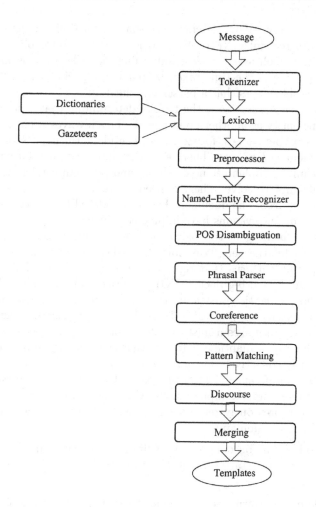

Fig. 3. An IE System Architecture

Some of the most frequently used methods are Hidden Markov Models and finite state automata patterns. With the help of dictionaries these techniques are able to recognize that "John Smith" is a proper name, and "John Hopkins" is a University; or that "Austin Ventures" is a Company, "Austin, Texas" is a City and "Austin Thomas" is a name. Machine learning methods are sometimes used to train the Name Recognizer in a new domain. NE-recognition benefits by morphological analysis by looking up in a dictionary for all morphological variations of words.

Part of Speech Tagging is useful for subsequent text analysis stages. This involves specifying the part of Speech of each word. POS taggers are rule-based or statistical and achieve an accuracy around 95%. The *Parser* identifies simple noun phrases (NP), e.g. "the fast red car", verb phrases (VP), e.g. "is being observed daily", and also particles that may be significant in subsequent text analysis. In many MUC systems only shallow parsing was used. It was more important to recognize NP or VP and less important to solve the attachment of prepositional phrases, or close subordination. The reasons for avoiding full syntactic parsing is the time taken by parsers, especially if sentences are long, and the possible errors that a parser may introduce.

Coreference Resolution is the task of determining that a noun phrase refers to the same entity as another noun phrase. This involves equating various forms of personal proper names, for example "President Bush", "George Bush", "the 43rd President of US", etc. There are other more complex forms of coreference such as definite or indefinite noun phrase and pronoun coreference that some IE systems attempt to solve. There is need for temporal coreference resolution in which "today" from one document has to be related to "a week ago" in another document, but few systems have implemented this.

Pattern Matching is the basic method for extracting domain-specific information to fill the template slots. Considerable effort is put in developing domain-specific patterns that represent events specific to a domain. Typically these are subject-verb-object (SVO) patterns that are tailored to a domain by specifying semantic constraints that each component must meet. For example "Greenspan makes a recession" fits the pattern <human, causes, entity> while "Greenspan makes a mistake" does not fit the above pattern. This is decided by checking semantic constraints that the subject, verb, and object would have to satisfy collectively for pattern matching.

Domain Coreference is typically part of a *discourse analysis* module and attempts to fill empty template slots, which can be retrieved from the context of the pattern previously recognized. Consider the following example from the "natural disaster" domain:

> ... flooding has become a way of life in Guerneville in the last several years. This gas station along the Russian River gets hit nearly every time. ...

The domain pattern recognition module matches the <disaster, destroys, artifact> pattern over this text. Based on the semantics associated with this pattern, the following template is constructed:

```
<NATURAL_DISASTER> :=
    AMOUNT_DAMAGE: "this gas station"
    LOCATION: "Russian River"
```

Note that due to the inherent complexity of the natural language not all template slots can be covered through patterns. In this example a very important slot: the disaster type ("flooding") is not recognized by the pattern. In such situations the domain coreference module inspects the pattern context for possible fills for the empty slots. In the above example the resulting template is:

```
<NATURAL_DISASTER> :=
    DISASTER: "flooding"
    AMOUNT_DAMAGE: "this gas station"
    LOCATION: "Russian River"
```

Merging is the task of combining and consolidating the information that refers to the same event by combining the templates that refer to the same events. Merging is a multi-step process. For example, first the templates that refer to the same events found in one sentence are merged, then the same is done at the document level, then at the collection level.

3   Question Answering

A QA system accepts questions in natural language form, searches for answers over a collection of documents and extracts and formulates concise answers. As shown in Figure 4, the three essential modules in almost all QA systems are *question processing, document retrieval,* and *answer extraction* and *formulation.*

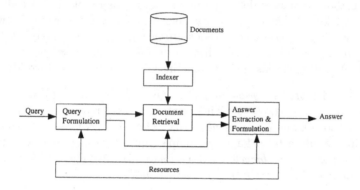

Fig. 4. A generic QA System architecture.

Just like MUC has boosted the IE technology, the Text Retrieval Conference (TREC) QA track has stimulated considerable interest and research in Question Answering in the last few years. In 2001, the US Government has initiated a new research program in QA, called Advanced Quest ion Answering for Intelligence (AQUAINT).

Since modern QA systems are open domain, the performance of a QA system is tightly coupled with the complexity of questions asked and the difficulty of answer extraction. For example, in TREC many systems were quite successful at providing correct answers to simpler, fact-seeking questions, but failed to answer questions that required reasoning or advanced linguistic analysis [Voorhees 1999]. From the combined set of 1460 evaluation questions, 70% of the participating systems answered successfully questions like Q1013: *"Where is Perth?"*, but none could find a correct answer to complex questions such as Q1165: *"What is the difference between AM radio stations and FM radio stations?"*

In order to put the QA technology into perspective, we first provide a broad taxonomy of QA systems. The taxonomy is based on several criteria that play an important role in building QA systems: (1) linguistic and knowledge resources,

(2) natural language processing involved, (3) document processing, (4) reasoning methods, (5) whether or not answer is explicitly stated in a document, (6) whether or not answer fusion is necessary.

Classes of Questions

Class 1. QA systems capable of processing factual questions

These systems extract answers as text snippets from one or more documents. Often the answer is found verbatim in a text or as a simple morphological variation. Typically the answers are extracted using empirical methods relying on keyword manipulations.

Class 2. QA systems enabling simple reasoning mechanisms

The characteristic of this class is that answers are found in snippets of text, but unlike in Class 1, inference is necessary to relate the question with the answer. More elaborate answer detection methods such as ontologies or codification of pragmatic knowledge are necessary. Semantic alternations, world knowledge axioms and simple reasoning methods are necessary. An example is Q198: *"How did Socrates died?"* where *die* has to be linked with *drinking poisoned wine*. WordNet and its extensions are sometimes used as sources of world knowledge.

Class 3. QA systems capable of answer fusion from different documents

In this class the partial answer information is scattered throughout several documents and answer fusion is necessary. The complexity here ranges from assembling simple lists to far more complex questions like script questions, (e.g. *"How do I assemble a bicycle?"*), or template-like questions (*"What management successions occurred at IBM in the past year?"*).

Class 4. Interactive QA systems

These systems are able to answer questions in the context of previous interactions with the user. As reported in [Harabagiu et al. 2001], processing a list of questions posed in a context involves complex reference resolution. Unlike typical reference resolution algorithms that associate anaphorae with a referent, the reference imposed by context questions requires the association of an anaphora from the current question with either one of the previous questions, answers or their anaphora.

Class 5. Speculative questions

The characteristic of these systems is their ability to answer speculative questions similar to:

"Is the Fed going to raise interests at their next meeting?";

"is the US out of recession?";

"is the airline industry in trouble?".

Since most probably answers to such questions are not explicitly stated in documents, simply because events may not have happened yet, QA systems from this class decompose the question into queries that extract pieces of evidence, after which answer is formulated using reasoning by analogy. The resources include ad-hoc knowledge bases generated from mining text documents clustered by the question topic. Associated with these knowledge sources are case-based reasoning techniques as well as methods for temporal reasoning, spatial reasoning and evidential reasoning.

Table 1. Distribution of TREC questions

Type	Number (%)
Class 1 (factual)	985 (67.5%)
Class 2 (simple-reasoning)	408 (27.9%)
Class 3 (fusion - list)	25 (1.7%)
Class 4 (interactive - context)	42 (2.9%)
Class 5 (speculative)	0 (0.0%)

Table 1 illustrates the distribution of TREC questions into the question classes. In addition to 1393 main-task questions collected from TREC-8, TREC-9 and TREC-2001, there are 25 list questions (e.g., *"Name 20 countries that produce coffee."*) and 42 context questions (e.g., *"How long was the Varyag?"*; *"How wide?"*).

QA System Architecture

First we identify the main modules of a QA system architecture, then present some architectural features seen in advanced QA systems. The model boundaries may change as some systems rely more on one method than another. There are ten modules presented below, the first five modules correspond to question processing, the next two modules perform document and passage processing, and the last three modules perform answer processing.

<u>M1</u> The individual question words are spell-checked. Words like *Volkswangen* and *Niagra* are expanded into their spelling variants *Volkswagen* and *Niagara*. If necessary, questions such as Q885: *"Rotary engine cars were made by what Company?"* are rephrased into a normalized form where the wh-word (*what*) appears at the beginning, e.g. *"What company were rotarg engine cars made by?"*.

<u>M2</u> The input question is parsed and transformed into an internal representation capturing question concepts and binary dependencies between the concepts [Harabagiu et al. 2000]. Stop words (e.g., prepositions or determiners) are identified and removed from the representation. For illustration, the representation for QO13: *"How much could you rent a Volkswagen bug for in 1966?"* captures the binary dependency between the concepts *rent* and 1966.

<u>M3</u> The mapping of certain question dependencies on a WordNet-based answer type hierarchy disambiguates the semantic category of the expected answers [Pasca and Harabagiu 2001]. For example, the dependency between *How much* and *rent* for Q013 is exploited to derive the expected answer type *Money*. The answer type is passed to subsequent modules for the identification of possible answers (all monetary values).

M4 Based mainly on part of speech information, a subset of the question concepts are selected as keywords for accessing the underlying document collection. A passage retrieval engine accepts Boolean queries built from the selected keywords, e.g. *Volkswagen* AND *bug*. The retrieval engine returns passages that contain all keywords specified in the Boolean query. Therefore keyword selection is a sensitive task. If the wrong question word (e.g. *much*) is included in the Boolean query (*much* AND *Volkswagen* AND *bug*), the retrieval is unsuccessful since the passages containing the correct answers are missed.

M5 Before the construction of Boolean queries for actual retrieval, the selected keywords are expanded with morphological, lexical or semantic alternations. The alternations correspond to other forms in which the question concepts may occur in the answers. For example, *rented* is expanded into *rent*.

M6 The retrieval engine returns the documents containing all keywords specified in the Boolean queries. The documents are then further restricted to smaller text passages where all keywords are located in the proximity of one another. Each retrieved passage includes additional text (extra lines) before the earliest and after the latest keyword match. For illustration, consider QOO5: *"What is the name of the managing director of Apricot Computer?"* and the associated Boolean query *Apricot* AND *Computer* AND *director*. The relevant text fragment from the document collection is *"Dr Peter Horne, managing director of Apricot Computers"*. Unless additional text is included in the passages, the actual answer *Peter Horne* would be missed because it occurs before all matched keywords, namely *director*, *Apricot* and *Computer*.

M7 The retrieved passages are further refined for enhanced precision. Passages that do not satisfy the semantic constraints specified in the question are discarded. For example, some of the passages retrieved for Q013 do not satisfy the date constraint *1966*. Out of the 60 passages returned by the retrieval engine for QO13, only two passages are retained after passage post-filtering.

M8 The search for answers within the retrieved passages is restricted to those candidates corresponding to the expected answer type. If the expected answer type is a named entity such as MONEY, the candidates (*$1, USD 520*) are identified with a named entity recognizer. Conversely, if the answer type is a DEFINITION, e.g. Q903: *"What is autism?"*, the candidates are obtained by matching a set of answer patterns on the passages.

M9 Each candidate answer receives a relevance score according to lexical and proximity features such as distance between keywords, or the occurrence of the candidate answer within an apposition. The candidates are sorted in decreasing Order of their scores.

M10 The system selects the candidate answers with the highest relevance scores. The final answers are either fragments of text extracted from the passages around the best candidate answers, or they are internally generated.

Performance Evaluation

A QA system with this baseline linear architecture [Moldovan 2002] was tested on 1460 questions collected from TREC-8, 9 and TREC-2001. Answers were extracted from a 3 Gbyte text collection containing about 1 million documents from sources such as Los Angeles Times and Wall Street Journal. Each answer has 50 bytes.

The accuracy was measured by the Mean Reciprocal Rate (MRR) metric used by NIST in the TREC QA evaluations [Voorhees 1999]. The reciprocal ranking basically assigns a number equal to $1/R$ where R is the rank of the correct answer. Only the first 5 answers are considered, thus R is less or equal to 5. When the system does not return a correct answer in top 5, the precision score for that question is zero. The overall system precision is the mean of the individual scores. System answers were measured against correct answers provided by NIST.

Table 2. Distribution of errors per System module

	Module	Module definition	Errors (%)
QP	(M1)	Keyword pre-processing (split/bind/spell check)	1.9
	(M2)	Construction of internal question representation	5.2
	(M3)	Derivation of expected answer type	36.4
	(M4)	Keyword selection (incorrectly added or excluded)	8.9
	(M5)	Keyword expansion desirable but missing	25.7
DR	(M6)	Actual retrieval (limit on passage number or size)	1.6
	(M7)	Passage post-filtering (incorrectly discarded)	1.6
AP	(M8)	Identification of candidate answers	8.0
	(M9)	Answer ranking	6.3
	(M10)	Answer formulation	4.4

The inspection of internal traces, at various checkpoints inserted after each module reveals the system errors for each evaluation question. The goal in this experiment is to identify the earliest module in the chain (from left to right) that prevents the system to find the right answer, i.e.cCauses the error.

As shown in Table 2, question pre-processing is responsible for 7.1% of the errors distributed among module M1 (1.9%) and M2 (5.3%). Most errors in module M2 are due to incorrect parsing (4.5%). Two of the ten modules (M3 and M5) account for more than half of the errors. The failure of either module makes it hard (or impossible) for subsequent modules to perform their task. Whenever the derivation of the expected answer type (module M3) fails, the set of candidate answers identified in the retrieved passages is either empty in 28.2% of the cases (when the answer type is unknown) or contains the wrong entities for 8.2% (when the answer type is incorrect). If the keywords used for passage retrieval are not expanded with the semantically related forms occurring in the answers (module M5), the relevant passages are missed.

The selection of keywords from the internal question representation (module M4) coupled with the keyword expansion (module M5) generate 34.6% of the errors. Both these modules affect the output of passage retrieval, since the set of retrieved passages depends on the Boolean queries built and submitted to the retrieval engine by the QA system.

Modules M6 and M7 are responsible for the retrieval of passages where answers may actually occur. Their combined errors is 3.2%. In module M6 there are parameters to control the number of retrieved documents and passages, as well as the size of each passage.

Answer processing is done in modules M8 through M10. When the expected answer type is correctly detected, the identification of the candidate answers (module M8) produces 8.0% errors. 3.1% errors are due to named entity recognition (incomplete dictionaries) and 4.9% are due to spurious answer pattern matching. Modules M9 and M10 fail to rank the correct answer within the top 5 returned in 10.7% of the cases. Module M9 fails if the correct answer candidate is not ranked within the top 5, whereas M10 fails if the returned answer string is incomplete, namely it does not fit within 50 bytes.

A More Advanced QA System Architecture

The results presented in previous sections correspond to the serialized baseline architecture. Such an architecture is in fact a simplified version of our system which uses several feedbacks to boost the overall performance [Moldovan 2002].

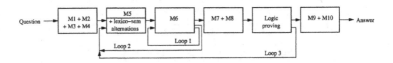

Fig. 5. Architecture with feedbacks

As shown in Figure 5, the architecture with feedbacks extends the serialized architecture in several ways. Keyword expansion (module M5) is enhanced to include lexico-semantic alternations from WordNet. A new module for logic proving and answer justification is inserted before answer ranking. In addition, three loops become an integral part of the system: the passage retrieval loop (loop 1); the lexico-semantic loop (loop 2); and the logic proving loop (loop 3).

Table 3. Impact of feedbacks on precision

Feedback added	Precision (MRR)	Incremental enhancement
none	$0.421 = b$	0%
Passage retrieval (loop 1)	$0.468 = b_1$	$b + 11\%$
Lexico-semantic (loop 2)	$0.542 = b_2$	$b_1 + 15\%$
Proving (loop 3)	$0.572 = b_3$	$b_2 + 5\%$

As part of loop 1, the Q/A system adjusts Boolean queries before passing them to the retrieval engine. If the output from the retrieval engine is too small, a keyword is dropped and retrieval resumed. If the output is too large, a keyword is added and a new iteration started, until the output size is neither too large, nor too small. When lexico-semantic connections from the question to the retrieved passages are not possible, loop 2 is triggered. Question keywords are replaced

Table 4. Summary of the main modules in IR, IE and QA

Subsystem	Module	IR	IE	QA
Question processing	keyword preprocessing	x		x
	question representation			x
	answer prediction			x
	keyword selection	x		x
	keyword expansion	x		x
document indexing and retrieval	document indexing	x	y	x
	document search and retrieval	x	y	x
	document ranking	x	y	x
document processing	morphological and lexical proc		x	x
	extract relevant passages		x	x
	syntactic parsing		x	x
	name entity recognition		x	x
	coreference		x	y
	discourse processing		x	x
	semantic analysis			x
use of world knowledge	WordNet		x	x
	dictionaries		x	x
use of domain knowledge	domain ontologies		x	x
	domain patterns		x	
	domain coreference		x	
	domain event merging		x	
output extracting	patterns		x	x
	complex nlp techniques		x	x
	merger		x	x
	answer ranking			x
	logic prover			x
	answer justification			x
output formatting	template filling		x	
	answer formulation		y	x

with WordNet-based alternations and retrieval is resumed. Loop 3 relies on a logic prover that verifies the unifications between the question and logic forms. When the unifications fail, the keywords are expanded with semantically related alternations and retrieval resumes.

Table 3 illustrates the impact of the retrieval loops on the answer accuracy. The knowledge brought into the question answering process by lexico-semantic alternations has the highest individual contribution, followed by the mechanism of adding/dropping keywords.

4 A Global View of IR, IE, and QA

As we have Seen, there are some modules common to more than one technology. A global view of this is shown in Table 4. We marked with x features that are fully supported, and with y features that are only partially supported. For example, advanced QA systems have answer formulation and generation features, whereas IE systems have only some limited form of text generation based on the template fills (see the COMMENT template fields in Figure 2).

5   Trade-Offs in QA Systems

As Table 4 indicates, Question Answering systems use modules common with IR and IE. The recent QA literature contains reports on QA systems that emphasize either IR or IE, which indicates a rich possibility of trade-offs in implementing these systems.

IR-Based QA
An IR-based QA system is built on top of an IR engine. In this case, the Question Processing is reduced to question classification. Two basic methods were used to build IR-based QA systems:

- QA systems that retrieve relevant *documents* and extract answers directly from those documents [Kwok 20001. The IR module extracts and ranks documents using: coordinate matching, stemming, synonyms, identifies important words, proximity of question words, order of question words, capitalizations and quoted query words. Answer extraction and formulation is reduced to heuristic pattern matching which identifies entities such as person, places, dates, units (length, area, time, currency, population) by using some heuristics.
- QA systems that retrieve only relevant *passages* from documents and then extract answers by further processing those passages. The advantage of passage retrieval over full document retrieval is that the amount of text that needs to be processed is significantly reduced. The systems in this category used various techniques to retrieve passages ranging from statistical methods [Ittycheriah 2001], to identifying passages based on answer category determined from the question [Clarke 2000], or conceptual indexing coupled with relaxation ranking [Woods 2000].

QA Based on IE
IE-based QA systems use IE methods, such as named entity taggers and surface patterns, to extract answers. Not having an IR engine, these systems rely on an outside source to supply relevant documents. Answers are extracted by matching the question keywords to the documents supplied from outside. The system described in [Srihari 1999] uses a preliminary ranking of documents to find the most probable answers by counting how many unique keywords are contained in a sentence. A secondary ranking of documents is done based on the order in which the keywords appear in the question. Yet, a third ranking is used to allow for matching variants of key verbs. A QA system that is based exclusively on IE patterns is described in [Soubbotin 2001].

6   Applications

Each of the three technologies has been implemented in commercial applications systems. In this section we will explore a few ways of combining two of the technologies for the purpose of building more powerful knowledge management (KM) application systems.

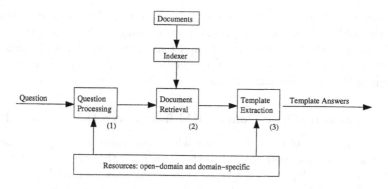

Fig. 6. IE Architecture extended with question processing and document retrieval

6.1   Domain Specific KM from Large Document Collections

This application answers domain-specific questions by finding domain specific events or entities from large document collections. From a technical point of view this system injects QA features into an IE system, such that: (a) the IE system understands natural language questions, and (b) large collections are accessed using passage retrieval techniques. For example, imagine a car insurance agency investigator who wants to find details about a certain accident:

"What accident took place in Dallas, at 3:30pm?"

The envisioned system architecture is shown in Figure 6. The system behavior is the following:

1. First the question must be processed. From the question answer type ("accident") the system identifies that the user is interested in an accident event, hence it will later enable only pattern rules relevant to this domain. The keywords are then selected just like in the QA system: "accident", "Dallas", "3:30pm".
2. The system retrieves paragraphs based on the set of keywords (similar to QA).
3. Answer processing is basically IE. Based on the question answer type, the corresponding domain (here "accident events") is enabled. Using IE techniques, the system fills in the templates extracted from the previously retrieved paragraphs, which become the answer as shown below.

ACCIDENT
            TYPE: "two cars collided"
            LOCATION: "NW Highway"
            TIME: "3:30pm"
            DAMAGE: "broken light, damaged fender"
            . . .

Such a system can be applied to any domain-specific application where the answers tan be represented in a template form. There are many such applications:

a news agency agency could use the "bombing domain" to track the latest events in the Middle East, an intelligence agency could use the "people movement" domain to track the movements of important people, etc. These domain-oriented applications are very hard to be handled by open-domain QA systems, which might miss domain-specific information.

6.2   Advanced Open-Domain KM from Large Document Collections

This idea enhances the QA systems with some useful techniques implemented in IE systems. We refer mainly to the framework that identifies syntactic patterns, such as SVO (subject-verb- object) patterns or complex noun groups. This framework can be ported to a QA system to help extract answers that can be identified through syntactico-semantic patterns. Currently, some QA systems handle definition (e.g. *"What is anorexia nervosa?"*) and author (e.g. *"Who wrote the declaration of Independence?"*) questions by using patterns. But the pattern recognition mechanisms implemented are more primitive than the ones implemented in advanced IE systems. Besides these types of questions, many other questions tan be identified through patterns as demonstrated by [Soubbotin 2001].

While information extraction provides the syntactic framework for pattern identification (i.e. all the forms in which a SVO patterns can be expressed) the semantic constraints for the patterns are provided by question processing. For example, for the question:

"What is a petabyte?"

The QP module constructs the semantic constraints for the SVO pattern as follows:

SUBJECT: *"petabyte"*
VERB: any *"be"* verb
OBJECT: anything

The answer extraction module identifies all the matches for this pattern, and extracts the answer as the object field of the SVO pattern. Note that the advanced pattern matching techniques implemented in state-of-art IE systems allow for broad coverage of possible syntactic forms of any given pattern. The template in the above example matches not only SVO patterns in active form, e.g. " *a petabyte is . . .* ", but also relative forms, e.g. " *a petabyte, which is . . .* ", or gerund verb forms *". . . the petabyte being . . .* ".

This approach allows the transfer of the pattern matching technology developed in IE systems for more than 10 years, to open-domain QA systems, which until recently have relied only on surface-text techniques for answer detection.

6.3   QA on the Web

Until recently, QA systems have focused on extracting answers from locally-indexed collections of documents. In many real world applications, the Web

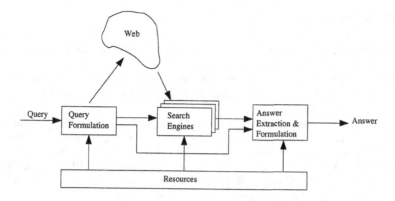

Fig. 7. Web-based Question Answering System

is a valuable source of information. With millions of anonymous contributors continuously adding new content, the Web has been growing into a huge, unstructured and diverse information resource, covering virtually every topic of interest. Search engines now offer access to over two billion Web documents [Sullivan 2000], but most of this information remains inaccessible to users, as the search engines are often incapable of pinpointing the specific information desired. The recently emerged web-based QA systems provide a natural language wrapper to search engines that: (a) provide a more intuitive interface for question formulation, and (b) extract and report natural language answers instead of a set of document URLs.

The architecture of a generic web-based QA system is shown in Figure 7. The system architecture is similar to a regular QA system, except that the static collection of documents is replaced with one or more search engines. Nevertheless, additional features have to be added to each of the three QA system modules. First, the query formulation module must understand the search engine syntax when formulating a query. For example, some search engines accept advanced boolean operators such as OR and NEAR, some do not. Second, the document retrieval module must handle the network latency when retrieving documents, and must also consider the fact that some indexed documents might not be available at all. And third, web documents are stored in various formats which must all be translated into a canonical form before being passed to the answer extraction module.

Besides these problems, the natural language wrapper around search engines offers some attractive advantages. Unlike meta-search engines, for web-based QA systems it is relatively painless to integrate multiple search engines under a single umbrella. The answer extraction module provides an elegant framework for ranking answers independently of their originating document, which means that multiple search engines can be queried in parallel and their documents merged before answer extraction and formulation.

Despite their young age and all the difficulties mentioned above, web-based QA system have approached commercial maturity [LCC].

References

[Brill 2001] E. Brill, J. Lin, M. Bnako, S. Dumais, A. Ng. Data-Intensive Question Answering. *Proceedings of the TREC-9*, 2000.

[Clarke 2000] C. L. A. Clarke, G. V. Cormack, D. I. E. Kisman, T. R. Lynam. Question Answering by Passage Selection (MultiText Experiments for TREC-9). *Proceedings of the TREC-9*, 2000.

[Harabagiu et al. 2000] S. Harabagiu, M. Pasca, and S. Maiorano. Experiments with open-domain textual question answering. *Proceedings of the 18th International Conference on Computational Linguists (COLING-2000)*, 2000.

[Harabagiu 2000] S. Harabagiu, D. Moldovan, M. Pasca, R. Mihalcea, M. Surdeanu, R. Bunescu, R. Girju, V. Rus, P. Morarescu. FALCON: Boosting Knowledge for Answer Engines. *Proceedings of the TREC-9*, 2000.

[Harabagiu et al. 2001] S. Harabagiu, D. Moldovan, M. Pasca, M. Surdeanu, R. Mihalcea, R. Girju, V. Rus, F. Lacatusu, P. Morarescu, and R. Bunescu. Answering complex, list, and context questions with LCC's question answering server. *Proceedings of the 10th Text REtrievai Conference (TREC-2001)*, 2001.

[Harabagiu and Surdeanu 2002] S. Harabagiu and M. Surdeanu. Infrastructure for Open-Domain Information Extraction. *Proceedings of Human Language Technology 2002 (HLT 2002)*, 2002.

[Hobbs et al. 1996] J. Hobbs, D. Appelt, J. Bear, D. Israel, M. Kameyama, M. Stickel and M. Tyson. FASTUS: A cascaded finite-state transducer for extracting information from natural-language text. Finite State Devices for Natural Language Processing, 1996.

[Hovy 2000] E. Hovy, U. Hermjakob, C-Y Lin, M. Junk, L. Gerber. The Webclopedia. *Proceedings of the TREC-9*, 2000.

[Ittycheriah 2001] A. Ittycheriah, M. Franz, S. Roukos. IBM's Statistical Question Answering System. *Proceedings of the TREC-2001*.

[Kwok 2000] K. L. Kwok, L. Grunfeld, N. Dinsti, and M. Chan. TREC-9 Cross Language, Web and Question Answering Track Experiments using PIRCS. *Proceedings of the TREC-9*, 2000.

[LCC] Language Computer Corporation web site: *languagecomputer. com*

[Mihalcea 2001] R. Mihalcea, D. Moldovan. Semantic Indexing using WordNet Senses. *Proceedings of ACL-2001 Workshop on Recent Advances in Natural Language Processing and Information Retrieval*, Hong Kong, 2000.

[Moldovan 1999] D. Moldovan, S. Harabagiu, M. Pasca, R. Mihalcea, R. Goodrum, R. Girju, V. Rus. LASSO: A Tool for Surfing the Answering Net. *Proceedings of the Eight Text REtrieval Conference (TREC 8)*, National Institute of Standards and Technology, 1999.

[Moldovan 2001] D. Moldovan, V. Rus. Logic Form Transformation of WordNet and its Applicability to Question Answering. Proceedings of the ACL, 2001.

[Moldovan 2002] D. Moldovan, M. Pasca, S. Harabagiu, M. Surdeanu. Performance Issues and Analysis in an Open-Domain Question Answering System. *Proceedings of the ACL*, 2002. Error

[Pasca and Harabagiu 2001] M. Pasca and S. Harabagiu. The informative role of WordNet in open-domain question answering. *Proceedings of the 2nd Meeting of the North American Chapter of the Association for Computationai Linguistics (NAACL-01)*, 2001.

[Soubbotin 2001] M. M. Soubbotin, S. M. Soubbotin. Patterns of Potential Answer Expressions as Clues to the Right Answers. *Proceedings of the TREC-2001*.

[Srihari 1999] R. Srihari and W. Li. Information Extraction Supported Question Answering. *Proceedings of the TREC-8*, 1999

[Sullivan 2000] D. Sullivan. Search engine sizes. searchenginewatch.com, November 2000

[Voorhees 1999] E. Voorhees The TREC-8 Question Answering track report. *Proceedings of the 8th Text REtrieval Conference (TREC-8)*, 1999.

[Voorhees 2001] E. M. Voorhees. Overview of the TREC 2001 Question Answering Track. Proceedings of the TREC-2001.

[Woods 1997] W. A. Woods. Conceptual Indexing: A Better Way to Organize Knowledge. Technical Report SMLI TR-97-61, Sun Microsystems Labs, Mountain View, CA, 1997.

[Woods 2000] W.A. Woods, S. Green, P. Martin, and A. Houston. Halfway to Question Answering. Proceedings of the TREC-9, 2000.

Natural Language Communication with Virtual Actors

Marc Cavazza

School of Computing and Mathematics, University of Teesside
TS1 3BA, Middlesbrough, United Kingdom
m.o.cavazza@tees.ac.uk

Abstract. The development of realistic virtual actors in many applications, from user interface to computer entertainment, creates expectations on the intelligence of these actors including their ability to understand natural language. Based on our research in that area over the past years, we highlight specific technical aspects in the development of language-enabled actors. The embodied nature of virtual agents lead to specific syntactic constructs that are not unlike sublanguages: these can be used to specify the parsing component of a natural language interface. However, the most specific aspects of interacting with virtual actors consist in mapping the semantic content of users' input to the mechanisms that support agents' behaviours. We suggest that a generalisation of speech acts can provide principles for this integration. Both aspects are illustrated by results obtained during the development of research prototypes.

1 Introduction

The increased visual realism of virtual agents naturally creates expectations on their intelligence and, as many of these are either interface agents or virtual actors, their ability to understand human language. In this paper, we focus on some key technical problems aspects in the design of language-enabled virtual agents.
We will largely base this discussion on our own recent research in the field, which covers several different kind of virtual agents [1] and virtual actors in interactive storytelling [2], and has resulted in the development of several prototypes.
Virtual agents are embodied in a physical (although virtual) environment: apart from the properties of any specific task they have to carry, this embodiement is at the heart of understanding the requirements for NLP. The embodiement of virtual agents requires that their understanding of language is entirely translated into actions in their environment. Although this problem has been described as early as 1970s in the SHRDLU system, no systematic account has been attempted until the mid-90s [3].
The most generic representation of an agent behaviour is a *plan*. This is why the semantics of actions can be described as relating the utterance content to plans to be executed by the agent. Previous work from Webber et al. [3] has classified various forms of language statements in terms of the complexity of actions that should result from them. This classification distinguishes, among others, doctrine statements, purpose clauses and procedural instructions. *Doctrine statements* express "general policy

M.T. Pazienza (Ed.): SCIE 2002, LNAI 2700, pp. 148–162, 2003.

regarding behaviour in some range of situations" [3], such as avoid confrontation as much as possible. These very high-level statements can only be understood by an agent possessing sophisticated reasoning mechanisms.

Purpose clauses are instructions that convey the goal of an action. One example in a computer games corpus is shoot a barrel to get rid of most of the pink demons. It is not so much the explanatory nature of this statement that matters as the implicit instructions that it carries. In other terms, it means that the character should wait for the pink demons to come in close proximity to the barrels before opening fire. Both doctrine statements and purpose clauses require complex inference mechanisms that can only be implemented within autonomous agents with intentions.

Procedures correspond to actions to be taken immediately or in the near future, subject to specific pre-conditions being met. These can however relate to complex action sequences, including some variability due to specific configurations or changes in the virtual world.

In this paper, we investigate two main aspects of interacting in natural language with embodied virtual actors. We do so through different research experiments we have been conducting over the past few years, whose evolution reflects the progress in the integration between natural language processing and the agents' behavioural mechanisms. The first one deals with the basic requirements of linguistic processing and explores how traditional parsing problems should be approached in this context. The latter attempts to relate the semantic content of natural language input to the mechanisms that support agent behaviour.

2 Linguistic Processing and Sublanguages

There are still few real-world applications in which a user would interact with a virtual actor. In order to study the corresponding technical requirements in a realistic environment, we explored the possibility for a human player to control the characters in a computer game using natural language instructions. Computer games provide large scale environments and limited but well-defined tasks; we selected a classical game at the time of our experiments, DOOM™, for which many on-line resources were available, and designed a natural language interface for part of the game. The first step was logically to carry a corpus study in order to establish a list of the most relevant linguistic phenomena. The DOOM™ "spoiler" corpus we used was an on-line corpus available from http://www.gamers.org. It described in natural language the traversal of DOOM™ levels. Typical spoilers alternate the description of landmarks, item locations, and describe sequences of actions to be taken by the player. Here is a typical excerpt from a DOOM™ spoiler:

Enter the door with the skull on it and push the switch. Walk out of the room and turn right. There are now stairs going into the wall, which is fake. Enter the teleporter, you're now in a circular room; find the secret door (the wall with the face on it) to go to the next circular room and enter the teleporter.

Fig. 1. Natural Language Instructions to a DOOM™ game Emulator

Most importantly, they correspond to some kind of briefing that would be given to a player before his gaming session. Such a briefing incorporates advice along a description of a temporal sequence of actions to be taken, including the consequences of previous actions (e.g. "Enter the teleporter, you're now in a circular room"). These actions are in limited number and essentially include various displacements, collecting objects as well as combat moves. Yet, there is a great deal of variability in issuing instructions to carry out these elementary actions, which justifies the use of linguistic processing.

This corpus shows many regularities suggesting sociolectal aspects, which could be characterised as a sublanguage [4]. This would bear significant implications in terms of natural language processing. On the other hand, a common method to design natural language interaction is by means of habitable languages [5]. These are formally defined controlled languages, which are designed to facilitate language processing in a given application by making parsing tractable. They approach natural communication by defining a sufficient number of formally specified variants of standard expressions that can be encountered in the task domain. In habitable languages, the practical approach consists in identifying the system actions targeted, investigating the most frequent surface variants for the associated commands, and generating a set of variation rules. More specifically, habitability indicates how easily and effectively users can express themselves within the constraints of a system command language. A command language is considered habitable if users can express everything that is needed for a task using language they would expect the system to understand [5]. Lexical habitability is achieved by providing appropriate synonyms for the main domain concepts. Syntactic habitability refers to the number of paraphrases of a given command that the system understands. In practical terms, it involves describing enough syntactic variants of a given construction so the user does not realise the underlying constraints or can adapt to these with minimal effort. Habitable languages are widely used in multimedia systems [6] [7] [8].

Communication with virtual actors finds itself in-between these two paradigms: on one hand, depending on the nature of the application (e.g. computer games), it is possible to recognise the emergence of actual sublanguages. On the other hand, limitations in speech recognition and parsing might make recourse to habitable language a necessity. In the next sections, we describe the design of a simplified parser based on the above principles. It is common that sublanguages should show a high frequency of specific constructs related to the domain at hand. In this case, as natural language interaction has to refer to situations in the agent's world, it is quite logical that there should be a predominance of spatial expressions ("the door near the stairs on the right", "the blue circle in the middle of the room"). Other very frequent phenomena are definite descriptions ("the door with a skull on it"), and instrumental relations ("shoot the baron with the plasma gun"). These arise from the need of designating objects that might be outside the current focus or field of vision, or for which no physical pointing at is available in the environment. It should be noted that all these expressions involve prepositional phrases (PP). That is to say, syntactic analysis will be faced with many PP-attachments problems, which are a main source for syntactic ambiguities in parsing for all but the simplest commands.

The existence of some complex syntactic phenomena such as those reported above is a rationale for making use of actual syntactic formalisms in the design of the parser. We have based our parser on a simplified variant of Tree-Adjoining Grammar (TAG) [9], Tree-Furcating Grammar (TFG) [10]. TFG have been shown to be less powerful than TAG, as some constructs cannot be represented in TFG [11]. This, however, does not affect our parser whose coverage is meant to be limited to the habitable language we have defined.

Our main objective was to achieve a good level of integration between syntax and semantics, which is essential for real-world applications. Simplifying basic tree structure and operations was also intended to speed up the parsing process itself.

Like TAG, TFG are based on larger syntactic units, which facilitate parsing while achieving a first step in the integration of syntax and semantics. These syntactic units can group verbs with their arguments or directly represent idiomatic expressions in an integrated fashion. Parsing in TFG consists in combining trees according to their categories, until the set of trees corresponding to the sentence (called a forest) is reduced to a single parse tree. This process is detailed in the next sections. Lexical trees can be characterised by the part-of-speech category associated with their root note (S, V, N...). Trees of root S (sentence) are generally the most important trees, since they group together a main verb with placeholders for its subject and objects, and most instructions tends to follow this generic pattern. Other categories reflect the syntactic category of the main word grounding the tree (its anchor). Trees of root S, V, N are called initial trees. In TFG, like in TAG, there is a specific category of trees, called auxiliary trees that combine with initial trees on the basis of their syntactic category. For instance, N* is the root of a right auxiliary tree, e.g. the red adjective in the red door. A sentence comprising two such prepositions would thus generate four forests, notwithstanding the duplications arising from other phenomena.

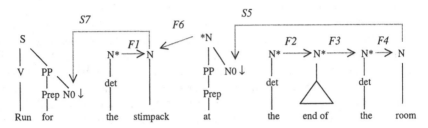

Fig. 2. Parsing in the TFG Formalism

On average, we have observed that an input sentence generates between one and four forests. These are parsed in sequence, and every forest not reduced to a single tree of root S after parsing is discarded. Generating multiple forests provides a principled yet efficient way to cope with syntactic ambiguity.

2.1 The Parsing Algorithm

Parsing consists in combining all trees in a forest until a single tree of root S can be produced or no further operations are possible. In the TFG formalism, trees are combined through two elementary operations: substitution and furcation. Substitution replaces a pre-defined substitutable node, acting as a placeholder (e.g. the N0 node in Figure 2.) with a compatible tree of similar category (e.g. a N tree). From a semantic perspective, the substitutable nodes are often placeholders for action parameters. For instance in the tree Run-for-N0, N0 stands for the object to be collected. As an example of tree fusion operations, in Figure 2, the nominal phrase the stimpack, of type N, will be substituted in the initial tree at leaf N0. Furcation adjoins an auxiliary tree to its target tree, thus adding an extra branch to it. It is a simplified variant of the adjunction operation that was initially described by De Smedt and Kempen [12]. While substitution can only take place at determinate node, nodes for furcation are determined dynamically. For instance, furcation of an auxiliary tree of type N takes place on the rightmost N leave of the target tree [10]. One of the advantages of furcation is that it results in trees of moderate depth, which speeds up tree traversal at further stages of parsing for successive furcations. As we have seen, furcation generally involves modifiers such as adjectives (of N* root), which can add their semantic information to the tree they modify during the furcation process. The "flatter" trees obtained with furcation evidence the prevalence of dependency over constituency structures.

Our parsing algorithm is a simplified bottom-up parser. The first step consists in assembling all the lexicalised trees compatible with the word sequence and to generate a set of candidate forests. Each forest is then scanned left to right and each pair of adjacent trees is considered for fusion on the basis of their generalised type compatibility.

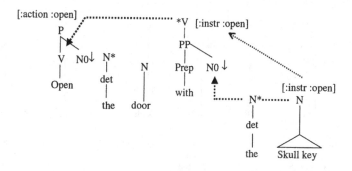

Fig. 3. Syntactic Disambiguisation with Selectional Restrictions

Adjacent trees in a forest are thus combined left-to-right, until the forest is reduced to a single tree of root S, or no further operations are possible (in the latter case the parsing exits on failure). Part of the parsing algorithm is actually compiled into a compatibility table that states for each pair of adjacent trees the kind of fusion operation that can be applied to them. Figure 2 shows the sequence of operations involved in parsing the command "run for the stimpack at the end of the room". The numbers associated with the operations indicate the order in which these operations take place. This shows that the sentence undergoes several passes as a result of the constraints imposed on substitution and furcation operations. The first pass is mainly dedicated to the constitution of nominal groups through furcation (F1-F4). Once these have been assembled, it is possible to substitute the prepositional group (S5), which will then modify the nominal group the stimpack (F6). This makes possible to attribute the correct target object (the stimpack at the end of the room) to the main action, through substitution operation S7.

We have previously described the frequency and importance of prepositional phrases for natural language instructions to virtual actors, and the associated syntactic ambiguities they generate. Spatial prepositions attachment (e.g. N-at-N0, see Figure 2.) is based on a nearest-neighbour heuristic that states that the attachment should relate to the closest compatible noun phrase. The case of the with preposition is a classical case of PP-attachment where two different trees have been produced in two different forests. So, considering this specific implementation, it should be determined at parsing time whether the two candidate trees for PP-attachment are semantically compatible, using traditional selectional restriction. Semantic restrictions are defined in terms of compatible pairs of semantic features for both *N attachments and *V attachments. Semantic restrictions for *N-PP groups correspond to part-whole relations or spatial relations, while *V-PP groups generally correspond to instrument semantic relations. Figure 2 shows the selectional restriction process for the sentence shoot the baron with the plasma gun. The ambiguity is between *N-with-N0 (the Skull key would be on the door, e.g. an ornament like in "the door with a Skull on it") and V-with-N0 (the key's telic is to open the door, Figure 3). Only the latter is consistent with the semantic properties of the candidate trees. The semantic relation is between opening and the instrument category to which the key belongs.

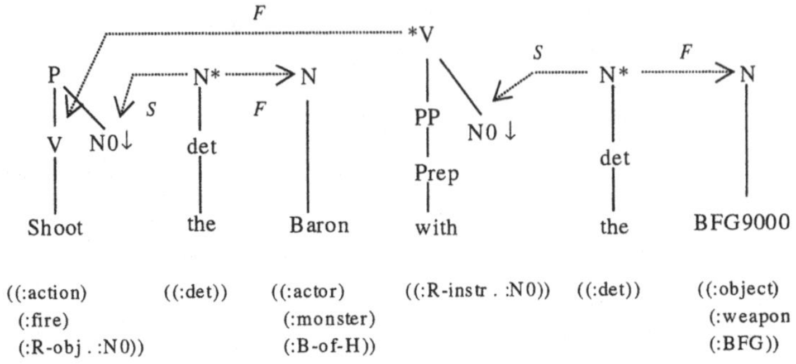

Fig. 4. Syntax-Semantics Integration

On the other hand, there are no such semantic relations between baron and rocket launcher, like would be the case with the door with a skull on it, as there exists part-whole relationships between doors and icons, or between pillars and icons, switches, etc. The parser maintains two lists of selectional restriction pairs, describing pairs of compatible features, one for verbal attachments and one for nominal attachments.

2.2 Integrating Syntax and Semantics

Semantic processing is carried out in parallel with syntactic parsing. Two elementary semantic operations support the construction of semantic structures. The first one is the establishment of semantic relations: it mainly corresponds to substitution in verb phrases or furcation of *V groups such as *V-with-N0, which associate actions with their instruments. The other one is the aggregation of semantic content through furcation operations, e.g. for the processing of nominal descriptions.

Semantic structures produced by the parser are structured according to semantic relations established during parsing. More specifically, substitution operations will establish functional relations between the semantic structures associated with the combined trees. Furcation operations will propagate the semantic content of auxiliary trees, which often correspond to qualifiers (adjectives, adverbs...), on the initial tree that these qualifiers modify. However, furcation operations corresponding to prepositional groups are associated with the establishment of semantic relations, which can be either functional or non-functional. One example of functional relation is the instrument relation that is established as a result of furcating a *V-with-N0 auxiliary tree on a verb node, for instance when processing shoot the baron with the rocket launcher. Non-functional relations are mostly represented by part-whole or spatial relations. These are introduced by spatial prepositions such as on, near ... or with prepositions in *N-with-N0 trees. These establish spatial or part-whole relations within the feature structure.

There is one additional reason why semantic and syntactic analysis should be carried in parallel and that is that some of the semantic features required for selectional restrictions are indeed propagated through other tree combination operations. This is clearly the case for e.g., *V-with-N0 attachments, where the tree root acquires all its semantic features only after substitution has taken place at the N0 node (Figure 3). As a consequence, it is required to delay operations involving PP-attachments until the corresponding trees have been fully substituted, to ensure that their semantic descriptions are complete and include all information need to enforce selectional restrictions. This simplified bottom-up parsing has however to be enriched with a certain number of control heuristics, in particular to cope with multiple-type trees. These heuristics, which are part of the integrated semantic processing, ensure that multiple-types trees are not considered for left-side operations prior to consideration of right-side operations that would e.g. provide the required semantic information for disambiguation. These heuristics impose constraints on the order in which furcation and substitution operations can take place.

While the semantic relations in the semantic representation provide the argument structure for the message, there is a need to identify system actions and objects from the set of semantic features in the initial semantic representation. System actions are usually straightforward to identify on the basis of their feature descriptions, which appear on top of the semantic representation. Most of the interpretation is hence dedicated to the identification of discourse objects. The main specificity of reference resolution in this kind of agents' environment is that it cannot be entirely performed on a sole linguistic basis, as it contains indexical elements or elements referring to the agent's situation in its environment.

Objects can be identified by aggregating the semantic features of their nominal description, such as the door with a skull on it or more simply the large red door. As we have seen, these features are initially part of the semantic structure for each lexicalised tree, which represents the semantic content of the main anchor (see Figure 4). The integrated parsing process produces more complex feature structures, as features are aggregated from nominal descriptions, adverbial phrases, etc. Upon reference resolution, the NLP module can thus pass directly relevant object identifiers to the animation module. This is mainly the case for landmark objects whose designation is unambiguous (doors of a given colour, with specific patterns, specific walls or stairs, etc.). For instance, when processing the command go to the door with a skull on it, the reference resolution process can unambiguously return a single object identifier. It is thus passed to the animation system through its identifier. Reference resolution is not always possible on the basis of linguistic information only. Some designations are highly contextual, depending for instance on the relative position of the character in the virtual world. This is for instance the case for spatial expressions such as the barrel near the door on the right, which refer to the relative orientation of the character and can only be computed by accessing its actual position. As a consequence, reference resolution is a dynamic process, which is shared by the natural language interpreter and the animation system.

The overall goal of parsing is to produce a semantic structure rather than a syntactic one. In most of the cases, this semantic structure describes an action to be carried out by the agent, i.e. a case structure with the action arguments and parameters. These can be used to trigger corresponding scripts to be executed by the virtual actors.

Fig. 5. Interacting with Virtual Actors with Speech Recognition

However, providing direct instructions for procedural actions is somehow limited, and does not relate properly natural language semantics to the behaviour of intelligent characters. Webber et al. [3] have advocated that, in contrast with direct procedural instructions, natural language should influence the agents at an intentional level, for instance in a BDI framework. To be properly investigated, these assumptions also require more sophisticated applications than the one we have just described above.

In the next sections, we describe how natural language can be used to influence virtual actors in interactive storytelling. In this application, the behaviour of each character is determined dynamically by executing a plan corresponding to their role in the story. For us, this will be an opportunity to discuss the more sophisticated integration of natural language techniques and characters' behaviours implemented in these experiments.

3   From Semantics to Agents' Behaviours

The interactive story is inspired from a popular sitcom and consists for the main character "Ross" to invite the main female character ("Rachel") on a date [12]. Each character's role is based on a plan, which is implemented using Hierarchical Task Networks (HTN) Planning [13]. HTN planning is a knowledge-based formalism supporting forward-search refinement planning and is well-adapted to applications that have a strong knowledge content. This means that they accommodate the baseline authoring of the story rather than generate agents' behaviours from first principles. The baseline plans for the characters contain the sequence of tasks that constitute their role, though the actual choice of tasks as well as their outcome is determined dynamically and underlies story variability. For instance, Ross' tasks to invite Rachel out consist in gaining information about her, gaining her friendship, finding a way to talk to her in private, etc. The system is implemented as a real-time 3D animation using a computer game engine (Unreal Tournament™). The user can interfere with the unfolding of the story by issuing natural language advice to the characters, making use of a speech recognition engine integrated in the system (Figure 5).

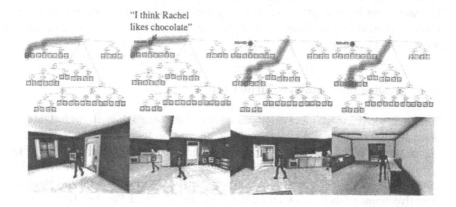

Fig. 6. Providing Virtual Actors with Information

The storytelling dimension of speech influence mostly consists in either contrasting or favouring the perceived actions of the virtual characters. In that sense the spoken input should take the form of realistic advice rather than commands and be embedded within the story. For instance, rather than saying "go talk to Phoebe" the user will say something like "Phoebe has the information you need". These more natural forms of expression, based on implicit background information, characterise the influence paradigm of speech interaction as another implementation of speech acts. The speech act nature of spoken advice can be illustrated by considering the meaning of the same sentence in different contexts. An utterance such "Phoebe is in Rachel's room" will convey different information depending on the context in which it is uttered. If Ross is trying to reach Phoebe in order to obtain information about Rachel, it will give him Phoebe's location (information provision). However, if Ross is trying to acquire the same information by stealing Rachel's diary in her room, it can also signal to Ross that he won't be able to do so, because Phoebe will object to that (warning).

The identification of speech acts from a user's utterance is compatible with many parsing techniques provided these generate an appropriate semantic representation from which the utterance's content could be matched to the pre-conditions of various operators in the HTN. This is why we should not detail here the parsing mechanism: it can be similar to the one described in previous sections or can take the form of a simplified template-matching approach. It can be noted that there is no obvious mapping between the surface form and the interpretation in terms of narrative influence. For instance, "talk to Monica" is interpreted as a direct suggestion for action (which will solve a sub-goal such as obtaining information about Rachel, see below), while "don't talk to Phoebe" is more of a global advice, which should generate situated reasoning whose result is to try to avoid Phoebe. There is no clearly established procedure for the identification of speech acts. In recent years, some methods have been proposed based on the semantic content of the utterance rather than on its surface form. This approach seems well adapted to the recognition of speech acts that should affect specific tasks in an agent's plan, as these could be identified by mapping the semantic content of an utterance to descriptors associated to a task (e.g. preconditions) [14]. However, user input might correspond to a great diversity of speech acts and as such require different interpretation mechanisms that we outline below in conjunction with a provisional classification

3.1 Providing Information to Virtual Actors

The direct provision of information can solve a character's sub-goal: for instance, if, at an early stage of the plot, Ross is acquiring information about Rachel's preferences, he can be helped by the user, who would suggest that "Rachel prefers chocolates" (Figure 6). The provision of such information has multiple effects: besides directly assisting the progression of the plot, it also prevents certain situations that have potentially a narrative impact (such as an encounter between Ross and Phoebe) from emerging. From an implementation perspective, sub-goals in the HTN are labelled according to different categories, such as information_goals. When these goals are active, they are checked against new information input from the NL interface and are marked as solved if the corresponding information matches the sub-goal content. In that sense, both the recognition of the speech act and the computation of its effect can be carried out by mapping the semantic content of the natural language input to the semantic atoms occurring in some HTN's operators' pre or post-conditions. Provision of information can also be used to trigger action repair. If for instance, Ross is looking for Rachel's diary and cannot find it at its default location, he can receive advice from the user ("the diary is in the other room") and repair the current action (this restores the executability condition of the read_diary action). In this case, spoken information competes with re-planning of another solution by Ross. The outcome will depend on the timing and duration of the various actions and of the user intervention (once a goal has been abandoned, it cannot, in our current implementation be restored by user advice).

Finally, it is possible for the user to lie to the character. The actual effects of such lies will depend on the overall context: if the user lies about the location of an object, this would result in a simple re-planning at a further stage, unless by doing so the user triggered specific situations, such as encounters with other actors, to which the character must react. On the other hand, if he lies about user preferences, this can have more adverse consequences though these would only appear towards the end of the plot [15].

3.2 Direct Instructions

Direct instructions for action is used mostly to create situations, for instance by provoking encounters between actors ("go to the shop", "talk to Phoebe", etc.) (see Figure 7). Once again, the outcome of these situations, i.e. whether Ross gets information from Phoebe or whether Rachel becomes jealous, depends on the overall context. The actions expressed in natural language are directly interpreted in terms of narrative actions and the current plan is interrupted. Once the action is completed, any additional post-conditions resulting by the situation created are returned to the original plan, which is resumed.

However, direct instructions can also solve narrative sub-goals by the situations they create. One example consists in Ross needing to talk to Rachel in private when she is busy with her friends. The player, by instructing them to leave, will solve Ross' sub-goal without exposing him to blunders, such as rudely interrupting Rachel, which could have upset her. In this case, the natural language instruction addresses other characters than the main character (e.g. Phoebe or Monica rather than Ross). Plan interruption is generally less problematic with secondary characters, whose plans are generally based on generic goals (such as "spending time" or "working").

3.3 Advice and Warnings

Advice is most often related to inter-character behaviour and social relationships. We have identified three kinds of advice. Generic advice is related to overall behaviour, e.g. "don't be rude". This can be matched to personality variables, which in turn determine the choice of actions in the HTN. Such advice can be interpreted by altering personality variables that match the heuristic functions attached to the candidate actions in the HTN. For instance, a "nice" Ross will refrain from a certain number of actions, such as reading personal diaries or mail, interrupting conversations or expelling other characters from the set. This of course relies on an a priori classification of actions in the HTN, which is based on static heuristic values being attached to nodes of the HTN to be used when searching the HTN for a solution plan. Specific advice involves behaviour towards a given character or situation.

For instance Ross can be advised not to upset Monica because this would in turn upset Rachel ("Ross, be nice to Monica"). In this case the advice generates a rule that is triggered for every action interacting with the character referred to in the advice. This rule will suspend the executability conditions of that action (for instance, interrupting Phoebe and Monica), triggering a repair action more compatible with the advice given (in the above example: waiting for them to finish their conversation). The generic class of warnings consists in preventing certain situations to happen in the story. We consider here that warnings aim at avoiding adverse situations only, hence being rather helpful to the character they are directed to.

We can further specify warnings into anticipating action failure or avoiding negative outcomes. One example of the former case consists in warning Ross, who intended to steal Rachel's diary to get information about her, that Rachel is currently writing in her diary. This form of advice avoids the negative impact of action failure. Another possibility consists in creating rules for behaviour that will be checked against dynamic situations. Examples of such advice would be "don't leave Rachel alone" or "don't let Rachel see you with Phoebe". These will generate small-size, situated plans, triggered by the emergence of the corresponding situation (more precisely detecting specific pre-conditions).

Fig. 7. Giving Advice to Virtual Actors

Another example of a *warning* speech act will illustrate the principle of semantic mapping: the user can warn Ross that Rachel is approaching while he tries to steal her diary or when he is talking to another female character (e.g. "Ross, Rachel is coming"). Both these actions have as their pre-condition the fact that Rachel should not be at the location where the action is taking place. At the same time this corresponds (ignoring the modality) to the semantic content of the warning. Such a warning will thus terminate the task by altering the pre-conditions for the corresponding operator (or, at a lower level, altering the executability conditions of the corresponding actions).

Finally, another mode of influence consists in engineering the social relations between characters (through gossip), which will affect any further interactions between them (e.g., "Phoebe, Monica said that your songs are daft" or "I heard Monica say horrible things about you"). This can have a variable impact on the story: it can for instance cause Ross to avoid seeking information from Phoebe. Or it can result in avoidance behaviour between certain characters, which can play a substantial role in the situations generated during the plot. The result is cause premature termination of all sub-tasks that involve interacting with a disliked character, with associated re-planning. For instance, if Ross dislikes Phoebe he will rather find another source of information about Rachel, even if his current plan initially prescribes getting this information from Phoebe. The mechanism by which this is implemented again consists in activating specific situated reasoning.

4 Conclusions

Natural language interaction with autonomous virtual actors is a complex process in which the semantic content of user utterances has to match an agent's representations for actions. The linguistic processing benefits from the description of appropriate sublanguages, in which spatial expressions play a significant role. This makes possible to design efficient parsers integrating syntactic and semantic processing, as the ultimate goal of parsing is to produce a semantic structure for the user instruction.

The original work of Webber et al. [3] has provided a first classification of natural language interaction with an agent's plan. We have extended this work by actually relating the semantic content of linguistic input to the implementation of agents' plans. In doing so, we have however considered plans as control structures rather than as resources as initially suggested. The latter approach, while useful as a descriptive tool for analysis, is still open to too many interpretations to support a proper implementation. We have introduced a speech acts approach to the interpretation of linguistic input, which also opens several research directions for the mapping of semantic content to descriptions of the plans' operators.

Acknowledgements. Research in natural language instructions and the development of the natural language interface to DOOM™ were carried out in collaboration with Ian Palmer (University of Bradford). The (ongoing) research in Interactive Storytelling is joint work with Fred Charles and Steven J. Mead at the University of Teesside.

References

[1]   Cavazza, M. and Palmer, I.J., 1999. Natural Language Control of Interactive 3D Animation and Computer Games. *Virtual Reality*, 3, pp. 1–18.

[2]   Cavazza, M., Charles, F. and Mead, S.J., 2001. AI-based Animation for Interactive Storytelling. *Proceedings of IEEE Computer Animation*, Seoul, Korea.

[3]   Webber, B., Badler, N., Di Eugenio, B., Geib, C., Levison, L., and Moore, M. 1994. Instructions, Intentions and Expectations. *Artificial Intelligence Journal*, 73, pp. 253–269..

[4]   Sager, N., 1986. Sublanguage: Linguistic Phenomenon, Computational Tool. In: R. Grishman and R. Kittredge (Eds.), *Analyzing Language in Restricted Domains*, Hillsdale (New Jersey), Lawrence Erlbaum Associates.

[5]   Ogden, W. C. and Bernick, P., 1996. Using Natural Language Interfaces. In: M. Helander (Ed.), *Handbook of Human-Computer Interaction*, Elsevier Science Publishers (North-Holland).

[6]   Zoltan-Ford, E. 1991. How to get people to say and type what computers can understand. *The International Journal of Man-Machine Studies*, 34:527–547.

[7]   Microsoft. Guidelines for Designing Character Interaction. Microsoft Corporation. Available on-line at
http://www.microsoft.com./workshop/imedia/agent/guidelines.asp

[8]   Wauchoppe, K., Everett, S., Perzanovski, D., and Marsh, E., 1997. Natural Language in Four Spatial Interfaces. *Proceedings of the Fifth Conference on Applied Natural Language Processing*, pp. 8–11.

[9] Joshi, A., Levy, L. and Takahashi, M., 1975. Tree Adjunct Grammars. Journal of the Computer and System Sciences, 10:1.

[10] Cavazza, M. 1998. An Integated TFG Parser with Explicit Tree Typing, *Proceedings of the Fourth TAG+ Workshop*, Technical Report, IRCS-98-12, Institute for Research in Cognitive Science, University of Pennsylvania.

[11] Abeillé, A., 1991. *Une grammaire lexicalisée d'arbres adjoints pour le francais: application a l'analyse automatique.* These de Doctorat de l'Université Paris 7 (in French).

[12] De Smedt, K. & Kempen, G., 1990. Segment Grammars: a Formalism for Incremental Sentence Generation. In: C. Paris (Ed.) *Natural Language Generation and Computational Linguistics*, Dordrecht, Kluwer.

[13] Nau, D.S., Smith, S.J.J., and Erol, K., 1998. Control Strategies in HTN Planning: Thoery versus Practice. *Proceedings of AAAI/IAAI-98*, pp. 1127–1133.

[14] Cavazza, M., Charles, F. and Mead, S.J., 2002. Interacting with Virtual Characters in Interactive Storytelling. *Proceedings of Autonomous Agents and Multi-Agent Systems 2002*, Bologna, Italy, in press.

[15] Cavazza, M., Charles, F. and Mead, S.J., 2002. Sex, Lies and Video Games: an Interactive Storytelling Prototype. *AAAI Spring Symposium in Artificial Intelligence and Interactive Entertainment*, Stanford, USA.

Author Index

Lecture Notes in Artificial Intelligence (LNAI)

Lecture Notes in Computer Science

Vol. 2708: R. Reed, J. Reed (Eds.), SDL 2003: System Design. Proceedings, 2003. XI, 405 pages. 2003.

Vol. 2709: T. Windeatt, F. Roli (Eds.), Multiple Classifier Systems. Proceedings, 2003. X, 406 pages. 2003.

Vol. 2710: Z. Ésik, Z, Fülöp (Eds.), Developments in Language Theory. Proceedings, 2003. XI, 437 pages. 2003.

Vol. 2711: T.D. Nielsen, N.L. Zhang (Eds.), Symbolic and Quantitative Approaches to Reasoning with Uncertainty. Proceedings, 2003. XII, 608 pages. 2003. (Subseries LNAI).

Vol. 2712: A. James, B. Lings, M. Younas (Eds.), New Horizons in Information Management. Proceedings, 2003. XII, 281 pages. 2003.

Vol. 2713: C.-W. Chung, C.-K. Kim, W. Kim, T.-W. Ling, K.-H. Song (Eds.), Web and Communication Technologies and Internet-Related Social Issues – HSI 2003. Proceedings, 2003. XXII, 773 pages. 2003.

Vol. 2714: O. Kaynak, E. Alpaydin, E. Oja, L. Xu (Eds.), Artificial Neural Networks and Neural Information Processing – ICANN/ICONIP 2003. Proceedings, 2003. XXII, 1188 pages. 2003.

Vol. 2715: T. Bilgiç, B. De Baets, O. Kaynak (Eds.), Fuzzy Sets and Systems – IFSA 2003. Proceedings, 2003. XV, 735 pages. 2003. (Subseries LNAI).

Vol. 2716: M.J. Voss (Ed.), OpenMP Shared Memory Parallel Programming. Proceedings, 2003. VIII, 271 pages. 2003.

Vol. 2718: P. W. H. Chung, C. Hinde, M. Ali (Eds.), Developments in Applied Artificial Intelligence. Proceedings, 2003. XIV, 817 pages. 2003. (Subseries LNAI).

Vol. 2719: J.C.M. Baeten, J.K. Lenstra, J. Parrow, G.J. Woeginger (Eds.), Automata, Languages and Programming. Proceedings, 2003. XVIII, 1199 pages. 2003.

Vol. 2720: M. Marques Freire, P. Lorenz, M.M.-O. Lee (Eds.), High-Speed Networks and Multimedia Communications. Proceedings, 2003. XIII, 582 pages. 2003.

Vol. 2721: N.J. Mamede, J. Baptista, I. Trancoso, M. das Graças Volpe Nunes (Eds.), Computational Processing of the Portuguese Language. Proceedings, 2003. XIV, 268 pages. 2003. (Subseries LNAI).

Vol. 2722: J.M. Cueva Lovelle, B.M. González Rodríguez, L. Joyanes Aguilar, J.E. Labra Gayo, M. del Puerto Paule Ruiz (Eds.), Web Engineering. Proceedings, 2003. XIX, 554 pages. 2003.

Vol. 2723: E. Cantú-Paz, J.A. Foster, K. Deb, L.D. Davis, R. Roy, U.-M. O'Reilly, H.-G. Beyer, R. Standish, G. Kendall, S. Wilson, M. Harman, J. Wegener, D. Dasgupta, M.A. Potter, A.C. Schultz, K.A. Dowsland, N. Jonoska, J. Miller (Eds.), Genetic and Evolutionary Computation – GECCO 2003. Proceedings, Part I. 2003. XLVII, 1252 pages. 2003.

Vol. 2724: E. Cantú-Paz, J.A. Foster, K. Deb, L.D. Davis, R. Roy, U.-M. O'Reilly, H.-G. Beyer, R. Standish, G. Kendall, S. Wilson, M. Harman, J. Wegener, D. Dasgupta, M.A. Potter, A.C. Schultz, K.A. Dowsland, N. Jonoska, J. Miller (Eds.), Genetic and Evolutionary Computation – GECCO 2003. Proceedings, Part II. 2003. XLVII, 1274 pages. 2003.

Vol. 2725: W.A. Hunt, Jr., F. Somenzi (Eds.), Computer Aided Verification. Proceedings, 2003. XII, 462 pages. 2003.

Vol. 2726: E. Hancock, M. Vento (Eds.), Graph Based Representations in Pattern Recognition. Proceedings, 2003. VIII, 271 pages. 2003.

Vol. 2727: R. Safavi-Naini, J. Seberry (Eds.), Information Security and Privacy. Proceedings, 2003. XII, 534 pages. 2003.

Vol. 2728: E.M. Bakker, T.S. Huang, M.S. Lew, N. Sebe, X.S. Zhou (Eds.), Image and Video Retrieval. Proceedings, 2003. XIII, 512 pages. 2003.

Vol. 2731: C.S. Calude, M.J. Dinneen, V. Vajnovszki (Eds.), Discrete Mathematics and Theoretical Computer Science. Proceedings, 2003. VIII, 301 pages. 2003.

Vol. 2732: C. Taylor, J.A. Noble (Eds.), Information Processing in Medical Imaging. Proceedings, 2003. XVI, 698 pages. 2003.

Vol. 2733: A. Butz, A. Krüger, P. Olivier (Eds.), Smart Graphics. Proceedings, 2003. XI, 261 pages. 2003.

Vol. 2734: P. Perner, A. Rosenfeld (Eds.), Machine Learning and Data Mining in Pattern Recognition. Proceedings, 2003. XII, 440 pages. 2003. (Subseries LNAI).

Vol. 2741: F. Baader (Ed.), Automated Deduction – CADE-19. Proceedings, 2003. XII, 503 pages. 2003. (Subseries LNAI).

Vol. 2743: L. Cardelli (Ed.), ECOOP 2003 – Object-Oriented Programming. Proceedings, 2003. X, 501 pages. 2003.

Vol. 2745: M. Guo, L.T. Yang (Eds.), Parallel and Distributed Processing and Applications. Proceedings, 2003. XII, 450 pages. 2003.

Vol. 2746: A. de Moor, W. Lex, B. Ganter (Eds.), Conceptual Structures for Knowledge Creation and Communication. Proceedings, 2003. XI, 405 pages. 2003. (Subseries LNAI).

Vol. 2748: F. Dehne, J.-R. Sack, M. Smid (Eds.), Algorithms and Data Structures. Proceedings, 2003. XII, 522 pages. 2003.

Vol. 2749: J. Bigun, T. Gustavsson (Eds.), Image Analysis. Proceedings, 2003. XXII, 1174 pages. 2003.

Vol. 2750: T. Hadzilacos, Y. Manolopoulos, J.F. Roddick, Y. Theodoridis (Eds.), Advances in Spatial and Temporal Databases. Proceedings, 2003. XIII, 525 pages. 2003.

Vol. 2751: A. Lingas, B.J. Nilsson (Eds.), Fundamentals of Computation Theory. Proceedings, 2003. XII, 433 pages. 2003.

Vol. 2752: G.A. Kaminka, P.U. Lima, R. Rojas (Eds.), RoboCup 2002: Robot Soccer World Cup VI. XVI, 498 pages. 2003. (Subseries LNAI).

Vol. 2753: F. Maurer, D. Wells (Eds.), Extreme Programming and Agile Methods – XP/Agile Universe 2003. Proceedings, 2003. XI, 215 pages. 2003.

Vol. 2759: O.H. Ibarra, Z. Dang (Eds.), Implementation and Application of Automata. Proceedings, 2003. XI, 312 pages. 2003.